America's Army

AMERICA'S ARMY

A Model for Interagency Effectiveness

Zeb B. Bradford, Jr., Brig. Gen. USA (Ret.)
Frederic J. Brown, Lt. Gen. USA (Ret.), Ph.D.

Foreword by Gordon R. Sullivan, Gen. USA (Ret.)

PRAEGER SECURITY INTERNATIONAL
Westport, Connecticut • London

Library of Congress Cataloging-in-Publication Data

Bradford, Zeb B.
America's Army : a model for interagency effectiveness / Zeb B. Bradford, Jr. and Frederic J. Brown.
p. cm.
Includes bibliographical references and index.
ISBN-13: 978-0-313-35024-5 (alk. paper)
1. United States. Army—Reorganization. 2. United States—Military policy. 3. National security—United States—21st century. 4. Interagency coordination—United States. I. Brown, Frederic Joseph. II. Title.
UA25.B64 2008
355′.033573—dc22 2007043644

British Library Cataloguing in Publication Data is available.

Library of Congress Catalog Card Number: 2007043644
ISBN-13: 978-0-313-35024-5

First published in 2008

Praeger Security International, 88 Post Road West, Westport, CT 06881
An imprint of Greenwood Publishing Group, Inc.
www.praeger.com

Printed in the United States of America

The paper used in this book complies with the Permanent Paper Standard issued by the National Information Standards Organization (Z39.48–1984).

10 9 8 7 6 5 4 3 2 1

We are in debt to many who have assisted us in producing this book. Especially we wish to acknowledge the contributions of the Association of the United States Army, and in particular the Institute for Land Warfare, the U.S. Army Infantry School, the Georgia National Guard, and HQ, U.S. Army Reserves. We are deeply in debt to our lifetime partners, Inge Bradford and Anne Brown, for their unflagging support of our efforts and their keen judgments of our work at every step of the process.

Contents

Foreword

Frederic J. Brown and Zeb B. Bradford, Jr., have been involved in the profession of arms as well as being keen observers of the national security policies of the United States. Through military service in peace and war, education, and interests, these two concerned citizens have devoted themselves to involvement in strengthening the security of our republic.

The strategic force for the 21st century is landpower, supported by airpower and seapower. A key component of landpower is America's Army—active duty forces, Army National Guard, and Army Reserve. The men and women who serve are focused in special forces, conventional forces, and as specialists in too many functions to enumerate. It is, however, in this relatively small commitment of available manpower that the means of achieving success during these demanding times reside.

Global issues related to national security seem to revolve around the environment, ideology, and resource allocation. While soldiers are in no sense the only resource available to address such a complex world buffeted by physical, climatological, or human-generated crises, it certainly is possible to hypothesize that organized, trained, equipped, and available manpower will be needed to play a role in securing and maintaining the national security of the United States.

This is not a new idea, given that we have had an Army since 1775, and for most of this time it has consisted of an active duty force and a militia. In modern times this force is known as "The Army": Active, National Guard, and Army Reserve.

Armies are complex organisms with the capability to change quickly when challenged while being painfully slow to adapt to new requirements.

In spite of these tendencies, America's Army has—given intellectual stimulus as well as the appropriate resources—responded remarkably well to the demands imposed by external threats.

This important work gives substance and definition to America's Army, a shorthand expression used informally within the Army to stress the fact that the institution is uniquely American, responsible, and adaptive to the demands of the nation. Our nation's history, in war and peace, in international crises or domestic disturbances, has been shaped by—and shaped—America's Army.

—Gen. Gordon R. Sullivan, U.S. Army,
Retired (former Chief of Staff, Army)

Preface

VIETNAM AND ITS AFTERMATH

We wrote our first book, *The United States Army in Transition,* in the waning days of the Vietnam War.[1] Both of us served in combat units in that conflict. Our purpose then was to describe the difficult problems the Army would face in an uncertain post-Vietnam future and to give our views on how it should deal with them. The war in Vietnam was the longest in our history. It dominated the Army's efforts and consumed its human and materiel resources for over a decade. The challenge facing our armed forces and the United States at that time was to restore our capacity to meet the security needs of the Cold War. These had been eroded by our long preoccupation in Southeast Asia. This was no easy task. But the fundamentals of the international environment were basically unchanged since the early post–World War II era.

The Soviet Union and the Warsaw Pact remained the primary threats to American and Western security. Our system of alliances, NATO in particular, was intact and provided a framework for our efforts. The problem then was primarily restoring the Army's strength and health, which had been sapped by years of ultimately unsuccessful warfare. The Army rose to the challenge. A generation of gifted and dedicated leaders rebuilt the Army and created the world-class learning organization that exists today. Most apparent, its equipment was modernized. Less apparent was the rebuilding of the Army's human materiel—its morale, its leadership, its doctrinal concepts of warfighting, its self-confidence, and a superb noncommissioned officer corps. The nation will always owe a great debt to those who labored to recreate the United States

Army, bringing it to today's historically high level of professional competence and effectiveness.

A NEW ERA

We believe that the nation faces a challenge no less daunting than it confronted after Vietnam. Unlike the world of the 1970s, the international landscape has been altered almost beyond recognition since the Berlin Wall came down and since 9/11. There are no familiar landmarks. The Soviet Union is a thing of the past. Our relations with traditional allies have altered radically as Europe has been reunited and the military threat to it has subsided. While the United States has achieved near-absolute dominance in objective military terms and is an economic powerhouse, it is confronted with a threat to its security and its interests every bit as dangerous as any it has faced in the entire post–World War II era.

Today we face a more complex set of challenges. While the United States retains its obligations and requirements as a global power, it now faces a much more amorphous enemy in the form of international extremism and terrorism as nonstate rivals grow and hostile regimes threaten our interests. And unlike past eras, this immediate threat is directed at the American homeland as well as our international interests. National security has now become a personal matter for ordinary American citizens in a way not seen since the Civil War. We are not alone in facing this threat. Moderate regimes throughout the world, East and West, share our risks. Yet the world has become both more fragmented as old relationships have diminished, and more intimate through globalization. Interests have diverged. Forging a common defense is difficult.

TRIBAL SOCIETIES

Compounding this is the "tribal" character of many of the societies in which the terrorist threat is most acute, such as Pakistan, Lebanon, and Afghanistan. We have extensive experience with tribes in the past on the North American continent. But in the twentieth century we became accustomed to the nation-state model in shaping our security programs.

Our intervention in the Middle East has revealed the shortcomings of this "top down," centralized approach, appropriate as it may be when facing nation-state peer competitors. We have learned that we must work with the most fundamental wellsprings of human identity and loyalty. These are the core, "bottom up," tribal sources of human conduct, such as combinations of religious affiliation, geographic region, ethnic grouping, or race.

This is not confined to the Middle East. Kosovo, India, and Belgium are examples of tribal identification below recognized state identities elsewhere in the world. Elections in such societies tend to reveal and exacerbate divisions rather than heal them. We must face this abiding yet uncomfortable reality. We have to respect and not fear such tribal realities globally as we pursue flexible, decentralized, external "bottom up" strategies appropriate to each of the many diverse environments—and simultaneously provide direction for continuous learning and adaptation to this new situation by our government as a whole.[2]

The potential impacts of extremism and the terrorism it produces go far beyond the direct destruction and loss of life that may result, costly as that has been and may be in the future. It has the potential of undermining the world order. The fall of moderate regimes to extremists could threaten the world's energy supply, disrupt longstanding alliances, undermine the resolve of nations that seek to escape the wrath of terrorists, inhibit common defensive efforts, create debilitating divisions within societies over civil liberties, and poison political life. For these reasons, the threat of extremism is much more serious than simply defending ourselves against attack. It is a battle for the future in the broadest sense.

We are attempting to contribute to effective responses to this unprecedented security dilemma while maintaining needed capabilities (conventional and nuclear) beyond those required for countering extremism. This is more than a military problem. All elements of national strength must be marshaled. But as always, the principal guardian of the American people, their "first responder," is the United States Army—all of it, including the National Guard and the Reserves, which together form "America's Army" (as expressed uniquely by visionary Army Chief of Staff Gen. Gordon R. Sullivan). Its task is to support and safeguard a democracy, a nation, a state, a federal republic, and a continent.[3] This instrument of the American people is our focus.

Military professionals of America's Army have clear obligations. They are to make their best efforts realistically to assess the problems facing the country and then to suggest solutions, both within America's Army and for other departments and agencies that need to be strengthened, drawing on organizational best practices institutionalized highly successfully in the rebuilding after Vietnam. This is not easy in an uncertain environment and facing enemies we do not fully comprehend with federal, state, and local governance organizations of varying competence.

INTERAGENCY INEFFECTIVENESS

We express considerable angst about the inability of many public-service agencies in this country to perform with consistent competence. Examples include the flawed response to Hurricane Katrina, the reorganizations of the U.S. intelligence community, and the faltering organization of the Department of Homeland Security.

The recent difficulties of the Department of State in deploying additional foreign service officers to Iraq have highlighted the growing inadequacies of the nonmilitary agencies of the government in contributing to international operations. Agencies such as the U.S. Agency for International Development are severely underfunded, while others such as the U.S. Information Agency and the Arms Control and Disarmament Agency have folded. And it is more than a question of inadequate funding. State's operational culture focuses more on policy development than implementation. As a result, the department relies more and more on contractors to carry out policies in the field. This has raised additional problems of supervision and accountability.[4]

Nor should bad examples be limited to other agencies of government beyond America's Army. The Army has its share recently, including the abuses at Abu Ghraib, the serious lack of support to wounded soldiers at Walter Reed Army Medical Center, incompetent oversight of reconstruction contracts in Iraq, and the misrepresentation of the killing of Ranger Corporal Tillman. These are unacceptable failures of command. We have a problem in competence of governance—federal, state, and local. The good news is that this problem is beginning to be recognized and addressed, for example by the substantive, bipartisan Project on National Security Reform, led by James R. Locher.

CHALLENGES TO AMERICA'S ARMY

As in the aftermath of Vietnam, our Army faces not only strategic security challenges, but profound institutional ones. The Vietnam War was fought with a draftee army led by a professional officer corps. It is unlikely that the decade-long effort in Vietnam could have been sustained without the draft. This provided a continuing stream of replacements deployed as individuals to the combat zone. But even that system could not be maintained in the face of widespread discontent with the war. Despite a declining budget deficit while at war, American tenacity found its limits. We may be finding them again as the war in Iraq enters its sixth year.

America's Army today is a product of the transformation from a system of conscription to one of volunteerism. It was recognized at its inception that this was more than a mere change in personnel systems, and that it would have profound strategic and institutional implications for the Army and the United States. It was widely anticipated that it would affect how the nation would fight its wars and provide for security generally.

America is now experiencing some of the consequences of this transformation after constant, near-total mobilization of our ground forces since 9/11. The nation—or more accurately, America's Army—has been engaged in sustained, large-scale ground operations for the first time since the end of the draft. The strains and limitations of this are becoming evident. In an editorial, the *New York Times* put it this way:

> America's all-volunteer military was simply never designed to be deployed as it has been for the past few years: unilaterally, indefinitely, and at peak strength in the middle of a raging civil war.... Beyond Iraq, the Army needs to move out of crisis mode—with almost every available division deployed, just returned, or preparing to be shipped out. It needs forces large enough to be able to devote time and resources to develop skills it is chronically short of and is sure to need in the post-Iraq future.[5]

An additional unintended consequence of our intervention in Iraq has been the extraordinary use of civilian contractors employed for a wide variety of tasks. The magnitude of the contractor presence is enormous. There are some 180,000 contractors in Iraq. This is a result of an unanticipated nation-building requirement being attempted in a hostile environment concurrently with combat and counterinsurgency operations. It also reflects the inability of the nonmilitary agencies of our government to contribute sufficiently to the overall effort, which requires far more than military capability.

It is not our purpose to pass judgment on decisions made in the past. But the consequences of the unprecedented efforts America's Army has been required to undertake are of enormous concern to us. It is vital that America's Army is capable in both human and material terms to fulfill the arduous tasks assigned to it by the nation. An essential element is the continued trust and confidence of the American people. In welcome contrast to Vietnam, the public has remained steadfast in support of our troops although divided over the conflicts in which they are engaged. This is why any indications of breakdown in leadership and professional behavior are of enormous potential consequence. There have been worrisome situations that distress us greatly and outrage our professional consciences. The failure of leadership in the Abu Ghraib scandal, for example, was a devastating blow to the moral standing of both the Army and the nation.[6]

There are other worrisome developments. We see the Walter Reed fiasco as a serious symptom of overload. It is a delayed effect of extraordinary overcommitment with incrementally decreasing resources over at least a decade while undergoing tumultuous change—described to one author by a very senior Army staff leader as "like trying to build an aircraft in flight." The magnitude and intensity of the current Army Plan governing transformation would be staggering even if the Army were at peace. But it is not: it is engaged in a war that has lasted longer than World War II, and it has been systematically underresourced by senior national leadership—before and after both the Secretary of the Army and the Chief of Staff were fired for accurately describing major problems.

These and other problems demonstrate that some of our institutions have failed us in recent years in the formulation and execution of policy. America's

Army as an instrument of policy can be and we believe has been held hostage to dysfunctional planning and execution within the government as a whole. It is all but impossible to overcome the constraints of a flawed strategy relying only upon the dedication and innovative tactics of soldiers compensating for inept governance and interagency ineffectiveness.

THE WAY FORWARD

The emerging era has prompted numerous analyses of the changing threats we face and suggested remedies the United States should take. We draw on many of these in our work. But we will go beyond describing challenges on a strategic level. Our experience is that concepts and strategies are all but meaningless if they cannot be translated into action and implemented effectively. For this reason, we discuss in detail specific programs that we believe to be key to achieving our recommended security goals in the years ahead. Policies must in the end be implemented by the strengths and inadequacies of the actual human resources we have at our disposal—certainly for the warriors in America's Army and also, we believe, for the leaders who implement policies and programs across federal, state, and local public-service organizations.

We suggest that the Army family of institutions and its programs can serve as a useful model for other American institutions that must contribute to national security, both domestic and abroad. There is a synergistic "cascade of excellence" within it that multiplies relevance and capability. This should be exploited and emulated within the cultures and practices of other experienced and justifiably proud agencies of federal, state, and local governance.

We come away from our analysis convinced that America's Army today is overcommitted, undermanned, and underfinanced. This has to be corrected. But in spite of the serious problems we face, we possess an enormous asset: never in our history has the United States been blessed with American soldiers of such caliber and professionalism. However stressed the Army may be, its core values and strengths have never been greater. Severely bent but not broken—the depth of the bench of experienced, motivated, and trained officers and noncommissioned leaders built after Vietnam holds. It should be a source of great confidence to the American people. It is to these heroes, past and present, that this book is dedicated.

1

National Security in a World Transformed

> The international system is in a period of change like we haven't seen for several hundred years because of the declining power of nation states. We are used to dealing with problems that have a solution, but Americans have to realize that we are at the beginning of a long period of adjustment.
>
> Henry Kissinger, quoted in the *Washington Post*, June 24, 2007

THE UNITED STATES entered the new millennium with supreme power. Militarily and economically it had no serious rivals. Victorious in the Cold War, it had won more than a military contest. It had prevailed in an extended conflict between social systems, values, and ideologies. It enjoyed great moral authority.

America remains immensely powerful today, nearly two decades after the collapse of the Soviet Union. With only 4.6 percent of the world's population, it accounts for 27.5 percent of the world's gross domestic product (GDP) and for nearly half of global spending on defense.[1] Its economy remains vibrant and growing. By any traditional measure, its military is the most powerful on the planet, perhaps in history. Clearly, American security policies since the end of World War II succeeded and were right for their time. They served us well. But it is our belief that transformations in the international environment require major changes in our security policies and how they are implemented if the nation is to successfully meet the demands of the future.

In spite of its enormous power, America faces great difficulty in translating its strengths into influence and acceptable results in the conduct of policy. We need both appropriate adaptations of national security policy and significant alterations in how it is implemented. There is no question that the nation possesses the inherent strength and adaptability to achieve these. But this will require recognition of the demands of the new era and changes in attitudes and practices. The evidence is overwhelming to us that the United States must move to a security strategy of much greater adaptability. It will require much more decentralization in execution on a multilevel basis, and it must possess the appropriate policies and the effective instruments for doing so. The purpose of this book is to propose solutions to this challenge.

In our view, the United States has an instrument at hand that can offer a model and a vehicle for major improvements in how the United States can approach the future and become much more effective in policy implementation. This is the institution we term "America's Army." This is the full community of the components of the United States Army: the active duty forces, the Army National Guard, and the Army Reserves, as they have evolved responsive to the changing requirements for important national military landpower in a democracy, a state, a nation, a federal republic, and a near-continent. America's Army has undergone continuous and fundamental change to adapt to new requirements since the Vietnam era, while bearing the brunt of meeting the complex and lethal challenges facing the United States around the world. We are convinced that America's Army has been, can, and should be a major instrument of positive change and model of effective, timely innovation "how to" in the development of a more effective national security policy. In the course of this book, we will discuss how we believe this can be achieved. This chapter discusses the dynamic international environment, which we believe requires new approaches.

A PERFECT STORM

The international environment is being shaped by the convergence of four major developments and events. These are interrelated, and in the aggregate produce a "perfect storm" of turmoil and change in the world order and America's place in it. These are globalization, the collapse of the Cold War order, the emergence of new powers on the world scene, and the rise of a global Islamic insurgency. Taken together, these make our policies, which have been effective since World War II, now inappropriate.

Globalization

Globalization has brought prosperity and benefits to millions of people as barriers to trade, travel, and information have fallen. But it has also created forces and developments that threaten the traditional capacities of nation states to fulfill their traditional sovereign responsibilities of providing security and protecting the interests of their publics. Globalization and its effects recognize no national borders. Today, nations throughout the world face mass migrations of people, AIDS epidemics, potential international pandemics such as avian flu, economic competition disruptive of local economies, and most ominously, global terrorism. Nation states, including America, face unprecedented challenges. Citizens look to their national authorities to promote their interests and to protect them from the adverse impacts of globalization, in an era when many problems are beyond purely national solutions. As in efforts to confront climate change, nations must seek collaborative approaches and policies and rely on or create international institutions to address transnational issues. As a truly global power, the United States inevitably is involved in this effort, and its security is affected by local developments elsewhere. For example, an insurgency in one locale may potentially reinforce broader movements, which can pose a threat to our nation in the future.

The End of the Cold War

The collapse of the Soviet Union and the end of the Cold War fundamentally altered the bipolar world order, and the relationships between the United States and other nations, particularly those of Western Europe. For a century, America was preoccupied with seeking stability and peace in Europe. In the new era, Europe does not occupy such a central position in our national security strategy. It does not constitute a security threat to the United States, nor is it an arena of threatening instability. But the "new" Europe poses new challenges to the United States. It is less dependent upon American power for its security. The nations of Eastern Europe, formerly within the Soviet bloc, require a more nuanced and flexible approach by the United States to Europe than in the past.

Clearly, we can expect that European and American interests on the global stage will diverge on many issues, as demonstrated by the divisiveness over Iraq. But there are also common interests between some or all European nations and the United States that a flexible security policy can accommodate and exploit. These include a concern over climate change and over a more assertive and truculent Russia regarding relations with its former satellites in Eastern Europe. Most compelling is a common interest in defeating global terrorism. Europe has played an important role in stabilization efforts in Afghanistan and is a potentially highly important partner with the United States in stabilization efforts elsewhere, such as Africa. An ability to team with European and other partners on a regional or local basis would be a valuable asset in stability efforts.

The end of the Cold War also affected American relations with other nations throughout the world beyond Europe. Virtually all nations took sides, for various reasons. This is not the case now. We can no longer have a centrally directed "one size fits all" security policy with a common template for operations. The world is more diverse, more complex, and more fluid. We have to adapt to a world where catchy U.S. electoral statements such as "free trade," "democracy whatever," or "no abortions" can become confining if not dysfunctional to responsive policy execution.

New Powers

The rise of new powers adds to the complexity of the security environment. The extraordinary emergence of India and China, in particular, introduce new security issues for the United States. It is in the mutual interest of all that we remain on friendly terms although fiercely competitive. It is also important that we identify and act in concert in areas of common interests to strengthen forces of stability in the world. But it is a truism that nations do not have friends, only interests. Economic power can be and usually is accompanied by military power. In the case of China, it is embarked on a continued strengthening of its military capabilities. This is not necessarily a threat to our interests. But America must maintain its ability to deter and if necessary to counter actions against us and our allies, Taiwan for example. This underscores the continued need for maintenance of robust conventional power prepared for conventional midintensity conflict in the event of conflicts, and the continuation of a powerful nuclear deterrent.

Russia represents a special case among important nations. Although not an enemy, it is clearly uncomfortable with its erosion of influence in the post-Soviet era, particularly in Eastern Europe. A flexible security policy must attempt both to counter divisive Russian efforts to undermine American interests and engage it in becoming a constructive partner in defeating terrorism and in halting the further proliferation of nuclear weapons. The challenges posed by these and other emerging and rising powers must also be accommodated in an effective national security policy adapted to the realities of today.

Global Terrorism

Amidst the uncertainties accompanying globalization, the end of the Cold War, and the rise of new powers, global Islamic terrorism has exploded onto the scene. While there was abundant evidence that terrorism was a growing global threat long before 9/11, that attack was a traumatic wake-up call to the American people and its leaders. The course of events since the destruction of the World Trade Center and the strike at the Pentagon is well known. But countering and containing this continuing threat has become a central concern of our national security policy. It is a formidable challenge. The dimensions and seriousness of it was summarized in a *Financial Times* editorial:

> The roll call of atrocities, from Casablanca to Istanbul, Bali to Mumbai, Riyadh to Amman, London to Madrid, is bloody indeed. Now, however, jihadi extremism is sprouting like poisonous mushrooms in the darkness enveloping the Middle East. . . .
>
> The totalitarian jihadism peddled by Osama bin Laden and his growing following is emerging in new chapters all over the Middle East, including in some places it has never before been seen. . . .
>
> Virulent jihadism seems to be seeping out of Arab soil almost everywhere. It is spreading into Gaza and northern Lebanon, into Iraqi Kurdistan (and southeastern Turkey), into Jordan, Yemen and across north Africa. The region's political immune system, such as it was, is collapsing.[2]

Grim as that assessment is, it is not the full picture. Extremist insurgency goes far beyond the Middle East itself. It is active in Indonesia, the Philippines, Thailand, and a number of other countries. Terrorist attacks within Europe are ominous harbingers of growing extremism in the West itself.

Global terrorism brings into sharp relief, more than any other challenge, the urgent need for new and more effective security policies and practices. We will describe in more depth this threat, this "Long War," later in our work. It is a major focus of our efforts.

BROKEN PARADIGMS

Any national security strategy for the future must be appropriate for the environment shaped by the major elements of the "perfect storm" described earlier. They are fundamental. But national policy must take into account more specific factors that bear directly on our ability to operate effectively within that environment. It must be recognized that any new strategy, and any new missions assigned to our forces, particularly the Army, must realistically acknowledge that many of the assumptions underlying previous national security policies are no longer valid. There have been major paradigm shifts that make the problems facing the military more difficult and complex. Some of these are both part of and consequences of the major changes we have described. Some are painful to acknowledge, but we cannot proceed as if many of the old "givens" still apply. The following are "broken paradigms" that have important impacts on the formulation and conduct of American security policy in the future.

Realignment and Conflict Within Islam

There has long been conflict within Islam, as illustrated by the Iraqi invasion of Kuwait, and the eight-year conflict between Iraq and Iran. And rivalry between the major branches of Islam, Sunni and Shia, has existed for centuries. But these took place within an established framework, or paradigm, which has now been radically altered. For a millennium, there was Sunni domination of most of the Middle East. Only in Iran, which is Persian, had there been Shia rule. Even in Iraq, the Sunni minority was the governing class. The invasion of Iraq and the overthrow of the Saddam regime has brought an end to this established order and has created a realignment in the region, and has been the catalyst for escalating sectarian violence between Muslims.

An unintended consequence of our overthrow of Saddam and the destruction of the Sunni-led Taliban regime in Afghanistan has been the empowerment of Iran. This has led to a major change in the distribution of power throughout the Middle East. Iran has moved aggressively to assert its influence among Shia communities, not only in neighboring Iraq, but in Lebanon, Palestine, Syria, and elsewhere. Its instruments have been nonstate proxies, such as Hezbollah in Lebanon and Hamas in Palestine. This phenomenon, which we address further in this chapter, is a major new factor in the development of security strategy. For their part, the Sunni powers, traditional allies of the United States, fear an Iran dominated "Shia Arc" in the region, which challenges their interests. For the United States, this creates dilemmas. Rather than choosing sides, it must attempt a difficult balancing act between mutually hostile regimes.

Escalating and barbaric sectarian has been another unintended consequence of our intervention. It should have been anticipated. Similar conflict within societies was seen also in the Balkans when the pressure of a totalitarian government was released in the former Yugoslavia, triggering unimaginable sectarian violence. We should not have been surprised when the same happened in Iraq. With all of our good intentions, clearly we did not fully understand the nature of the conflict we entered into with Operation Iraqi Freedom. In *The Shia Revival*, Vali Nadr writes: "The conflict that mattered to the mobilization of extremists and support for them was not the one Washington was focusing on—it was not the battle of liberty against oppression but rather the age-old battle of the two halves of Islam, Shias and Sunnis. This was the conflict that Iraq has rekindled and this is the conflict that will shape the future."[3] As a consequence of this, we have now become a major factor in an accelerated struggle within Islam, which promises to be of very long duration, with or without our direct involvement—a competitive struggle dividing Islam that may or may not be in the strategic interests of the United States.

The radically altered state of affairs in the Middle East has serious consequences for American security policy and America's Army. It has been a major consideration in convincing us that our nation needs a new, more adaptable strategy, and must become far more effective in implementing policy in general. Our travails in the occupation of Iraq dramatically demonstrate our operational shortcomings in a complex environment. We believe we can do better. We must.

Decline of American Credibility

A major shift has occurred in the vital area of perceptions. While the tangible features of American national power such as defense spending, manpower under arms, and weapons systems give us superpower status, in the intangible area of perceptions we face growing difficulty. Fairly or accurately or not, our problems in Iraq over an extended period undermine the credibility of American power. We are perceived as being stretched thin, with little capability to take on new challenges. This is reflected in the increased willingness of secondary and even third-rate powers to defy the United States. Adding to this credibility problem was the response to Hurricane Katrina, which brought into question the abiding competence of our government in dealing with an unexpected crisis of whatever nature. This not only encourages our enemies but also undermines our influence with traditional allies. Opinion polls reflect growing disenchantment with American policies in many parts of the world. This underscores the importance of policies, which engages partners in common endeavors wherever possible. This should apply especially in collaborative teamwork approaches to the implementation of policy.

The Wounded Israeli Defense Force (IDF)

A separate but parallel paradigm shift is of particular importance to our interests in the Middle East. This is the loss of the aura of invincibility of the IDF, a perceived alter ego of military competence to America's Army. Fear of drastic and successful retribution against those who would attack Israel was worth any number of divisions as a deterrent. Iran and Hezbollah were masterful in destroying this image in the Lebanese conflict, which left Hezbollah bloodied but unbowed. In the aftermath of the campaign, the IDF was portrayed as a "paper tiger," not the highly competent "western" military we were accustomed to. It was seen as inept in command, in training, and in logistics. This affects the United States as well, as Israel's primary patron. We had relied upon this intangible element as an extension of our own influence in the Middle East.

The Rise of Nonstate Actors

Hezbollah, Hamas, and Al Qaeda illustrate another major departure from the past. This is the rise of nonstate actors operating outside the nation state system that has been the framework for international security policies for centuries. Hezbollah represents the military arm of a transnational political system clearly able to erode the power of Israeli and western conventional capabilities. Both Hezbollah and Hamas are terrorist organizations with important political roles in support of extremist movements, but largely beyond the reach of traditional international diplomacy and sanctions. Politically competent, they win democratic elections, multiplying their influence in countering U.S. national policy.

National sovereignty has in the past legitimized the employment of national military power. International conventions, such as the Geneva Conventions, assumed nation state monopoly on the instruments of violence and conferred singular status on national armed forces and their personnel. International law and convention also clearly distinguished between civilian noncombatants and those taking up arms on behalf of a state. In today's world, as we have seen, movements outside the traditional international structure are now major players. Dealing with this major new reality will require a high level of sophistication and knowledge by our policy makers and those who must counter these threats. A primary need is continuous learning by our organizations and the people within them, particularly America's Army and hopefully extended into other federal departments and agencies who together must fight this complex challenge as a team. Knowledge and understanding must be translated into effective actions on the local level where conditions and circumstances vary and are unique to each locale. This requirement figures prominently in our approach to the Long War.

Asymmetric Threats

The use of "asymmetric" means to challenge the power of modern states and their armed forces is a primary strategy of insurgent movements we face. This brings into question the relevance of traditional instruments of power such as weapons systems, defense spending levels and the like. Nonstate forces have struck lethal blows against numerous modern countries and societies. The aim often is to destabilize and weaken the power of regimes to govern by attacking the infrastructure that holds societies together. These have been and are occurring both in western cities such as New York, London, and Madrid, and in active theaters such as Iraq and Afghanistan. The battle for Iraq is being fought largely in the streets using suicide bombers and relatively primitive but increasingly complex weapons and explosives. Our organized defense forces were not designed to counter this type of threat and are hard pressed to respond effectively. This also is an important feature in the Long War. It is extraordinarily important that we develop means appropriate for this phenomenon, rather than continue to operate as we have in the past with tools designed for another era.

Threats to the Homeland

With the attacks of September 11, 2001, the home territory of the United States was revealed as vulnerable and a new front in the war being waged with global terrorism. This is new, and is in part a consequence of globalization exploited by nonstate terrorist actors. The creation of the Department of Homeland Security constituted both an historic departure for the nation and an additional large claim on national financial, law enforcement, and military resources. National security is no longer only an overseas problem. It has become personal for our citizens. The specter of possible use by terrorists of nuclear weapons against the homeland has added to the importance of this new paradigm. The devastation caused by Hurricane Katrina, and the unsatisfactory response by government at all levels, further elevated this new dimension of national security policy. The threat of both weapons of mass destruction (WMD) attacks and catastrophic natural disasters creates large new demands on those responsible for the security of the American people. We devote a chapter to this subject, which proposes major changes in how the United States should deal with this issue, entailing a leading role for America's Army.

Transformation and Stability Operations

A final paradigm is of particular importance for America's Army. The Department of Defense intensified a major ongoing transformation of the armed forces at the beginning of the Bush administration. The objective was to make our military more flexible and interactive across the military services. This was to facilitate rapid, lethal, and effective operations within a given reduced force structure. The brilliant successes of the Afghan and Iraqi interventions were at least in part testimony to the wisdom and success of this program. But, as we have seen, a long occupation and nation building was not anticipated, either in operations or in the assumed employment of the reserve components. For the Army, this has meant that we must succeed in a major nation-building project of uncertain duration with a force designed for striking fast and hard, not for pacification and reconstruction—a force that has had to improvise faced with expected but inadequate support from other departments of the federal government. The Army has been heroic in coping with this development, but it is faced with the challenge of adapting to the new era in which it has become our primary instrument for bringing stability to areas of postconflict and insurgency. Stability operations have now been defined as integral to all operations and as important as offense and defense. We will address the specifics of what this requires of the Army going forward.

These broken paradigms add complexity to the challenge of providing national security to the American people. We must accept them as part of today's reality and take them into account as we go forward.

PREPARING FOR THE UNCERTAIN—HEDGING FOR CONTINGENCIES

We do not have the luxury of preparing only for those things we know with certainty. Nor can the nation or America's Army plan only for those requirements that can be met with current, existing resources, which are finite and fully engaged in current operations. This places major demands on America's Army. Its institutional and human capabilities can be leveraged and multiplied to cope with threats beyond its existing forces. Later we discuss the importance of hedges and how we must plan for contingencies (response to domestic emergencies being one of them). At this point, we believe it appropriate to consider two threats that must be given full consideration in any national security policy, although they may not currently be at critical points of decision. One is the possibility of a crisis on the Korean Peninsula, which among other things could possibly require major new demands for conventional forces. The other is the threat of further proliferation of nuclear weapons into the hands of hostile states or terrorists.

While these contingencies are of immediate concern, there is a range of other potential threats that must be considered. A number of these must be taken into account in our overall national security posture and strategy. In particular, a broad range of potential challenges to American security and interests could result from the extraordinary growth of the Chinese economy and the voracious appetite for natural resources that sustains this demand. We cannot know the path that China will take as its drive for growth continues. Hopefully, this will be in the form of peaceful participation in the world economy. Yet there are already troubling developments as China intervenes in virtually every continent in the global competition for resources—oil, timber, minerals, and others. To maintain its monopoly of political power, the Chinese regime could resort to the exercise of military power to achieve its goals. The full spectrum of conflict could be postulated. We touch upon this again later in this chapter in our discussion of climate change and the large negative impact China is having on this important issue.

Instability on the Korean Peninsula

Major international efforts have been underway to prevent North Korea from continuing its nuclear weapons program. We believe, however, that another potential threat exists on the Korean Peninsula that should be of great concern to the United States and to the United States Army in particular. This is the possibility of collapse of the North Korean regime.[4] The Kim Jong-Il regime retains its control on power by totalitarian repression, while its population suffers drastic deprivations and starvation. North Korean armed forces are the central pillars of support for the government. They have a privileged place in life and are shielded from food and other shortages that face the civilian population. These forces are also formidable. An estimated one million men under arms are positioned in the areas adjacent to the South Korean border. Without moving from position, some estimated 12,000 artillery pieces, some with chemical and biological capabilities, are in range of the Greater Seoul area with its 20 million people. The capital city region and its people are thus hostage to North Korean intentions, with or without nuclear capabilities.

Our concern is the potential disintegration of the central government, which could lead to any number of nightmare scenarios including massive refugee migrations within North Korea and into South Korea and China, civil war between rival factions, and some form of aggression against South Korea and American forces. Indeed, some or all of these might occur simultaneously. The prospect of such a horrendous development preoccupies its neighbors, including China and Japan, as much as North Korea's nuclear program. Indeed, some observers believe its nuclear program is a consequence of the fragility and insecurity of the regime.

The Korean peninsula has been a target of hostile powers and rivals since antiquity, to include the Soviet Union, China, and Japan. The United States Army has for over half a century been a lynchpin for stability in northeast Asia, accepted, however grudgingly, by all parties. The potential collapse of order in the armed camp that is North Korea threatens this stability. No foreign power with vital interests in the area could avoid becoming involved should the peninsula become chaotic. The United States Army would bear the brunt of any consequences were this to happen. For this reason, we believe that our military leadership should seriously plan for worst-case scenarios in Korea, and prepare accordingly, to include possible mobilization of reserve elements. Our ongoing commitments in the Middle East complicate this. We must also support international efforts aimed at preventing catastrophic collapse of the regime. Necessary responses to chaos on the peninsula would be an unprecedented challenge.

Nuclear Proliferation and Extremism

We assume that more nations, some hostile to the United States, will become nuclear powers within a few years. Eventually, these will also develop some means of delivering nuclear weapons to their intended targets. The most prominent contenders at present are North Korea and Iran. Successful establishment of a nuclear capability by either of these nations prompts others to seek this capability as well. In the case of North Korea, Japan or South Korea could feel it necessary to create their own nuclear deterrent capabilities. Regarding Iran, a nuclear capability could lead to an arms race in the Middle East. With nuclear Israel and nuclear Pakistan (Sunni) next door, it seems inevitable that Iran (Shia'a) will develop nuclear weapons as a regional power. The proliferation of nuclear weapons would have significant effects on how the United States would view its security interests and its options. It is possible that these WMDs would in fact embolden some nations to undertake aggressive actions under their own nuclear umbrella, deterring intervention by the United States or anyone else. It is also possible that rogue nuclear states would make nuclear weapons available to extremist groups hostile to the West in general and the United States in particular. Either or both cases would obviously introduce great uncertainty and perhaps instability in volatile regions of U.S. interest. This would argue for a continuing and enhanced American full-spectrum conventional warfighting capability, within a potentially nuclear environment.[5]

But there is an additional, and perhaps more troubling, possibility. It has been the assumption and the operating principle since the dawn of the nuclear era that nations possessing nuclear weapons could be deterred from using them by the threat of retaliation. National survival was the supreme, overriding interest of nations. Many wars have been fought in the nuclear era, Korea and Vietnam to name only two. Conventional wars were not deterred, but limits were imposed by fear of mutual destruction. The likely imminent possession of nuclear weapons by extremist states such as Iran directly or indirectly supporting proxy global terrorism introduces an entirely new calculus to international security. What if nations or multistate global terrorists are willing to accept apocalyptic destruction and loss of life in the millions in pursuit of what they consider to be a higher cause? Suicide bombing, once unthinkable, has now become ordinary in the arsenal of Islamic extremism. What if this principle, that self-destruction is justified, becomes applicable to the state—directly or by proxy—as well as to the individual? Although the regime of

North Korea does not appear suicidal, it is not clear that Iran or other states, if under the control of extremists, would not be prepared regardless of the consequences to employ nuclear weapons against Israel, or other nations.

We cannot know if this is the case. But if it is, the bedrock principle of deterrence will have been undermined. If that were to occur, we would be entering a period of maximum danger and instability. This would have profound implications for defense planners, especially for our ground forces. The entire nuclear picture opens a range of unsettling possibilities, with an increased likelihood of conventional aggression if adversaries believe that we will not respond to hostile actions through fear of a retaliatory nuclear attack. Or it could mean the possible use of nuclear weapons against ourselves or our allies regardless of the consequences if the deterrent principle does not apply. The possibility of these dismal developments cannot be wished away. We have to be prepared for them as best we can. America's Army must plan for this era of heightened danger at home and abroad.

We do not propose major alterations in how the Army should operate. But we do believe that the possibility of conducting operations in a nuclear environment should be acknowledged and its implications examined for any changes in doctrine and training that might be appropriate. As we will point out in Chapter 6, virtually no attention is paid to this issue in our doctrine or training. We recall, as junior officers in the pre-Vietnam era, routine integration of simulated nuclear attacks in maneuvers in 7th Army in Europe. At service schools, selected officers were given special training and assigned an additional occupational specialty as "Nuclear Weapons Employment Officer." Consideration of nuclear warfare was as routine as constantly carrying a gas mask. Measures such as these might be appropriate today. We are fully aware that additional missions or training requirements carry real costs in resources, and most importantly time, which is a scarce commodity for leaders and soldiers. Allocation of these at the margins is a tough issue. What threats are important enough to accrue the opportunity costs associated with hedging against them? This will be the subject of later discussion.

Climate Change

Another great uncertainty facing us is the potential consequence of climate change. There is mounting evidence that global warming is beginning to impact on the environment. This is a transnational phenomenon beyond the control of individual national governments. Ultimately, climate change could have profound geopolitical effects. Preliminary indications are that northern regions may benefit somewhat, as areas now unsuitable for habitation and agriculture become more temperate. Siberia, Canada, Alaska, and other sparsely populated regions could be transformed. It appears that the areas that would suffer the worst adverse effects are those already disadvantaged by poor climate and demographic problems. Areas such as sub-Saharan Africa could face even less favorable circumstances. These effects would likely translate into alterations in the relative power of nations, for better or worse. This could raise new security issues for all nations, including the United States. This would require security policy adaptation. We are very much aware of this evolving environmental issue and considered addressing it in this work. We have concluded, however, that the potential impacts of climate change cannot be predicted with any certainty with the present state of knowledge and understanding, and that in any event these will occur gradually and over an extended period of time. Our purpose in this book is to address the clearly defined issues that we face in the present and in the foreseeable future. For this reason, we do not include it in our analysis. We believe, however, that responsible planners should remain informed and vigilant on this issue as knowledge increases and be prepared to incorporate its potential effects into their policies as they become better understood in the future.

This is not to minimize this important issue. We are particularly concerned over the real and potential impacts on international security by the ongoing environmental crisis taking place in China. A recent analysis describes the growing disaster: "China's environmental problems are mounting. Water pollution and water scarcity are burdening the economy, rising levels of air pollution are endangering the health of millions of Chinese, and much of the country's land is rapidly turning into desert. China has become a world leader in air and water pollution and land degradation and a top contributor to some of the world's most vexing environmental problems such as the illegal timber trade, marine pollution, and climate change. . . . the Chinese people and the rest of the world will pay the price."[6] The consequences are alarming, as illustrated by a few examples:

- Levels of airborne particulates are now six times higher in Beijing than New York City.
- The Gobi desert is spreading by about 1,900 square miles annually; about one-quarter of the country is now desert.
- More than 75 percent of the river water flowing through China's urban areas is considered unsuitable for drinking or fishing; nearly 700 million people drink water contaminated with animal and human waste.[7]

The effects of this disaster are not confined to China:

- The U.S. Environmental Protection Agency estimates that on some days 25 percent of the particulates in Los Angeles originated in China.
- Reportedly, 25–40 percent of all mercury emissions in the world come from China.
- China has already surpassed the United States as the world's largest contributor of carbon dioxide to the atmosphere.[8]

China's demand for resources is expected to grow rapidly even beyond current levels. By 2020, China is expected to have 130 million cars, and by midcentury to have more than the United States. In it plans to relocate 400 million people by 2030, and in the process to erect half of all the buildings constructed in the entire world, China's demand for timber, paper, and pulp will likely increase by 33 percent between 2005 and 2010. The effects of China's relentless economic expansion go beyond impacting the environment and the climate. As we stated earlier, it leads to growing competition for resources, which can potentially raise serious security issues. Vast illegal Chinese timber operations in Myanmar and elsewhere and efforts to secure oil and mineral sources in Sudan and globally could lead to confrontation with others in the world community. Students of history will recall that Japan's drive to industrialize and realize its imperialist ambitions in the 1930s led to aggression in Southeast Asia under guise of "The Greater Southeast Asia Co-Prosperity Sphere," and ultimately to World War II. This was driven in large degree to secure resources to fuel its economy. We must hope that history will not repeat itself.

This discussion concerning China in connection with climate change reflects our belief that this phenomenon is multidimensional and cannot be addressed in this work as a national security issue in isolation from its fundamental causes and diverse effects. This being said, responsible military planners must be prepared to respond to challenges to American security as appropriate. America's Army may contribute to the challenges of climate change, but as a part of a much broader global effort.

THE NEED FOR A NEW NATIONAL SECURITY STRATEGY

The transformations in the international environment since the end of the Cold War make planning for the future exceedingly difficult. We have not seen such radical alterations in generations. These circumstances must be understood and taken into account. Today, a national strategy appropriate for this turbulent new world is yet to be articulated. Although we are responding on many fronts to threats facing us, we lack an overall strategy that can serve as an organizing principle and a comprehensive framework for sustained and coherent responses across a broad array of programs and actions. "The Global War on Terror" describes our general response to a new threat, but is inadequate to serve as a long-term strategy. An effective strategy defines both the desired end and the means of achieving it. It must also provide for the full range of security needs across a broad spectrum. It also goes beyond military considerations alone. It must encompass diplomatic, economic, and other instruments as well. All need to be brought into a coherent relationship under a concept that relates them to a common objective. As we stated at the outset, we believe that the United States requires a more adaptable and flexible approach, and one that decentralizes appropriate authority to the levels charged with executing policy. We also believe that any national strategy should take advantage of the strengths of America's Army in meeting these challenges. We offer in the next section a strategic concept that we believe can accommodate these requirements.

CONTAINMENT REVISITED

We should reflect upon our successful response to an earlier global challenge. During the Cold War, our strategy was "containment." Soviet expansionism, directly or by proxy, was opposed. Allies formed coalitions in the common defense. All instruments of power were enlisted in the struggle. The ultimate objective was to achieve the collapse of the Soviet system from its internal contradictions and failures when denied external successes. It worked. While the national security strategy was containment, "massive retaliation" and "flexible response" were military elements of it with which to implement containment and give shape to our efforts. Documents such as NSC 68 provided operational guidance.

We believe that the United States should use the concept of containment, updated as necessary, as an overarching strategy for the future. The conflict with militant Islam would be a major component of an overall national security strategy that must continue to take into account the other enduring vital interests of the United States around the globe in other regions and with different security challenges.

There are important differences in this era from that of the Cold War. There are no front lines or clear territorial boundaries. And as we have discussed, many problems facing nations today do not respect national boundaries or sovereignty. The principle military threats are more asymmetric and unconventional. With regard to militant Islam, the competing ideologies are not based upon opposing views of social organization but upon cultural and spiritual identity, past opposed to future. A revised containment would be characterized by less formal alliances, and be more opportunistic in dealing with threats and challenges that will vary and require different responses.

Containing Global Terrorism and Conflict Within Islam

An important purpose of this strategy would be to prevent militant Islam from achieving ascendancy in the Muslim world and undermining the interests of the larger community of nations. A primary objective is to shield the American people from the effects of extremism directed against them and from the ongoing conflict within Islam. Ultimately, the goal is to erode the strength and appeal of extremism while defending against it. This would come about by denying it successes and through the moderating influences of globalization and modernization. This may take generations.

The internal contradictions and schisms within Islam cannot be resolved by the United States. Accommodation must be reached within Islam itself. We see this in the increasing sectarian violence in Iraq, over which we have only limited influence, and in the violent confrontations between Hamas and Fatah in Palestine. These may be microcosms of the future in the Muslim world at large.

Containment should not be construed as passive acquiescence or isolationism. During the Cold War, both the Korean and Vietnamese conflicts were active enforcements of a containment strategy as was vigorous diplomacy. Although we would confront extremism directly with arms as necessary, we would also actively encourage those elements within Islam who can be allies in modernization and moderation. In practice, this would require collaborating with some who do not share our form of government or values, although we must remain true to our ideals in our own conduct. The challenge is far more than military. We must demonstrate that we offer a more promising future than those who are at war with modernity and other nations in the region and beyond.

A major goal of an updated containment strategy would be to defuse and internationalize issues that are sources of conflict and hostility in this troubled region. To the extent that the international community can take ownership of these issues, it reduces the profile of the United States as the global hegemon, primary target, and enemy of Islam. This process is underway already as demonstrated by NATO in Afghanistan, the European Union in Bosnia, a diverse group of nations creating a buffer zone in Lebanon, and allied diplomacy addressing the Iranian nuclear issue. Other tasks fall more directly on the United States. It must continue to lead the effort to establish a viable government in Iraq, and as a minimum, prevent it from falling under the control of extremists or hostile states such as Iran.

Our intervention in the Middle East did not create the crisis in Islam. It did unleash pressures that were already building as the forces of modernity and globalization threatened and undermined the prevailing order in the region. Iran was a clear beneficiary. This is now a global long-term threat. We can and must adapt our thinking and rise to this new challenge. This will take decades. But if as a result the Muslim world and the larger family of nations reach peaceful accommodation, all of our efforts will have been worth it. As a minimum, we must reduce the threat to the American people. We believe that a strategy of updated and active containment of it is needed to reach that goal.

Richard Haas, president of the Council on Foreign Relations and former head of policy planning for the State Department, has recently expressed a similar concept regarding the Middle East: "No quick or easy fixes exist to solve the problems of this critical region. The Middle East will remain a troubled and troubling part of the world for decades to come. The challenge will be to contain the effects and to hasten the arrival of something better."[9]

An "active" containment of extremism would not be the sum total of our national security policy. As indicated, this would be in parallel with meeting our security needs through actions in other areas of the world, from countering a North Korean assault on South Korea, to hedging against Chinese aggression, to intervention to shore up threatened regimes in Latin America, to support of disaster relief as we did in the wake of the tsunami in Indonesia, and a wide range of other contingencies across the spectrum of conflict.

In view of the global demands on American power, we find troubling the use of the U.S. Marine Corps for extended occupation duty in Iraq, and possibly Afghanistan in the future. While the Marines have performed heroically, the United States will require the conventional expeditionary capability of the Corps for numerous other contingencies. The planned increase in Army forces should be taken as an opportunity for the Marines to revert to their more traditional role.

Containment as a Global Strategy

To focus excessively on Islam would be a mistake and would detract from the potential of containment as a common approach for working with others on issues of mutual security. Other nations have their own priorities and interests. The European Union, for example, has a compelling interest in the stability of the Balkans and is more directly affected by Russian efforts to reassert its influence in Eastern Europe than is the United States. The Eastern European nations themselves continue to view the United States and NATO as guarantors of their own security more so than those of Western Europe. India has its own perspectives on relations with Pakistan and China that may differ from ours, although we may share common overall goals. Latin American nations have their own hemispheric and national interests.

Potential rivals such as Russia and China would not be excluded. Both competition and collaboration on an issue-by-issue basis would characterize the relationships with them in a revised containment strategy. In other words, containment should not be considered as simply a vehicle for an expanded "War on Terror." It will obviously encompass efforts to confront terrorism, but should be seen as a flexible strategy that engages a broad range of nations and organizations that perceive that their security interests are served by working with the United States, not just ours. This will require far more flexibility and adaptability of American policy makers and institutions than we have demonstrated in the past.

Resources for America's Army

In this discussion we have described some of the extraordinary changes that have taken place in the environment the nation and the Army faces. Taken together, these present enormous challenges. It is important to acknowledge that, great as America's power is, it has limits. America's Army itself has and will continue to have finite resources with which to meet the demands placed upon it. Nevertheless, it goes forward with enormous strengths and capabilities. Of greatest importance is its human materiel. Today's Army is the most experienced, battle-hardened, and best-equipped and led armed force on the planet, perhaps in the history of warfare. The unprecedented demands placed upon it in recent years have not weakened it but have made it stronger in will, cohesion, morale, and leadership.

But this should not obscure the reality that the Army has been required to operate with what we believe are inadequate resources. It was underfunded and reduced in strength before it went into the commitments in the Middle East. At the end of the Cold War, it was assumed that the resources needed to protect the American people and their interests would be substantially reduced in a less dangerous world. Without fanfare, the United States began to undertake substantial force reductions, especially in ground forces. In the decades preceding the attacks of September 11, 2001, more than 425,000 soldiers were cut from the total Army end strength. Army outlays in real terms had fallen to levels not seen since the late 1940s. Investment accounts were underfunded by approximately $100 billion, producing about $56 billion in equipment shortages.[10]

Now America's Army faces even greater resource demands as it continues to consume materiel and equipment in major amounts in Operation Iraqi Freedom and elsewhere. In addition to this, the Army must prepare for the future. It must develop new systems and weapons to maintain its effectiveness beyond its current operations. We will discuss this in Chapter 3. The Army Game Plan identifies major resource requirements not only to replace losses and reequip the existing force, but also to field new, more advanced materiel. These latter are described in the Future Combat System (FCS) program, a major element of the Army Plan.

In contrast to other national institutions, America's Army, all components of it, have retained the admiration and respect of the American people. It is this nexus between the soldier and the public that is the bedrock foundation of the United States as a world power. America's Army will play a critical part in national security going forward. But it cannot carry the burden alone, or be cast in roles that should be the responsibility of others. The entire security establishment must immerse itself in the security challenges of our time.

The following chapter will examine more closely the significant changes in the nature of warfare as we face the demands of the Long War. This will further underscore the need for greater flexibility and effectiveness in the conduct of operations in support of national policy.

2

The Long War

One of the difficulties in creating an adequate strategy for the future is an evolution in the nature of warfare itself, within the context of the new challenges and broken paradigms mentioned in Chapter 1. Gen. John Abizaid, the former commander of Central Command, responsible for operations in Iraq, has characterized the struggle with militant global terrorism as the "Long War." This war is of enduring and indeterminate duration, is global in scope, and will assume many forms shaped by local conditions and causes. It will require a mixture of many elements, both military and nonmilitary. While this war was shockingly brought home to the American people with the attacks of 9/11, it had already been raging for several decades. The attacks on the marine barracks in Lebanon, on the Khobar Towers, on the USS *Cole*, an earlier attack on the World Trade Center, attacks on embassies in various countries, the ascendancy of the Taliban in Afghanistan, and numerous other incidents of terrorist activity were battles in this war long before American military intervention in the Middle East. We were at war were but only dimly aware of it.[1] Our response has been, naturally enough, to confront this new threat with our existing forces and attitudes. As we have seen in Iraq, these are only partially relevant to these new circumstances. In this chapter, we will examine the nature of the global threat of terrorism and suggest approaches we should take in waging this Long War within the context of an overall containment strategy.

While our superb conventional forces made short work of the Iraqi military, their stunning victory in 2003 did not result in victory, which would have been the achievement of the political goal America was seeking: a new democratic beginning in the Middle East that would deal a decisive blow to the forces of extremism and tyranny. Whether or not we reach that goal, it has become clear that we must reconsider how the United States must engage this threat. We need better understanding of what we face and how in fact our enormous power can be employed effectively.

NEW FORMS OF WARFARE

This must begin with recognizing that forms of warfare new to our times are emerging. Gen. Rupert Smith, the former UN commander in Bosnia and a veteran of numerous international peacekeeping operations, including Northern Ireland and Kosovo, addresses a major aspect of this challenge in *The Utility of Force: The Art of War in the Modern World*. Smith believes that we continue to view warfare and develop our forces for an era that has passed. In his view, we cling to a paradigm of "Industrial War," in which organized forces of nation states engage each other in a contest for traditional military objectives. This remained the dominant form of warfare throughout the Cold War. Smith characterizes the new form of warfare as "War Amongst the Peoples," in which the large "industrial" forces of modern states are largely inappropriate, even irrelevant. In this warfare, our goal is generally to establish a condition, a political outcome, rather than the destruction of enemy forces. As he puts it:

> Increasingly we conduct operations amongst the people. The people in the cities, towns, streets and their houses—all the people, anywhere—can be on the battlefield. Military engagements can take place against formed and recognizable groups of enemies moving amongst civilians, against enemies disguised as civilians, and unintentionally and intentionally against civilians. Civilians can be the target as much as the opposing force. First, this occurs because moving amongst the people is the guerilla fighter's proven method of neutralizing the strength of his stronger opponent. Secondly, civilians can be targeted because the will of the people is the objective, and the direct attack on the people is thought to assail that will. Finally, there are the media that bring the conflict into the homes of millions of people: people who vote and whose opinions influence their politicians—those who make the decision on using force.[2]

There are features of the evolving threat of global insurgency that Smith does not discuss, however.

At first glance, Smith's thesis may appear to be simply a restatement of the requirement for emphasis on counterinsurgency warfare and doctrine. Certainly much of that doctrine and practice do apply, but it is far more complex than that in the present era. In Iraq, for example, the United States appeared to consider the ultimate goal of the conflict—the will of the people—only as an afterthought, as an adjunct to the main event that was seen to be a conventional conquest of a state and a regime.

In addition, there are distinctly different features of what we face in the Long War than we did in earlier experiences with insurgency, as we did in Vietnam. A major element is the sectarian and religious nature of the roots of the current conflict. The insurgents in Vietnam were motivated by political and nationalist goals, ultimately seeking to control the apparatus of a nation state. This was a limited objective and had a definable end point. Once the goal was achieved, the conflict ended. And although there was legitimate fear of a "domino effect" if South Vietnam fell to the control of the north, this did not occur. The conflict in which we are engaged today is not limited in time or space. To a certain extent, Vietnam and Iraq were wars of "choice."

But the Long War is not a war of choice. We are compelled to fight it on behalf of our own security and interests and those of our allies, largely on battlefields of our opponents choosing.

THE CHANGING NATURE OF GLOBAL TERRORISM

Although Smith's analysis offers important insights, they only partially describe the nature of current global terrorism today. The phenomenon of rising global jihadism coincides and overlaps with the conditions he describes. This is characterized by several crucial new developments:

- The evolution of bin Ladenism and al Qaeda from organization to movement.
- The globalization of terrorism, which presents threats on a multidimensional basis across the globe far beyond the original, motivating source.
- The adaptation and refinement of conflict by asymmetric means.
- The decentralization and fragmentation of terrorism into "open source" warfare.

The Evolution of al Qaeda

Although al Qaeda conducted numerous terrorist attacks for many years, it became part of American public consciousness only with the attacks of 9/11. It was also perceived as, and was, distinguished by its character as a transnational nonstate organization, directing operations from a central authority. It had at its disposal the apparatus of a nation state—the Taliban-dominated regime of Afghanistan. "Six years after terrorists struck New York and Washington, al Qaeda as an organization has been severely undermined, its haven in Afghanistan destroyed and many of its leaders captured or killed. But the violent fanaticism promoted by al Qaeda has not only survived it has proliferated, many experts say, by the U.S.-led 'war on terror.'"[3] Christopher Heffelfinger, a senior analyst at West Point, says: "I actually think [bin Laden] may be dead. But it's irrelevant. His ambition was to set up an Islamic awakening. I think he's done that."

One should not assume, however, that as an organization al Qaeda has become irrelevant. It has become less operational, but is reaching out to jihadist groups elsewhere and provides inspiration and guidance to them even if not organically linked. A recent Associated Press report states that a surge in al Qaeda propaganda began in 2006. The terror network has accelerated its pace. In 2006 its media wing released 58 audio and video messages. By mid-2007 it had already released 62. Its response time has been dramatically reduced. It took only a matter of days to weigh in on Pakistan's crackdown on a radical mosque. It had taken nearly a month to blame Britain itself for the carnage when Islamic radicals killed 52 people in London three years ago.[4] Through this and other means, it motivates a worldwide constituency of disaffected Muslims and extends its reach. Through its identification as a movement, it now encourages groups to "rebrand" themselves as franchises.

The Globalization of Terror

This has the effect of actually expanding the reach of al Qaeda. An example is in Nigeria, where long-established terrorist fighters from the northeast part of the country and from Chad have recently rebranded themselves as "Taliban." Another is in Algeria, where a militant faction, which had been in decline, adopted both the al Qaeda name and its tactics.[5]

This ideological globalization is by no means limited to the Third World. Its effects are apparent in the West also. Individuals and small groups find inspiration to action even if they are remote from sources of jihadism in the Middle East and have resided in the West for extended periods or are even native-born Western citizens. In the globalized world of today, these elements can experience "vicarious" outrage and humiliation via the Internet and television.

Research conducted for the National Security Council reveals that top-down recruitment or brainwashing is not much in evidence. It is estimated that "about 70 per cent of terrorists enlist in groups through friendship, and about 20 per cent through kinship. The preferred cell is eight members and consists of males between the ages of 15 and 30."[6] A commonality of these individuals and small groups is self-isolation from the larger society around them. This fits a pattern of long standing, established well before the current era of the Long War. There is a deep psychological dimension involved in the motivation of the fanatic. In 1951, Eric Hoffer, the self-educated longshoreman philosopher, observed that the fanatic finds self-assurance and fulfillment by clinging passionately to whatever cause he embraces: "This passionate attachment is the essence of his blind devotion and religiosity, and he sees in it the source of all virtue and strength. Through his single-minded dedication he easily sees himself as the supporter and defender of the holy cause to which he clings. And he is ready to sacrifice his life to demonstrate to himself and to others that such indeed is his role."[7]

These insights bear remarkable resemblance to the analysis performed recently by the New York City Police Department on domestic terrorism:

> It is a phenomenon that occurs because the individual is looking for an identity and a cause and unfortunately, often finds them in the extremist Islam. There is no useful profile to assist law enforcement or intelligence to predict who will follow this trajectory of radicalization. Rather, the individuals who take this course begin as 'unremarkable' from various walks of life.... The image of the heroic, holy warrior or 'mujahedeen' has been widely marketed on the internet as well as

in jihadi tapes and videos. This image continues to resonate among young, especially Muslim, men 15–35 years old—men who are most vulnerable to visions of honor, bravery and sacrifice for what is perceived as a noble cause.[8]

This motivation is chillingly apparent today in the Islamist movement. According to official figures of the Palestinian Central Bureau of Statistics, 60 percent of the population of Gaza is 19 years of age or younger. Nearly 76 percent are 30 or younger. A Palestinian social worker commented, "I'm very worried about this generation. They are very pessimistic and very vulnerable to appeals for mastery, for meaning." What they want, she says, "is a sense that they can control their lives, and that their lives will have meaning. So they are susceptible to appeals from religious groups and armed groups. It is not hard to find young people at loose ends, jobless and bored, admiring of the gunmen, ready to be inspired or recruited or brainwashed into fighting for something larger than their own lives."[9]

The foregoing discussion of potential fanatics included isolation from society as a contributor to extremism. The Unites States has been fortunate in assimilating individuals and groups from diverse cultures, including Muslims. The Pew Research Center recently conducted the first survey of the United State's 2.4 million members of the Muslim community. Andrew Kohut of the Center states that "What this survey shows is that Muslim Americans are largely assimilated, happy with their lives and moderate—mostly in contrast to Muslims in Western Europe. They also reject Islamic extremism to a much greater extent than Muslim populations around the world."

While we in America must be grateful for this, we cannot be complaisant. Inclusiveness must be constantly sustained. This will be a challenge in face of the competing demands for security from global terrorism. There is a difficult tradeoff to be made between openness and measures required to protect the public safety. Both must be achieved. Nor should we assume that we are unaffected by the more troubling rise of extremism in Europe. It can cross the Atlantic. In the age of globalization, we are all in it together.

Systems Disruption by Asymmetric Warfare

There is an increasingly common strategy employed by jihadists worldwide. This is the disruption of society's normal functioning by attacking the critical social and economic networks that underpin modern life. The effectiveness of this has been immeasurably multiplied by the widespread adoption of the suicide bomber as a delivery system. In the case of Iraq, this has been aimed at preventing the emergence of effective government and economic reconstruction. This asymmetric warfare is very cost effective. In his book, *Brave New War*, John Robb uses the example of an attack during the summer of 2004.[10] A small group of Iraqi insurgents blew up a southern section of the Iraqi oil pipeline infrastructure.

The attack cost an estimated $2,000 to produce and no attackers were caught, while the explosion cost Iraq $500 million in lost oil exports—a return 250,000 times the cost of the attack. Attacks in the West can produce similar effects and returns. In his book, *Overblown*, John Mueller points out that the U.S. Postal Service will eventually spend about $5 billion on protective screening equipment and other measures in response to the anthrax threat, or about $1 billion per fatality.[11]

Although goals of various insurgent groups may differ, many do not seek to take over countries or regimes, as did twentieth-century guerrillas. They merely seek to weaken states so that they can prosper or pursue their other aims in the space created by the collapse of law and order. In Iraq, if successful, this would have twofold benefits. It would prevent the Iraqi government from providing security and services to its people, and it would undermine American support for a regime that appears incapable of governing and a war that appears unwinnable.

Decentralization and "Open Source" Warfare

In parallel with the evolution of al Qaeda itself, the insurgencies in Iraq, Afghanistan, and elsewhere have become decentralized. In Iraq, it is estimated that the insurgent movement is made up of at least seventy different groups.[12]

There is no apparent central command structure for the movement. Groups operate opportunistically and entrepreneurially. This makes it hard to put a name and a face to our enemies, and attacks are likely to be more numerous and carried out by smaller groups on targets of opportunity. Robb describes their modus operandi as "open source." Open source is a method applied to software development, in which all who wish to share in it may do so without restriction. This permits various groups to participate as they see fit. This is directly opposite from top-down hierarchical command structures typical of Western military organizations and governments. This introduces a flexibility and an elusiveness that are very difficult to counter with traditional tactics and procedures. This new characteristic of current insurgency movements, along with its other features, creates a daunting new challenge indeed in the Long War.

STRENGTHS AND VULNERABILITIES

The global insurgent movement poses an enormous threat. But the Long War is similar to all conflicts in that it consists of measures and countermeasures between opposing sides. Each seeks to take advantage of its own strengths and exploit the weaknesses of the enemy. In this contest, Jihadism has undoubted strengths. It has the inherent advantage of the initiative as it can seek out vulnerabilities in the systems infrastructure of the forces of order. It also has the strength of "true believers," groups and individuals who are fanatically dedicated to their cause. And it is unconstrained by the value systems of Western democracies, which honor the sanctity of human life and civil liberties. It can be ruthless. But it also has vulnerabilities.

A major vulnerability is actual and potential conflict within the Muslim world itself. We have mentioned the enduring conflict between Sunni and Shia Islam. This is at play now both between secular communities within Muslim nations and between Sunni-dominated and Shia-dominated states. There is also conflict between groups and organizations struggling for power. We see today numerous examples of this intra-Muslim conflict: the conflict between Hamas and Fatah for supremacy in Palestine; conflict between the Pakistani government and jihadists; virtual civil war within Lebanon among various Islamic groups, and the moves by Arab nations, such as Egypt, Saudi Arabia, and Jordan to counter Iranian supported movements in Gaza and elsewhere in the region. This struggle within Islam can sap the strength of the insurgent movement.

The depth and extremism of this conflict has been reflected in the recent struggle between Hamas and Fatah in Gaza: "Palestinians never used to do these things to one another. Putting bullets in the back of the heads of unarmed men on their knees. Shooting up hospitals. Killing patients. Kneecapping doctors. Executing clerics. Throwing handcuffed prisoners to their deaths from Gaza's highest apartment buildings. There is a madness in Gaza now. Hamas claimed it was fighting infidels, with a holy sanction to kill."[13] We have discussed this internecine conflict earlier as a strategic consideration in a policy of containment. It can work to our advantage and to the detriment of the jihadist cause.

On a more fundamental level, the very fanaticism of Islamic extremism, and its intolerance of others who do not share its vision, limits the potential of jihadism as a global movement and the cause it represents. We recognize that not all individuals share our value system, which separates church and state, and protection of individual liberties. But nevertheless even many of those who do not share our western values, would be unwilling to submit themselves to totalitarian domination if given a choice. Ultimately the inclusiveness of our value system can work to our advantage. But we must be prepared to defend and to fight for these values. The extremist movements we face have power. But it is negative power. It is the power to create fear, and to destroy and disrupt. It not the power to build or to uplift. It is an ideology of hatred, grievance, and resentment. It is not an inspirational vision of a brighter future.

In waging the Long War, our goal is to prevent this negative force from succeeding in destabilizing our lives and the infrastructure of civilization upon which we depend. This is a primary objective in this difficult struggle. But no war has been won only by defense. We must have a positive, forward strategy. This does not mean attempting to impose our values on others by force.

It does mean that we stand behind those who share our goals of stability and the rule of law. Our overarching objective is to promote the interests of the American people in contributing to worldwide prosperity, stability, and tolerance.

With our inherent strengths, the United States and moderate states elsewhere, coupled with enormous material and intellectual resources, can meet the challenges of the Long War. Where we are seriously lacking and are vulnerable is in the operational competence across various jurisdiction and agencies of governance to protect ourselves and engage in this conflict effectively. Developing this competence is one of the main tasks of this work.

DIMENSIONS OF THE LONG WAR

We have discussed our need for a more flexible national security policy that would be more decentralized in implementation and operate effectively at multi levels. The nature of the Long War demands this. A difficulty in developing an adequate response is the complexity of the challenge. On an ongoing basis, there is a bewildering array of events occurring across the globe: a bombing in London, conflict in Gaza, insurgent attacks in Iraq, and a variety of others. While are all a part of the Long War, its very complexity makes a coherent, coordinated approach difficult. We believe it useful to view these various dimensions of the Long War as "theaters." They are not primarily geographic, are not mutually exclusive, and are interrelated. Furthermore, there are some common elements to all of these overlapping theaters. These are conceptual, "virtual" theaters. We take this approach because each requires different responses, with different players, and at variable levels. There are at least five such dimensions, or theaters:

- The first is the area of direct, active conflict against forces of the West and its allies. This is centered currently in Iraq and Afghanistan, where there is advanced insurgency.
- Next is a theater of campaigns waged by organized nonstate actors, used as proxies by Iran and others to challenge existing political orders in seeking realignment of political power. These include struggles for power in Lebanon involving Hezbollah, in Palestine involving Hamas that has seized control of Gaza, and others, such as in Pakistan, where bin Laden-type jihadism is challenging the authority and rule of the national government.
- There is also a theater in which the contest is being waged to prevent states from failing and for insurgency to reach advanced stages as in Iraq, typified by efforts by the United States in the Horn of Africa to prevent Somalia from failing as a state and being dominated by Islamist elements. This is the arena of "preemptive nation building" and "pre-insurgency" operations. An excellent positive example of this theater has been the U.S.,

NATO, then European Community operations in Bosnia Herzegovina achieving currently stability that was unimaginable when Operation Deliberate Force started in 1995.

- There is the theater of terrorism directed against the West on western soil itself.
- Finally, there is the theater of virtual appeal. What compelling vision does the United States of America offer to the world? It is a conflict of images and perceptions. More fundamentally, it is a theater of conflict over values, both spiritual and secular. It is far more than clever and imaginative packaging and marketing, although these serve as weapons in this theater.

This means that we are fighting a multifront war. We must engage on all fronts concurrently as part of an overall strategy of containment. We must have integrated strategic and operational synergy employing all instruments of government. The first theater above impacts on all the rest. How it will be resolved will have long-lasting impacts on our own security and on the Middle East for years to come. We make clear our disappointment with how this war has been managed. But we cannot turn back the clock. Iraq and Afghanistan have become a crucible in which Western resolve and competence is being tested and is a lethal laboratory for learning some hard lessons, including how we must conduct the Long War in the future, especially for America's Army. Regardless of the outcome, we must absorb these experiences and apply them constructively as we go forward strategically, operationally and tactically.

The second theater brings into play the need for diplomatic and military adaptation to a rapidly changing region of great geopolitical significance. While not directly engaged militarily, we can play a large role in reinforcing the forces of moderation and order and striving to contain the effects of conflicts in the region.

The assassination of Benazir Bhutto and the widespread violence (largely along tribal lines) resulting from it reflect an ominous increase in instability in that crucial country and in that vital region. Pakistan has been an important ally in support of the United States in the Middle East. This relationship could be threatened should that nuclear-armed nation succumb to chaos and instability, which could in turn prompt adverse reactions from Iran, among other countries. This underscores the crucial role the United States plays in the region and indicates that it may well require a significant, open-ended presence in the region beyond the demands of the conflict in Iraq.

The third is one in which we are attempting to shape the future. Here we believe that America's Army can take the lead and serve as a model for effective integrated national policy implementation. For example, which we mentioned above, from their base in the former French colony of Djibouti, a small U.S. task force comprised of special forces, as well as other elements of the

American military, and with participation of nonmilitary government agencies has been operating covertly and overtly against the Islamic militias in neighboring Somalia, and recently assisted the Ethiopians in intervening to dislodge them from power. Later, we expand upon this concept and propose specific programs to institutionalize interagency operational effectiveness.

The aims and commitment level of America and of its NATO and Western European allies in the Middle East continue to diverge. Not only capability but political will is lacking. There is an ongoing thinning out of coalition forces in Iraq, and many NATO partners in Afghanistan are unwilling to subject their forces to serious combat. This is another harbinger that the United States in the future will continue to bear the principal burdens of waging the Long War nearly alone, far from the homeland. An American presence in the region to foster and ensure stability would be comparable to the role the United States has played in stabilizing the Korean Peninsula for over half a century.

The fourth theater consists of the homelands of the Western democracies. Primary responsibility for operations in this dimension of the Long War falls to national authorities, although intense international collaboration on intelligence and coordinated responses is essential. For our part, we believe that America's Army can and should be the key to effective response to major terrorist attacks and other domestic disasters. We devote a chapter to this subject later in this work.

The final theater of public diplomacy is one we should focus on much more seriously. One can wonder that a group of terrorist killers with a primitive ideology and with few resources can define the narrative and write the story line for the struggle of our time in much of the Muslim world. It does so while facing the West, which routinely dominates world wide media and manufactures instant celebrities of unknowns. Al Qaeda is far ahead of us in public diplomacy, or propaganda, if you will. Our country has been a force for good for at least two centuries. No other nation has such a universal appeal. We must learn to articulate this and project it. We must have an effective public diplomacy, backed up by our demonstration that we Americans live up to our own proclaimed ideals.

STABILITY OPERATIONS AND COUNTERINSURGENCY

Obviously, a clear understanding of the challenges we face in the Long War is essential to taking effective action. We will briefly examine two documents that describe the approaches being taken and provide guidance in the areas of Stability Operations and Counterinsurgency (COIN). One is Department of Defense Directive Number 3000.05: Military Support for Stability, Security, Transition, and Reconstruction (SSTR) Operations.[14] The second is the new Field Manual 3–24, Counterinsurgency.[15]

DOD Directive 3000.05 SSTR Operations

This directive establishes Department of Defense policy and assigns responsibilities within the department for planning, training, and preparing to conduct and support stability operations. It defines stability operations as: "Military and Civilian activities conducted across the spectrum from peace to conflict to establish or maintain order in States and regions." It acknowledges the multifunctional requirements of such operations and recognizes the need for participation of nonmilitary agencies, nongovernmental organizations, international participation, and the participation of indigenous elements. It also notes the importance of military–civilian teams as important tools on stability operations, including charging the Commander, Joint Forces Command, with developing organizational and operational concepts for them.

While this guidance reflects an understanding of the complexity and importance of such operations, we believe it is has shortcomings in meeting the challenges we face. Although it acknowledges a key requirement for nonmilitary participation, it states that "many stability operations are best performed by indigenous, foreign or U.S. civilian professionals. Nevertheless, U.S. military forces shall be prepared to perform all tasks necessary to establish or maintain order when civilians cannot do so." In our view, this simply makes American forces, particularly America's Army, the default organization for such operations in the continuing absence of effective participation by other national agencies. This is precisely what has occurred in Iraq. This must be avoided in the future.

Another shortcoming is that the expressed need for multiagency teams is made in the absence of an effective organizational mechanism or doctrine for creating such teams. Who are the other members of the teams? How will they be institutionalized? This reflects a core weakness of this guidance as national security policy, and of security policy as a whole.[16] The Department of Defense does not have authority over other agencies of government and it cannot impose requirements upon them. In addition, there is no operative concept for how such teams should be integrated into the fabric of the government-wide establishment. We address these problems in detail later in the book, with the concept of "Teams of Leaders" to fill the existing void, and by suggesting that guidance be provided to all agencies by appropriate authority.

Counterinsurgency

The recently published Field Manual 3–24 represents the first major revision of counterinsurgency doctrine in a generation. We do not presume to suggest specific tactical doctrine. That is not our purpose. We include a discussion of it to indicate where America's Army is today on a critical military challenge, and consider its contribution in light of what we believe are the requirements to counter the threat of global insurgency.

The manual has been rightfully acclaimed for placing needed emphasis on a subject that has been neglected since the Vietnam era. It stresses a pragmatic approach, distinguishing between "practices that work and practices that don't." Successful practices include focusing on the population, its needs, and its security; establishing and expanding secure areas; isolating insurgents from the populace; providing amnesty and rehabilitation for those willing to support the new government; embedding quality advisors with host nation forces; protecting key infrastructure, and others.[17] These are undeniably productive measures to be taken. Of course the ability of our soldiers to accomplish them depends largely on the circumstances they face and the pace at which the enemy can vary the circumstances.

Some critics of the manual believe that it was too heavily influenced by the "classicists" who attempt to apply the Maoist model of insurgency warfare used in "Wars of National Liberation" in the last century. This model assumed progressive stages of insurgent activity, from covert action, to overt action, and finally to conventional action. All were steps aimed at seizing political power.[18]

These critics believe that the insurgents we face do not fit this model, that many have no clearly defined goals, central organizations, or a unified strategy. Many seek simply to disrupt the forces of order or to promote the interests of their coreligionists. We share some of these observations based on our analysis we have presented. The new manual does not take these fully into account.

But there is one central theme with which we strongly agree. That is the requirement to "learn and adapt." A major difficulty in developing counterinsurgency doctrine for the Long War is that it is evolving, takes distinctly different local forms, and we have yet to fully comprehend the nature of our enemy. This does not mean that we will fail, but that it will require that we must learn on the job, led by the dedicated soldiers who are best positioned to devise appropriate counterinsurgency measures to defeat the enemies we face. Years ago we both served together under a remarkable leader, the first commander of TRADOC, who believed that "Army doctrine is what 51 percent of the Army does." The collective wisdom and experience of the men and women in its ranks will eventually be reflected in its doctrine. They will tell us what works. Their lives depend upon it.

America's Army has enormously experienced young leaders who reflect the character of our country and its strengths, including adaptability, individualism, and pragmatism. We have stressed the importance of decentralizing authority to those best positioned to operate effectively. We must listen to them "bottom up" and respond.

NEW COIN STRATEGY IN IRAQ

Whatever doctrinal arguments there are over counterinsurgency, the actual testing ground is our conflict in Iraq. The commander of coalition forces in

Iraq, Gen. David Petraeus, was instrumental in the development of the new manual previously discussed. His return to Baghdad signaled a new strategic approach to defeating the insurgency there. While clearly the ultimate outcome of our efforts cannot be predicted with any certainty, there has been undeniable success in countering those who would destabilize the country. There are distinct features of his approach, which offer promise in fighting the Long War.

During his testimony before congress in September 2007, he made an extremely important point: the defeat of al Qaeda in Iraq requires a combination of conventional forces, Special Forces, and local forces.[19] This is a departure from a strategy that places primary emphasis on targeted strikes against terrorist leaders, and the assumption that successful COIN operations can be achieved by Special Forces and precision weapons almost exclusively. While these remain critical components, of fundamental importance is the aggressive employment of conventional forces, both U.S. and local Iraqi forces, to protect the population from terrorist depredations against the Iraqi people and their leaders. The logic of the "surge" was to provide sufficient conventional forces to make this possible. The security provided by conventional forces enables local Iraqi leaders to assume traditional leadership roles. This has led to dramatic changes in various provinces, most notably Anwar, which was considered all but lost to the central government. This is now spreading to other provinces. There are now counter al Qaeda movements throughout Central Iraq, modeled on the Anwar pattern. Beyond Iraq itself, this has important implications for the future of America's Army. We cannot know the ultimate outcome, but it seems clear that an "either/or" choice between conventional and specialized forces for the Long War is not realistic.

Another significant feature of the new strategy is decentralization. This is a principle we believe is fundamental. While obviously much depends on reconciliation at the national level, a "bottoms up" movement in local areas where the population lives, if aligned with national goals for the nation, introduces a powerful new transformative dynamic. This decentralization is inherent in effective counterinsurgency operations and doctrine. Local units and commanders as well as local community leaders must be empowered to address the challenges as they see them.

This is a major feature of our Teams of Leaders concept. Cooperative and integrated efforts by those closest to the action are needed not only in direct conflict with insurgents, but across a wide spectrum of national security challenges, domestic and international, at all levels of government. As we have pointed out, the security of the homeland is a new "theater" of the Long War. The approaches discussed here are equally relevant and necessary for effective preparation and responses to a potential WMD attack on American soil, as well as for competence in dealing with natural disasters such as Hurricane Katrina. We explore this urgent requirement at length in Chapter 8.

WAGING THE LONG WAR

Its global nature, nontraditional features, and diverse dimensions make the Long War a challenge unique in our history. Can America successfully wage this war? We believe that it can. But it will require major changes in our attitudes and methods. Part of our difficulty is that we are still struggling to comprehend the nature of the new form of warfare and how to conduct it. It is not our purpose to propose tactics with which to combat a specific enemy. Our goal is rather to suggest means by which our national, state, and local institutions, including America's Army, can become more effective in this form of war and in implementing appropriate, effective policies necessary to be so. We believe that in order to be successful, the United States should incorporate the following guidelines into national security policy:

- Decentralize authority and responsibility, consistent with duly constituted legal authorization, and organize and empower regional and local teams of leaders to implement policy.
- Recognize the characteristics of America's Army and seek to achieve national, state, and local best practices comparable to those developed and proven for decades by America's Army. Exploit the capabilities of all U.S. agencies with roles in national security and organize their efforts in coordinated, integrated programs at regional and local levels.
- Apply the above to coordination and integration of national security policies and programs overseas. We must organize for a robust, competent, responsive multilevel, multifunction national overseas presence, again drawing upon post–World War II organizational innovations of the Department of Defense, reinforced by the Department of State as in Partnership for Peace.
- Exploit the capabilities of all U.S. agencies with roles in national security and organize their efforts in coordinated, integrated programs at regional and local levels.
- Work with and through local and indigenous groups, governmental and nongovernmental, to the maximum extent possible in formulating and implementing policies.
- Embrace the revolutionary advances in communications technology, master knowledge and information management technology, and exploit them as operational instruments and weapons. These would operate through high performing teams of leaders advantaging national strengths, including our religious and ethnic diversity, and world-class technological acumen.
- Stimulate local competency-based adaptiveness to new and changing opportunities and challenges at every level of government, throughout the security establishment.
- Understand the characteristics of insurgent elements and exploit their vulnerabilities.

- Foster continuous learning in leaders and organizations.
- Grow, educate, and train adaptive leaders.
- Consider homeland security as an integral part of the Long War.
- Consider media as an instrument of warfare and develop effective means of influencing public perceptions.

These "principles" should be applied throughout the government, establishment and applied as applicable in each agency as appropriate to their roles and capabilities. America's Army will have a large role in providing institutional expertise and muscle to an effective national security strategy, of which successfully waging the Long War is a central requirement. The demands of the Long War highlight a number of these requirements, which is why we emphasize them here.

We have stressed the importance of America's Army in contributing to national security. Does it have the capabilities it needs for the Long War? In our view, in many ways it is the American institution best positioned to live up to the demands of these guidelines, although it has much work yet to be done. But it cannot go it alone. Its strengths are essential, but must be replicated, blended with the strengths of others, and applied much more broadly throughout the government.

While waging the Long War is a major demand, the full national security challenge is broader and will require major changes to meet the full spectrum of defense needs, not only responding to known threats, but to provide hedges against contingencies that can range from unanticipated nuclear weapons in terrorist hands to large-scale conventional conflict with major nation states or domestic attack by weapons of mass destruction (WMD). These are significant requirements in an uncertain world. Successfully hedging against contingencies is a critical need. Failure to do so can have devastating consequences, as history has repeatedly demonstrated. America's Army must take the lead in preparing for many of these contingencies.

Increasingly, international security is put at risk by forces and elements outside the traditional nation-state framework. In numerous societies, people's primary allegiance is to the tribe or to other extranational groups. This is manifest in Afghanistan, Pakistan, Lebanon, and elsewhere. In Iraq there has been a recognition that tribal and religious identities must be part of any serious effort to achieve stability. The decentralized, "bottom up" strategy pursued by Gen. David Petraeus and his command makes tribal loyalty part of the solution rather than the problem. We must adapt to this reality.

We will address in some detail key areas in which America's Army is strengthening its capabilities to meet the full spectrum of security requirements, to include hedges and how they can be improved. The following chapter will describe and assess this institution.

3

America's Army Today

In the preceding chapters we described the radically changing environment the nation faces in providing for national security. Leading instruments for this are the active and reserve components of the United States Army. The Army is unique among American institutions and among the armed services in its complexity and depth. We will describe this institution in some detail—its main characteristics, how it is constituted, and how it is organizing its efforts for a daunting future. Subsequent chapters will deal with the implications of these challenges and efforts.

THE UNIQUENESS OF AMERICA'S ARMY

Landpower

The unique character of America's Army is ultimately derived from its nature as a ground force.[1] Although often at sea and in the air, man is essentially a land being. Responsibility to provide the enduring generational military force required to influence the actions of man on land in accordance with U.S. military policy rests, therefore, exclusively with landpower: the United States Army. Airpower and sea power are absolutely vital to national defense success but they come and go. Their presence is transitory. These forces rarely interact with the inhabitants of an operational theater. The orientation of these vital services is power projection, weapons systems, and the destructions of targets. While these are obviously essential to success, the ultimate goal in warfare is to influence human behavior at every level and across every function of society. Ground forces alone have the capacity to achieve this goal. Firepower and the systems for delivering it are but instruments for reaching this. History is replete with examples of overestimating the effects of bombardment and air strikes on an enemies' will to resist. The most recent was the failure of Israeli Defense Forces to break the power and will of Hezbollah in southern Lebanon. Landpower ensures possession of a capacity for an enduring presence prepared to enforce the national will, whatever force may be required, wherever, across vast continental landmasses. Landpower remains, when all other incentives fail, the bayonet at the throat that mandates human performance consistent with U.S. national objectives. The United States Army is unique as a military service in this country, as well as unique in relation to contemporary armies of all other nations. As such, the United States Army has responsibilities and requirements shared with no other military force, foreign or domestic.

Landpower must reflect the unique characteristics of the United States of America as a democracy, as a nation, as a federal republic, as a state, and as a continent. These characteristics are the practical sources of the nature and capabilities of America's Army—literally a citizen's army. Singly and in combination, these characteristics interact to become strengths molding a unique landpower force. Because of their fundamental importance, each of these strengths needs to be considered in detail—both how they serve to influence the nature of the Army itself and how they frame its responses to current and future challenges.

Democracy

Landpower exists with the consent of the governed. The institution reflects the "will of the people." The Army provides a particular public service—provision of a "citizens' army" governed entirely by civilian institutions.

The fundamental purpose of the Army is to fight and win our nation's wars with unlimited liability of the individual in service to state. Service to nation, up to and including death, sets the military aside as a profession and in the nature of service to the people it serves. It is the custodian of the nation's youth as it prepares them to go in harm's way. Officers, Sergeants, and Soldiers are equally at risk in attaining the military objectives of the United States.

The culture of the individual striving to excel as a member of a disciplined team performing under great stress prevails. Army slogans "Be All You Can Be," "An Army of One," and now "Army Strong" are more than recruiting ploys. They are fundamental expressions of both an individual desire to excel in an absolute meritocracy characteristic of Soldiers at all grades today. They are intended to project the essence of Army service and are aimed at the individual service person. Individual Soldiers are an important deployable strategic resource. By their presence (multiethnic, race, religion, gender) and their demonstrated competence and shared values of service to nation beyond self, they represent what America stands for. They serve and excel, however, as members of cohesive teams accomplishing the task or mission to standard, not letting their team members down. Individuals join, teams fight and win. The Army is teams of winners.

The Army is expected to support—to confirm the merit of if not to lead—national social programs within the framework of national landpower military readiness requirements to the state. After what many thought was a slow start, the Army has become a national leader in developing Soldiers without regard to race, ethnic origin, or (unless proscribed by law) gender. It and the other military services are national leaders in the assimilation of diverse nationalities into the national "melting pot." As a citizen's army, America's Army can be no less than the national model for execution of important national social programs as well as a model of support to domestic defense. It sets the standard.

From its creation the United States has constitutionally separated church and state, yet it is by far the most religious of modern nations. Tolerance of differing individual faiths is ingrained in the American tradition. There is a prevailing "civil religion" that stresses personal freedom and has historically accommodated various religions and beliefs. This is reflected in America's Army. It is diverse in its religious composition and provides opportunities for worship to all. While unofficial, the religious character of the United States and its army is a great source of strength. Samuel P. Huntington in his study of American immigration documents a very high correlation between religious belief and patriotism throughout the modern world. Some 80 to 90 percent of Americans identify themselves as religious. When asked, around 80 percent of Americans say they are patriotic. In contrast, only 25 to 30 percent of Germans claim to be religious. Only 20 percent say they are proud to be German. Similar patterns prevail throughout most of Western Europe.[2] This religious quality of the United States perhaps also makes it better able to understand movements motivated by religion, which is a powerful modern phenomenon.

The Army must be apolitical as an institution yet led by politically sensitive leaders prepared to express the requirements of the profession in a manner persuasive to political leadership while attentive to local political concerns. It must be proactively open to media at all echelons to better inform the citizenry.

Nation

Landpower reflects shared basic values, which in turn are born in national diversity. Reward of competent performance is practiced across boundaries of race, ethnic origin, gender, and religion. Landpower must be absolutely representative of the national population at all grades. The various national, religious, and ethnic elements of the United States as "a nation of nations" are absolutely represented in the Army. Leaders should be developed from all backgrounds and all regions in representative proportions. Landpower presence commits the nation more than that of any other military service because the Army is directly associated with people in their political milieu.[3] Once committed, these popular associations across economic and social strata, both within the United States and in the regions of deployment, are not easily withdrawn.

When American men and women are placed in combat, the nation commits itself far more powerfully than it does by applying air and sea power.

Planes and ships can be quickly and relatively painlessly deployed and withdrawn. Not so with ground forces. They become embedded in the battlefield environment and confront the enemy directly and personally. They are the proxies for the American people. For democracies, this has been historically true for ground forces. On the eve of World War I, Sir Henry Wilson, Chief of British planning, was asked how the British might become fully committed to hostilities. He replied, "Give me one British soldier at the front and I will see that he is killed on the first day of the war."

Federal Republic

The checks and balances of the Constitution—executive, legislative, and judicial—are reflected beneficially in reinforcing military jurisdictions: federal versus state, national versus regional, and individual versus unit as represented in active and reserve forces.

The strength of the United States Army is in the aggregate capabilities of the entire force—active and reserve components—reflecting both individuals and diverse teams and units in nationally and regionally composed organizations at both national and state levels of government, all reinforced by Department of the Army and state civilians and frequently teamed across agencies and service jurisdictions. The strengths of each component need to be drawn upon fully to reinforce strengths and minimize weaknesses such as citizen-soldiers' lack of time or active Army shortages of very focused, highly technical expertise.

Appreciating the unique and truly American institutions, the Army National Guard and the Army Reserve, is an important step to a broader understanding of the power of America's Army. Each component is different, but in a transcendent way all three unite in a common bond—the men and women of the Army in selfless service to the nation. We must, as a nation, preserve and nurture the enduring willingness of Americans to serve in uniform; we must not simply cast the abiding federal-state, national-regional, and individual-unit strengths of any of the three components aside to resolve some transitory contemporary budget or homeland defense challenge. Rather, the interlocking capabilities and practical interdependencies of all three should be reinforced at times of national trial.

If the United States Army did not already possess all three components, it would have to create them because they represent the diversity of governance that is the United States of America. The inherent competition for resources is healthy. Moreover, the "lowest common denominator" of "best landpower practice" for the future is not necessarily the active unit, justifiably dominant as the model for landpower during the Cold War. New threats, including defeating international terrorism, cyber warfare, radical religion, and weapons of mass destruction (WMD), mandate that each component provide capabilities that magnify unique strengths. The whole of landpower capability is much greater than the sum of the individual component parts. This potential must be advantaged in the larger Transformation.

Our focus on what we term "America's Army," the full range of army components as an integrated whole, is not to disregard the vital contributions of our other armed services and agencies to national security, but a conviction that America's Army, as we frame it, this institution, alone, has the essential core capabilities to meet the domestic and foreign needs of tomorrow. The foundation of these is the enduring culture of service to nation, sacrifice, and competence of America's Army. This is the bedrock upon which our efforts must be based. Its strength gives us confidence that in the end we will be serving the nation well.

State

The power of the state confers legitimate use of landpower, seapower, and airpower to win conflicts. The citizenry expects highly credible, disciplined, basic mission proficiency to fight and win, as the national civil leadership requires across a broad spectrum of potential conflict. New threats mandate new capabilities: military, political, economic, and social expertise. Terrorism and WMD are new "old" threats. Homeland security becomes an important landpower responsibility, not greatly different from the Army's practice during westward expansion in the 1880s. An abiding responsibility of America's Army is to look forward, to anticipate new threats, and to be ready when called upon. This responsibility has been reaffirmed since the aftermath of terrorism in New York, Pennsylvania, and Virginia. The possibility of rapidly emerging, unpredictable threats mandates that the Army sustain its mobilization capability to win against any combination of potential landpower threats while providing necessary support to U.S. seapower and airpower.

Continent

The essential global capability and perspective now present within the Army derived, in great measure, from the intensity of commitment overseas since the 1990s. Leaders at all grades possess an extraordinary range of service experience. The Army must be prepared for both inter- and intracontinental force projections under all circumstances of distance, terrain, climate, and population. Our continental character has conditioned our Army to "think big" and to readily identify our interests in global terms. In this, it is similar to the British in its heyday of empire. In our era, only the Soviet Union possessed a comparable international perspective. But now as we move past state to global terrorism (al Qaeda), we face another global perspective. While the most visible and publicly overt threat is continuation of world wide terrorist attacks, that is far from the sum total of what this new development means for our international security. The center of gravity of Islamic extremism lies in the heart of one of the most volatile and strategically significant parts of the world. Much of the world economy depends on access to oil from the Middle East. Furthermore, it constitutes a new form of hostility to our interests, one we have yet to fully comprehend. This is a cultural and religious challenge to our values and our way of life. Consider that even without another attack on our soil since 9/11, American foreign policy has been revolutionized by militant extremism. We are fighting two hot wars; our relations with traditional allies have been severely strained, and American preoccupation and difficulties with Iraq and Afghanistan have emboldened old and new adversaries. In the era of globalization, the perceptions of the strength and vitality of the power of the United States cannot be compartmentalized or confined to one region. We are in a struggle to preserve American preeminence. While the origins of this new threat come from a specific region, its effects on our interests are global. The United States must respond to this unprecedented development with a truly global response, as we did during the Cold War, using all instruments of our national governments and people.

OVERVIEW OF AMERICA'S ARMY: A TOTAL FORCE

Transition and Warfare

The elements of the family of Army components, while distinct in their organization and origins, form an integrated, complementary whole. The most visible and best understood of these is the United States Army, the full-time, combat unit preponderant force that provides the cutting edge of our national defense. A brief description of this component and how it is undergoing fundamental change will follow. How the active force can be made more effective will be an integral part of our analysis. We believe it appropriate, however, to describe the other elements, the Reserves, in some detail as they are less well understood and not adequately considered in security strategy and policy. Throughout the total force, America's Army is in transition, undergoing fundamental changes throughout its structure, while actively engaged in major combat on several fronts. Every component is powerfully impacted by these demands. Each faces major challenges.

The Active Army—Continuity and Change

It is not our purpose here to give a complete and detailed description of the active duty army. Its basic features are well known. It is important to point out that it is an army in transition while fighting. The Army has had a virtually fixed manpower ceiling of around 500,000 (currently it is at 503,000) and a budget constrained at just under $100 billion (not including supplemental appropriations). These fixed limits, given the Army's multiple tasks, have required it to optimize for itself to generate warfighting capability. Much of combat service support functions are placed in the reserve components. These constraints have also dictated an absolute premium on quality and high standards of personal and team performance in combat for every person wearing the uniform. Our volunteer manpower system has facilitated this. Within the resources available to it, the Army must extract the maximum capability possible. The Army has also until recently organized its combat forces around the division structure. It is now reconfiguring its organization around the brigade structure to facilitate greater flexibility in deployment and more efficient use of resources. This is a major change that will be described in a later section. Transformation is not limited to operating combat forces, but extends also to the other army force-generating functions, such as training, logistics, acquisition, accessioning, and financial management.

The consequences of unanticipated long occupations in the Middle East and a manpower-constrained force have placed the active force under great pressures. In Vietnam, the Army saw the debilitating effects of an individual replacement system on unit cohesion and morale and determined to never take that approach again. As a result, we have unit replacements for the force in Iraq and a personnel system designed to manage individual assignment by unit lifecycle. This has worked well, but it places great strains on the comparatively small rotation base. This affects the National Guard as well. In the case of the Reserves, there are limits on the length of time units may be deployed in a given time frame (24 months.) Many units are now approaching these limits. Without expansion of the rotation base, it would be exceedingly difficult to maintain a force of the current size (160,000) in Iraq for very much longer. There are a host of issues confronting the active Army in planning for the future. We will address a number of those we consider most significant in later sections of this book.

The Army National Guard

The reserve components of our armed forces, the National Guard and the Reserves, have their origins in the earliest days of the United States. The Army National Guard is derived from the various state militias of the revolutionary period. It has a dual role, both state and federal. It is subject to the authority of state governors and operates at his/her discretion in meeting the needs of the state in emergencies. Yet it is organically linked to the active military structure. The Guard is armed, equipped, trained, and inspected for competence by the active military. It is highly competent, probably the third or fourth most competent army in the world. It can be federalized by the President to perform national security missions under the command of the Department of Defense. The Army National Guard is represented at the national level by the National Guard Bureau in Washington, D.C.

Repeatedly throughout our history, the Guard has performed alongside active duty forces in times of war. During peacetime, they are integrated into contingency planning by the Department of Defense and undergo extensive joint training and coordination exercises under the direction of the active Army. Federalized Army National Guard units have served with notable distinction in the Balkans, Iraq, and Afghanistan. Today, over 50 percent of Soldiers in the Army National Guard are combat veterans who have trained and performed to identical task, condition, and standard as the active Army. Supporting "Partnership for Peace," the various state National Guards supported by their parent state administrations were the leading edge of influence as the Russian glacis was rolled back to the East after the Cold War. The National Guard made a major practical contribution to the spread of democracy and representative government after the end of the Cold War.

The contribution to the Long War could be equally significant—diverse, volunteer, combat-capable citizen-Soldiers can be powerful national representatives in a clash of civilizations. Their abiding local roots are profoundly nonkinetic; they "get" stability operations abroad and in disaster relief at home. The current Army active and reserve noncommissioned corps and the Army National Guard are arguably the greatest strengths of America's Army today. The Guard is that important.

Limitations were placed on deployment of both active duty and federalized Guard units for law enforcement within the United States as a result of experiences of the Reconstruction Era. The Posse Comitatis Act of 1878 limits intervention of either active duty or federalized reserves without agreement of state authorities to an executive order by the President. New legislation permitting instant call up by the federal government during an emergency is included in the 2007 National Defense Act to mitigate the problem of effectively employing Guard units. But this is highly controversial, and a number of governors are appealing this provision as an encroachment on their constitutional authority. An exception is when a state of martial law has been declared under the Insurgency Act.

This issue is often overblown or misunderstood. The need, exposed by Hurricanes Katrina and Rita, is to make federalized resources available to support local authorities, not to usurp them, including assisting in providing or restoring law and order if requested. In a later chapter, we will discuss at length what we believe is an appropriate role for the Guard and Reserves in major domestic disasters.[4]

The Army Reserve

While the National Guard is geographically and politically based in the states, the Army Reserves are directed federally, nationally by the United States Army Reserve Command. There are a wide variety of reserve commands throughout the country, all commanded by United States Army Reserve general officers. For example, there are regional readiness commands (about to become regional readiness sustainment commands), training divisions, support commands medical brigades, military police brigades, a transportation command, engineer brigades, signal units, and many others. These provide vital functional support backup to active duty and National Guard units.

The components of the total Army have varying jurisdictions derived from their histories and missions. The active Army is federal and national. The Army National Guard is state and regional and often local. The United States Army Reserve (USAR) is federal and regional. It is this unique combination of characteristics that creates America's Army and makes it well suited for providing land combat power to national defense capabilities, as well as for domestic emergencies for the Long War.

The distinctive characteristics of America's Army and its pervasive presence in America are described and illustrated in the Appendix. It is unique among all national institutions.

The contributions of the Reserves to our security have been enormous, although if not well understood. In Iraq, at times some 40 percent of our forces there have been federalized and deployed National Guard units and Army Reserves. In the case of the Georgia National Guard, for example, it recently had 4,500 men and women deployed in Iraq. In the wake of Hurricane Katrina, it dispatched some 2,500 Soldiers for service in disaster relief on the Gulf Coast. The total strength of the Guard is some 350,000. These are "citizen Soldiers" who normally pursue civilian lives and careers. They serve exceedingly well at great personal and often business sacrifice.

The business community itself is a national resource and one with which the reserve components have familiarity and often close ties. During the response to Hurricane Katrina, some firms, such as WalMart, made vital contributions to the effort to support victims and aid recovery. We will make further reference to this later in a discussion of dealing with major domestic emergencies.

Our history over the past decades since the end of the draft has shaped the role of the Reserves. It has been viewed primarily as an augmentation of active forces, providing not only additional residual combat power, but also essential service and support functions. In an era of constrained resources and manpower, this role has allowed the active forces to concentrate on maximizing the combat power of the units on active duty. The need for the Reserves to be combat ready demands that emphasis be placed on that combat readiness aspect, both in equipment and training.

Prior to deployment to a combat theater, guard units are often augmented with equipment, and combat units receive extensive training at the National Training Center at Ft. Irwin, California, the Joint Readiness Training Center at Ft. Polk, Louisiana, or the Joint Multinational Training Command at Hohenfels, Germany. These are very serious training exercises. Prior to Desert Storm, some significant National Guard units were unable to meet the training standards at Ft. Irwin and were not allowed to deploy to the Gulf. Since that time, through intensive training and improved leadership, many of those same units are now performing well in Iraq and Afghanistan after meeting the standards of America's Army at a training center. Increasingly, these are combat-seasoned, first-line Army units by any military standard.

The payoff for that competence is important—a substantial change in mission. In recognition of the abiding excellence of citizen Soldiers, recently they and their units were redesignated as operational forces as well as reserves. The average unit can expect to be deployed in harm's way one year in six.[5] These are not the reserves of the past America's Army—they are an important, uniquely American landpower capability, forged post-9/11.

The increased role of the Reserves on active duty missions raises a number of major issues. While landpower missions must remain transcendent, both 9/11 and Hurricane Katrina remind us that the equally essential role of domestic emergency response must be considered a vital national security requirement. It should be placed on a priority par with power projection abroad. 'Providing for the Common Defense' now faces new challenges. Not only does global terrorism present a new threat. The rapid growth of our major urban areas and increased reliance on motor transport make population control and evacuation far more challenging than even a few decades ago. With increased wealth, multiplication of services, and increasingly interlocking economic activity, our national infrastructure becomes more complex and vulnerable to new forms of disruption. Examples are the too-frequent failures of our electric power grids and the pressures placed on gasoline and natural gas supplies by Hurricanes Katrina and Rita. We are in the midst of change, and we must adapt our military priorities to support beneficial change.

Another issue faces our reserve components. Major, extended, overseas combat deployments raise questions about the sustainability of reserve manpower. In an earlier era, "draft pressure" provided an incentive to join the Reserves as an alternative to active duty. That no longer exits. One of the strengths of the Reserves has been its local character, with community-based units. This creates bonds with the population at large and deep roots within the populace. But it also can mean disproportionately large impacts on specific local economies. It unfortunately can also lead to greater concentration of combat casualties within a given community. Casualties within active forces are spread more generally throughout the population at large. All of these pressures and demands fall most heavily on the Army National Guard. Recruiting for the Guard is now more difficult but with aggressive leadership, both enlistment and reenlistment are holding up well with the force in combat. This vital asset must be preserved.

THE SOLDIERS OF TODAY'S ARMY

The Soldier as the Ultimate Weapons System

America's Army, more than any of the other armed services, is centered on individual Soldiers themselves. This results from the inherent character of land warfare and the almost numberless tasks that Soldiers must be prepared to undertake and that they alone can perform. The Air Force provides pilots to man aircraft. The Navy provides seamen to man ships. While the Army employs numerous weapons systems, its philosophy is to "arm the man (or woman)." It is not to man the system. It is also a team or group endeavor. A skilled pilot relies largely upon his own individual abilities. The commander of a warship must of course rely upon teamwork and leadership to have an effective crew. Yet he has far more centralized control over the environment in which his sailors must operate than does an Army leader. An Army leader, however skilled, must rely upon the performance of his troops for success. They are closest to the enemy and must often act on their own initiative. If they fail, the commander fails. If they succeed, he succeeds. This necessary outlook makes the human composition of the Army of vital importance. This is where one must begin in describing today's army. Who is serving to carry out the strategies outlined earlier?

Army Demographics

The total Army of today consists of just over 1,000,000 Soldiers. More than half serve in the National Guard and Reserve. The active force is 48 percent (503,000). The Guard is 33 percent (346,000). The Reserve is 19 percent (190,000). The social and minority make up of the force tends to reflect the larger society and the trends it undergoes over time. It is of interest to note that new entries into the force in recent years reflect the growing proportion of Hispanics in our nation. Hispanics are expected to soon be the largest single minority group wearing the Army uniform. The past decade has seen an acceleration of this trend. In 2000, black Soldiers amounted to 22 percent of new recruits, and Hispanics 6.5 percent. By 2005, new black recruits had declined to 13.5 percent, while Hispanics had increased to 11.7 percent. This also follows historic patterns of emerging immigrant groups finding opportunity in entering the service. Similar trends are reflected in the commissioned and warrant officer ranks. In terms of the Active Duty Army, the percentage of Hispanic Soldiers serving has more than doubled, while the percentage of black Soldiers has declined. Respectively, the percentages are 20.7 percent and 10.6 percent. The total minority presence in the active force is 38.4 percent. Yet blacks remain more highly represented in today's Army, both in the enlisted and officer corps than in the U.S. population (see Appendix).

Female representation has remained an important but relatively stable percentage of the force. Females are 14 percent of the active Army, 13.5 percent of the Guard, and 23.3 percent of the Reserves. Female Soldiers are less likely to be married than are male Soldiers (45.1 percent versus 56.3 percent overall), but far more likely to be married to someone who is also serving in the military. Male Soldiers are primarily married to civilian women. The male officer corps is overwhelmingly married (71.7 percent) while only about half of female officers are married.[6] In spite of family obligations, female Soldiers are performing exceptionally well in today's Army, including in the combat theater. There have been thousands of single mothers serving in the Mid East. As stated in a recent article: "When war started in Iraq, a generation of U.S. women became involved as never before—in a wider-than-ever array of jobs, for long deployments, in a conflict with daily bloodshed. More than 155,000 women have served in Iraq and Afghanistan. Among their ranks are more than 16,000 single mothers, according to the Pentagon, a number that military experts say is unprecedented."[7]

By historical standards, the active duty Army is well educated. Eighty-four percent of enlisted Soldiers have a high school or equivalent education, and some 7 percent have some college. Almost 60 percent of officers have college degrees, and over 40 percent have advanced degrees.

As mentioned earlier, America's Army is religiously diverse, with a vast majority of Soldiers expressing a religious faith. There are nearly 200 religious organizations represented in the Army, with the majority being affiliated with the Christian faith. In the active Army, 51 percent of Soldiers are Protestant and 21 percent are Catholic (71 percent Christian.) The remainder are affiliated with other religions (2 percent) or do not specify a faith group affiliation (26 percent). The figures for the Guard and Reserve are similar. Sixty-eight percent of Guardsmen are Christian or "other"; 32 percent are unaffiliated. Sixty-seven percent of Reservists are Christian or "other." Thus, the active force is slightly more religious, or claims to be, than the reserve components. As discussed earlier, the widespread spirituality of Americans is reflected in its Army and is a source of strength strongly related to love of country.

It should be understood that the composition and characteristics of the active duty force are ultimately reflected in the reserve components, but with some time lag. There are also features that vary across the components. The demographics of the Guard vary substantially among different state organizations, reflecting the local cultures from which they come.

We Americans are accustomed to the diversity of the Army and take it for granted. Yet it is a major source of strength in a multicultural world, especially during a "clash of civilizations." No amount of high-minded rhetoric can compare with the actual demonstration and practice of tolerance and respect for minorities and women. Consider the dramatic, even revolutionary, example that a black, female company commander provides to a tribal, male-dominated Afghan community. She has respect, authority, and real power over males. She portrays American values in reality. Similarly, the ethnic diversity of America's Army often demonstrates that opportunity is universal in our culture, especially when a Soldier is an immigrant from the culture in which he or she is operating.

Demographics are of course generalizations. A more substantive appreciation for the character of today's Army comes from more direct observation.

Table 1

Race	Number
Caucasian	137
Asian	45
Hispanic	26
African American	7
Native American	5
Other	1

Source: Infantry Training Brigade, Ft. Benning, Georgia, August 2006.

To take a microcosm of the Soldiers joining the force today, a look at an entering group of new recruits into the initial training experience is useful. A recent group of 221 new recruits entering Basic Individual Training at Fort Benning illustrate the larger demographics of the force as a whole, but also illuminate features that larger aggregates statistics may obscure. The group represented some 23 different religious groups (and 2 atheists). It also was consistent with the increasing presence of Hispanics noted earlier. A breakdown by race appears in Table 1. This reveals a somewhat new trend in the makeup of the Army, that of Asian Americans, which were the largest minority group in this particular cohort. While still small at around 4 percent of the force, this group has received little attention. It is expected to become a more significant proportion of the Army in the years ahead.

Soldier Training

After processing and orientation, these new Soldiers begin 14 weeks of basic individual combat training (OSUT, or One Station Unit Training), after which they will undergo further advanced individual and unit training with units at other stations. They are assigned to one of six training companies, each with 12 drill sergeants. The training covers those key critical skills required of the basic combat Soldier. The program is divided into every aspect of weapons employment that they can expect to encounter. This includes not only qualification on a number if weapons, but reaction to chemical or biological attack, man-to-man combat, first aid, preparation of fighting positions, and dealing with new conditions, which are prevalent in Iraq. They are taught land navigation both mounted and vehicular. Emphasis is placed on urban operations, such as entering buildings. Battlefield communications are taught stressing those required within small units in combat. All of these skills are tested and trained in numerous battle drills, which are conducted under realistic conditions. Lessons learned in current operations are rapidly incorporated into the training program. For example, today's Soldiers are trained to deal with improvised explosive devices (IEDs), which are used by Iraqi insurgents against our forces. The Army also exploits direct feedback from veterans of recent combat in leader training.

One measure of the intensity of initial training is the use of live ammunition. When a Soldier graduates from basic training at Ft. Benning, he will have fired his weapon at the human form with lethal intent more than 2,000 times in various marksmanship and live fire training exercises.[8] This is represents a major increase since before 9/11.

Given the demands placed on new trainees, it is remarkable that the success rate is so high. Approximately 95 percent of new recruits complete the program. This is due in part to strenuous efforts made to retrain and assist Soldiers having difficulty. And they came because they want to fight for their country. Many cite 9/11 as their motivation. Manpower is a vital resource and must be preserved whenever possible. An example is the new way in which sick or injured Soldiers are handled. Until recently, they were sent home on sick leave. But today, they are placed in a clinic at the training center until they have recovered. Fewer are discouraged or distracted from their goal of serving, thus fewer drop out.

Lethality

The Soldier in the Army of today is the best equipped in the history of warfare. He is virtually a one-man arsenal. Basic Soldiers are trained to employ some fourteen different weapons systems. One observer suggested that an individual combat infantryman of today has firepower greater than that of an entire 300-man rifle company of World War II. For example, the warhead of the AT-4, a shoulder-fired, antitank rocket can pierce a wall of steel from a mile away. Using the grenade launcher on his M-16, the Soldier can launch seven grenades a minute with enough explosive power to destroy a vehicle from blocks away. Yet the weaponry is becoming even more lethal. The replacement for the M-16 is the new M4. This has a night vision accessory that includes both infrared and thermal imaging within a single scope. Never in history has a Soldier been so armed as today's basic infantryman.

Values

Merely describing the training program, however, does not portray the essence of what the new Soldier is undergoing. The entire process is designed to transform young people from civilian life into highly disciplined and lethal fighters, from infantrymen to truck drivers and cooks. From the first day, the recruit is subjected to constant and relentless conditioning that subordinates individual preferences and desires to those of the unit. Day and night the Soldiers, male and female, are conditioned to consider their own performance as essential to the survival of the organization. Rewards and punishment are meted out accordingly. Frequent inspections require absolute adherence to standards. Physical activity is near constant.

Few Americans realize the intensity and depth of the conditioning that the young Soldiers undergo to become accepted as qualified members of the units they will join. He lives in a constant state of awareness that he is being observed and tested. His weapon becomes an extension of himself, almost literally. Long gone are company "arms rooms" where weapons were secured during off duty hours. In basic training today, the Soldier sleeps with his M-16. It is never out of his or her sight. There is strong emphasis on reinforcing a common value system among the diverse members of a training company. Indeed, the training command's "Big Five" are mental and physical toughness, marksmanship, first aid, disciplined teamwork (battle drills), and the Warrior Ethos—Army Values. These values are repeated endlessly and are memorized by the trainees. Each Soldier carries a card listing these values, derived from "The Soldiers Creed."

> I am an American Soldier.
> I am a Warrior and a member of a team.
> I serve the people of the United States and live the Army values.
> I will always place the mission first.
> I will never accept defeat.
> I will never quit.
> I will never leave a fallen comrade.
> I am disciplined, physically and mentally tough, trained and proficient in my warrior tasks and drills. I always maintain my arms, my equipment and myself.
> I stand ready to deploy, engage, and destroy the enemies of the United States of America in close combat.
> I am a guardian of freedom and the American way of life.
> I am an American Soldier.

This is the creed of all Army Soldiers, not only the combat arms. It applies equally to Soldiers in combat service support and combat support units. This reflects the necessity for a unified culture across the Army, as well as the nature of the modern battlefield where there is often no clear distinction between the "front lines" and the rear echelon. All are in it together.

Elite units and specialties of the Army in earlier periods were distinctive in their more rigorous standards and ethos. And today, individual Rangers and Ranger units do set a high standard for the Army as a whole. But these Rangers and others are older, with more time in service and rank than the ordinary young enlistee. The Ranger Creed includes the following: "A Ranger is a more elite soldier who arrives at the cutting edge of battle by land, sea, or air. I accept the fact that as a Ranger my country expects me to move further, faster, and fight harder than any other soldier."

What is significant is that Ranger-type values have been approximated across the total Army. This is a huge transformation. It is also to some extent the consequence of having an all-volunteer force. All Soldiers are there willingly and accept and expect high standards.

There is major emphasis placed on traditions and the valor of Soldiers of the past. Earlier, the diverse backgrounds of the recruits were described. The focus on values is one aspect of an organizational need to transcend disparate experiences and attitudes. Perhaps more important, the unremitting pressures placed on the new Soldiers to perform and meet the demands of the unit leave little time or inclination for pursuit of individual preferences. Actions and reactions become conditioned reflexes. But it is more than that. It is a functional necessity for the cohesiveness and unity need for survival and success on the battlefield whether kinetic combat operations or nonkinetic stability support operations.

It is hard to overstate the significance of the entry training being discussed. Each year the Army produces some 20,000 basic Soldiers from this process. This sets the tone for Army values as a whole. The Army is of course much larger and more diverse than the world of basic combat training. But this is the professional core of our ground forces and the ultimate key to American world power. Few nations of the world have the will and the human resources to field Soldiers in such numbers year after year, and employ them on distant battlefields. This is all the more remarkable given that we have an all-volunteer force in time of war. Willingness to serve has more than simply sustained the force. It has enabled us to increase the overall strength by some 30,000 Soldiers. And these values of service beyond self and expectations of competent performance to standard abide in thousands of retirees still eager to serve post-9/11 supporting federal, state, or local government—an important national resource post-9/11.

The Army in American Life

To many, if not most, Americans, the Army is an enduring but vague presence in their lives. While it is all-consuming for its members, its totality and complexity is not well understood by most citizens. It comes into visibility sporadically when it is thrust into prominence by events, or when it impinges directly upon the lives of individuals themselves or of those they know. Yet the public holds it in remarkably high regard, in contrast to the low esteem accorded to most other national institutions. In part, this is due to its long history of selfless service to country with virtually no hint of any challenge to civil authority, even during national crises.

America's Army is a true child of the people. It springs from the populace as a whole and generally reflects the demographic make up of the nation itself. Americans for the most part simply assume that it is a benevolent, trustworthy force that can be counted on serve the public interest without fanfare. It is above partisanship in a time if great political controversy in our nation. All of this is of course an enormous achievement and benefit both to the Army and the public. Yet this military institution faces enormous challenges in fulfilling its duties to the country in this time of extraordinary commitment.

TODAY'S ARMY'S GOALS

The Army Game Plan

The Army has identified four overarching, interrelated strategies for achieving its goals for the nation in its 2006 "Army Game Plan":

- Provide Relevant and Ready Landpower.
- Train and Equip Soldiers and Adaptive Leaders.
- Sustain an All-Volunteer Force.
- Provide Infrastructure and Support.[9]

In the preface to this plan, the Army leadership, the Army Chief of staff, the Sergeant Major of the Army, and the Secretary of the Army state the challenge directly: "We serve the nation in a time of great danger and unique opportunity. We are fighting an enemy determined to reduce America's presence in the world and to destroy the freedoms we enjoy.... This is a pivotal time. The progress we make over the next 12 to 18 months will determine our ability to continue to accomplish our mission and to position ourselves for the 21st century.... Our window of opportunity, however, is not assured. As support for supplemental funding diminishes, and budget pressures intensify, we will experience downward fiscal pressure."

The strategic goals stated above are quite general. They have to be to encompass the broad range of tasks facing our leadership. They also reflect the dynamic and fluctuating environment in which we find ourselves. What is "relevant" land power, and how do we provide it? We have seen the war in Iraq evolve from an initial conventional operation to a complex mixture requiring counterinsurgency and nation building. The same Soldiers must deal with both forms of conflict. We are seeing in Lebanon the emergence of non-state, highly armed militias conducting a nontraditional form of asymmetric warfare not previously faced in the Middle East. This may be a harbinger of the future.

Providing Relevant and Ready Landpower

The Army Game Plan for providing more relevant and ready forces is not merely rhetoric. In a radical departure from tradition, the Army is transforming to create an active and reserve component pool of 70 modular Brigade Combat Teams, reinforced by over 200 modular Support Brigades. In the future, brigades—not divisions—can "plug into" joint and coalition task forces in expeditionary and campaign settings.

This transformation is well under way. As of May 2006, some thirty-seven Brigade Combat Teams were converted to a modular form. The leadership also calls for an increase of 30,000 Soldiers. These reorganized forces will be equipped through an ambitious materiel development and acquisition program. The Game Plan calls for "over 350,000 pieces of equipment, including 615 aircraft; 7,000 combat vehicles; and 30,000 wheeled vehicles." The leadership commits itself to fully funding continuous modernization through the Future Combat Systems program that includes a new class of manned and unmanned air and land vehicles. Sustaining development of advanced technologies also is given a high priority. The program is vast, and larger because much of the existing Army is worn out and must be rebuilt (reset). That reset alone is expected to cost some $40 billion. The overall intent is to ensure that America's Army will retain its position as the preeminent landpower on earth prepared to respond to multiple global contingencies simultaneously.

Training and Equipping Soldiers and Leaders

The Army leadership fully recognizes the complexity of the challenges facing Soldiers of the future. This leads to the need to determine how best to train and equip our Soldiers, and to have leaders who can adapt to rapid change: "We are preparing our Soldiers for the rigors of war and leaders with skills to serve as multi-skilled 'pentathletes' amidst complexity and uncertainty." This is not easy for a large, hierarchical institution. It can only accomplish these tasks under leaders and trainers who themselves accurately envision the demands of future battlefields and put into place actual programs which help us to prepare for them. Measures underway affect every area of training: improving NCO training; junior officer education, to include more civil schooling; and stressing a "warrior first" approach using battle drills to ensure Soldiers are prepared for combat. The extensive training establishment is also undergoing major change. The traditional branch oriented character of service schools is being eliminated. For example, historically, Ft. Benning, Georgia, has been the Infantry Center. Ft. Knox, Kentucky, has been the Armor Center. These are being combined and transformed into "The Maneuver Center" to be located at Ft. Benning. Officers with infantry and armor affiliations will now be trained together. Branch identity is becoming less significant. Similar changes are taking place in the remainder of the training establishment following comparable refocusing and improvement of officer and noncommissioned officer professional development. All officers attend residential courses at the Command and General Staff College at its various campuses. There has been significant increase in opportunities for graduate school in humanities, increases in opportunities to attend foreign institutions to assimilate foreign cultures and increases in support to language proficiencies—all appropriate to leader development retuned for the Long War. These programs of continuing education are unmatched in any other agency of the federal government.

Sustaining the All-Volunteer Force

The Army Game Plan states, "We are sustaining the volunteer force being tested for the first time in history in a long war." The all-volunteer force has proven to be a remarkable success and is a key factor in the creation of the highly professional and quality Army serving America today. We were both field grade officers serving in command and staff positions at the inception of "VOLAR," the all-volunteer army. The draft was a casualty of the Vietnam War. The unpopularity of the war forced an historic change in manpower policy. The ending of college deferments resulted in widespread unrest on college campuses across the nation and lent support to those who opposed the war. In an unprecedented move, the United States fundamentally altered its manpower policy in the midst of a major war. Its success was not guaranteed. In addition to questioning whether adequate troops would be provided through volunteerism, there were also broader issues relating to how a volunteer "professional" Army would relate to American society and its values. There was some concern that a professional Army would become less a part of the fabric of American life and would remove constraints on policymakers in employing the Armed Forces in pursuit of security goals. There was also fear that a volunteer force would be less representative of the public and foster a culture of militarism.

None of these fears have been realized. Not only has this system provided adequate manpower; if anything, the Army and its Soldiers enjoy unprecedented esteem and support for the American people even as the nation is engaged in a highly controversial war in Iraq. This is tribute not only to the American people, but also to the Army leaders who led America's Army through this great experiment and its aftermath.

Perhaps unexpectedly, the change induced major changes in attitudes and psychology regarding enlisted Soldiers. The Army had to attract young people to its ranks and compete for them in the broader economy. It reinforces the powerful emphasis on placing the Soldier first and creating and maintaining an institution that will earn his or her loyalty and dedication. For example, the Game Plan includes "Promoting a sense of belonging-to units and communities-that build readiness, cohesion, and reduces uncertainty." Not widely recognized is how this system affects the qualitative character of the force. Earlier we pointed out the intensity of training and mastery of skills required of the enlisted persons of the Army. Were we to return to the draft, with perhaps shorter enlistments, and with at least a portion of service persons serving against their will, such demanding standards as now prevail would be difficult to sustain. It is our view that the Army and the nation are well served by the volunteer force and agree that major resources are justified in nurturing it.

The recruiting demands are large. The goals stated are to "Achieve an active component recruiting goal of 80,000 and retention goal of 64,000; an Army National Guard recruiting goal of 70,000 and retention goal of 34,900; and an army Reserve recruiting goal of 36,000 and retention goal of 16,900." With few exceptions, the Army has been successful in attaining these objectives. The enduring challenge for our leadership is to sustain the necessary level of resource commitment to continue to attract and retain the appropriate numbers and qualities of Soldiers needed in the face of relentless competition for resources for other programs which also have powerful claims on the Army budget.

Providing Infrastructure and Support

The Army Game Plan pledges "Full funding for Army installations and support to execute a carefully synchronized plan to achieve a new global basing posture, while fulfilling the requirements of the National Military Strategy." This is no easy task. The Armed Forces of the United States are undergoing extensive repositioning and realignment in adapting to the post–Cold War geopolitical situation and to accommodate the Army's own restructuring. This impacts not only our mission effectiveness, but is a significant element in shaping the quality of life vital to sustaining the volunteer force and the families of our service persons. For example, the 2007 Army budget allocates over $1 billion to family housing construction. This is only a small part of the overall effort. The Army operates bases, camps, posts, stations, and other installations worldwide that support all components. That is a massive management requirement.

An important innovation is a concerted effort to reengineer business practices throughout the service. In addition, in recent years installation management has been given increased professional status with greater recognition for those leaders who operate in this important area. This is another area that at times loses out to higher operational and material priorities in competition for resources. The Army leadership is correct in elevating it to one of the four "pillars" of its Game Plan. It is not glamorous, but it is vital.

PRIORITIES FOR THE FUTURE

These elements of the Army Game Plan represent the established priorities for the Army as it moves forward. They are reiterated with remarkable consistency throughout the institution. While general in nature, they encompass the full spectrum of programs that are essential to success in the future. In the chapters that follow, we will address in some detail a number of areas within these priorities that require special emphasis.

IMPLEMENTING THE ARMY GAME PLAN

The elements of the Army Game Plan represent the broad priorities for the Army as it moves forward.[10] To meet these priorities requires a fully integrated plan of initiatives—a number of carefully synchronized programs that all contribute to building tomorrow's Army. Like the strands of a rope, these are intertwined and mutually reinforcing. They are to translate goals into reality. These cover virtually every aspect of the total Army. They are briefly summarized here to provide substantive content to the Army Plan described earlier. In later chapters, we will address in more detail a number of areas within these programs and issues they raise that require special emphasis.

The Army Force Generation Model (ARFORGEN)

ARFORGEN is a readiness model for both active and reserve components. It is the central tool for integrating the Army's four overarching strategies. Its purpose is to enable the Army to provide rapidly deployable and employable forces to combatant commanders and civil authorities on a sustained basis. These tailored forces and capability packages will fill specific mission requirements.

Among the advantages AFORGEN will yield when fully implemented are:

- A continuous supply of eighteen to nineteen trained and ready modular brigades.
- Stabilized personnel to train, deploy, and fight together in the same unit.
- Assured, predictable access to reserve units to meet operational requirements.
- Reduced postmobilization reorganization and training time for reserve units.
- A system of cyclic readiness to allocate resources based on unit deployment schedules.
- More predictable unit deployments that will benefit Soldiers, families, and civilian employers.
- Deployment planning that will help to reduce the burden on high-demand, low-density units.
- The opportunity to synchronize a broad range of institutional Army processes.

Clearly, ARFORGEN is of central importance in an era of multiple deployments, extensive use of all Army components, and constrained resources. It enables units to deploy in more predictable patterns and helps to retain the ability to surge combat power to meet unanticipated strategic requirements. It also helps to retain the flexibility to provide units and capability to conduct State and Homeland Security operations and to provide military support to civil authorities (such as disaster relief).

In general terms, Army "Expeditionary" Forces fall into and potentially cycle through three categories:

- Deployed expeditionary forces
- Contingency expeditionary forces capable of rapid deployment
- Ready expeditionary forces designed to train and prepare for potential future operational requirements

All elements of America's Army fall into one of these categories and are trained and supported accordingly.

Future Combat Systems (FCS)

A transformed force, expected to perform across the range of military operations requires modern equipment for the Army to remain the preeminent landpower on earth. FCS is designed to replace forty-year-old equipment designed to defeat Cold War enemies. It extensively exploits advanced and emerging technologies, especially electronic. FCS plans four discrete "spin outs" of capabilities at two-year increments to the current force:

- *Spin Out One* is designed to increase situational awareness and provide actionable intelligence. It includes unattended ground sensors, non-line-of-sight launch systems, and intelligent munitions.
- *Spin Out Two* is to improve Soldier protection and weapons precision through the use of more unmanned sensors, primarily unmanned aircraft systems.
- *Spin Out Three* provides further increases in Soldier protection and precision with the emphasis on unmanned ground vehicles. Assault and reconnaissance, countermine and transport, and man-portable robotics are prominent features.
- *Spin Out Four* completes the total network of systems and equipment and is to improve the accuracy and responsiveness of joint systems supporting the Soldier.

The Army plans to equip fifteen new Brigade Combat Teams with the full complement of FCS by 2014 and to equip the remainder of the force with selected technologies and capabilities as appropriate.

Brigade Centric Modular Force

One of the most far-reaching Army programs is the conversion of its forces, both active and reserves, into a modular brigade-based structure. It is called "modular" because it will on self-contained, full-spectrum units that can be plugged in larger forces, including joint forces, providing the capability to respond quickly and effectively to meet the specific circumstances of a crisis. Traditionally, the Army has been a mixture of organizations, with the division as the basic formation consisted of multiple types of brigade combat teams (Heavy, Infantry, Airborne, or Air Assault). A number of active brigade combat teams were routinely not ready for immediate deployment, the twenty-seven Divisional and Separate combat brigades were designated for the Strategic Reserve and not ready or intended for immediate deployment. The

Army goal is to "fully man, fully equip, and fully train all of our units." One of the most striking changes involves the Reserves. "Our reserve component is no longer a reserve force requiring extensive time to prepare people and equipment for deployment. Our reserve is now an operational force." This conversion is intended to provide a more ready and flexible force to meet the demands of the new era.

Specifically, by 2010 the Army plans to field seventy Brigade Combat Teams and more than 200 Support Brigades of various types to meet requirements for expeditionary and expanded State and Homeland security operations:

- The Active component will maintain forty-two Brigade Combat Teams and seventy-five Support Brigades.
- The Army National Guard will continue to maintain 106 brigades. The new mix will be twenty-eight Brigade Combat Teams and seventy-eight Support Brigades.
- The Army Reserve will maintain fifty-eight Support Brigades.

Repositioning the Force

The stationing of Army forces in the United States and worldwide is largely the product of history. Abroad, most forces have been stationed based on the requirements of the Cold War and of the containment strategy that the nation implemented. Our forces in South Korea and Europe are prominent examples of this. Numerous factors have influenced domestic basing, including political and economic considerations, and again the forces of history, such as the Civil War and westward expansion. Increasingly, however, the need to more closely align our posture with the demands of a new security era has become more apparent. In the Army's words, "We are adjusting our global posture to better meet the needs of the combatant commanders.... Our effort will posture our forces, logistics activities, and power projection to respond to the demands of a complex, uncertain future and will enhance the flow of forces to and from current global commitments."

A number of influences and programs converge to shape the Army effort, and must be reconciled within a comprehensive stationing plan. The plan upon which the Army is embarked integrates and synchronizes Base Realignment and Closure (BRAC) mandated by Congress, the Integrated Global Presence and Basing Strategy (IGPBS), which Department of Defense initiated to transcend Cold War legacies, and the Army Modular Force (AMF) initiatives, described earlier. It also offers an opportunity to improve the quality of life for Soldiers and their families. The plan integrates initiatives to create the infrastructure required for the foreseeable future. Goals for funding are:

- Use existing infrastructure to reduce costs and excess capacity,
- Minimize use of temporary facilities,

- Place priority on barracks, housing, motor pools, ranges, and training facilities.

Starting in 2007, the Army is repositioning major elements of the operational force. Forces in the United States will be based on the factors of training facilities and power projection capabilities. In Europe and the Pacific, it will maintain a smaller forward presence. In the Middle East and elsewhere, a rotational presence will be maintained, eliminating many permanent bases.

Growing Adaptive Leaders—the "Pentathlete"

Army leaders must be multiskilled—"pentathletes"—if they are to succeed if the complex environment of today. Earlier, we mentioned the wide array of weapons systems the individual Soldier must master. Equally challenging is the range of operations and activities Soldiers and their leaders must perform. Consider that in the current era, Army forces are called upon to prevail in conventional combat, counterinsurgency, nation building, disaster relief, and many other contingencies, often more than one of these occurring simultaneously. The Army is continuing to evolve its training and education systems to grow adaptive leaders, military and civilian, who are comfortable with leading during times of change and uncertainty. Recognizing that intellectual change precedes physical change, the Army has chartered a task force to review education, training, and assignments for leaders. It will recommend changes to assess and improve all processes with a view toward producing "pentathletes"—leaders all.

The *characteristics* sought in adaptive leaders are:

- Strategic and creative thinker
- Builder of leaders and teams
- Competent full spectrum warfighter or accomplished professional who supports the Soldier
- Effective in managing, leading and changing large organizations
- Skilled in governance, statesmanship and diplomacy
- Understands cultural complexity and works effectively across it

The *attributes* required are:

- Sets the standard for integrity and character
- Confident and competent decision maker in uncertain situations
- Emphatic and always positive
- Professionally educated and dedicated to lifelong learning
- Effective communicator

Resetting the Force

Extended major combat operations have placed tremendous strains on Soldiers and equipment. The reset program is designed to address the effects of combat stress on equipment and to prepare equipment and Soldiers for future missions. The program has four major areas:

- Bringing all equipment to Army readiness standards.
- Upgrading capability from prewar levels based on Operation Iraqi Freedom and Operation Enduring Freedom lessons learned.
- Replacing battle losses and washed-out equipment.
- Reorganizing resetting units into a modular design.

The goal is to return active component unit equipment readiness to Army standards within 180 days after redeployment and reserve component unit equipment within 360 days. Numerous units are in various stages of the reset program. It is vast. The requirement for 2006 was for $5 billion to reset 350,000+ pieces of equipment including 616 aircraft, 7,000 combat vehicles, and 30,000 wheeled vehicles. The overall requirement is far larger and growing.

Rebalancing and Redistributing Forces

The emerging security environment requires adjusting the mix of capabilities within the total Army establishment. The aims are to:

- Divest Cold War structure to better fight the Global War on terror.
- Relieve stress on high-demand units.
- Improve readiness and deployability of units.
- Free up Soldiers to deploy by executing military to civilian conversion.

Altering the mix of units will see a reduction of units including Field Artillery, Air Defense, Engineer, Armor, and Logistic. There will be increases in units of Military police, Transportation, Petroleum/Water Distribution, Civil Affairs, Psychological Operations, and Biological Operations. Clearly, the Army's experiences in the Middle East has had a marked impact with greater resources being allocated to "nation-building" type capabilities.

Stabilizing Soldiers and Units

The unprecedented operational tempo since 9/11 has created enormous pressures on Soldiers, their families, and their units. In both the active and reserve components many individuals and units have served multiple tours in the combat theaters. The Army is making every effort to bring an order of stability and predictability to military life while meeting its national security obligations. This is one of the purposes of the transformation to a modular force.

It enables the Army to spread deployments over a wider array of units and allow them to be placed on more predictable rotations. It also plans to keep Soldiers assigned to units for longer periods of time. This will enhance unit cohesion and allow Army families deeper roots in their local communities.

The challenge is made more complex by the nature of the threat we face beyond that of conventional conflict with known potential adversaries. Non-state organizations using terrorist tactics may strike at any time, any place, retreating by blending into civilian population. Predictions are difficult. But the Army can and is attempting to normalize life within the unit and the Army, and at least mitigating the effects of this new era.

Lifecycle Management

The programs described above are being implemented concurrently with waging major conflicts thousands of miles from the United States. This places an enormous strain on the Soldiers and the units who must carry out their difficult missions. It is extremely important that the Army stabilize the force in the midst of multiple challenges and deployments. A major lesson of the Vietnam experience was the damage caused by sustaining the large presence in Southeast Asia through individual replacements. While divisions and separate brigades were stationed permanently in the theater, after the initial deployment of one year, the Soldiers within these units were rotated in and out as individuals. A Soldier would arrive at his assigned unit in Vietnam as an anonymous newcomer. His comrades and his leaders were strangers with no shared experience. This eventually had devastating effects on morale and unit cohesion. It took years to overcome this legacy in the post-Vietnam Army.

Today's Army has addressed this problem through Lifecycle Management. This synchronizes flow of officers, noncommissioned officers, and new Soldiers so that the right numbers of personnel, with the correct occupational specialties arrive at their unit at the same time. They are then stabilized for a three-year tour together. Obviously this must be integrated with the force generation program (ARFORGEN), which establishes the training, readiness, and deployment of the units to which they are assigned. All of this represents an extremely complex personnel issue. But it is worth it. The cohesion, discipline, and high re-enlistment rates reflect the improved morale and professionalism of today's Army in contrast to that of the latter days of Vietnam.[11]

The Army Game Plan, initiated in 2006, continues to be implemented vigorously. However, Army leadership is paying increased attention to the pressures borne by Army families as a result of continued extended deployments and the increased tempo of operations. Some remedies are incorporated in "The Army Soldier Family Action Plan." These include high-priority programs in a number of key areas: family housing, health care for Soldiers and their dependents, education and employment programs for family members, and family support and readiness programs that provide increased funding for

Army Community Services and other organizations. These are key requirements for sustaining the force and attracting and retaining quality Soldiers for the All-Volunteer Force. These programs extend to all components of America's Army, both active and reserve.[12]

THE CHALLENGES TO AMERICA'S ARMY

In the preceding two chapters, we described the unprecedented changes taking place in the global environment. As a premier instrument of our national security, America's Army is at the forefront of meeting the challenges of the future. In Chapter 1, we concluded that the United States requires major changes in our security policies and how they are implemented if it is to successfully serve the interests of the American people. We suggest a more flexible, comprehensive, security strategy that transcends the formulations of the Cold War. We propose an updated policy of active containment, which can embrace the full spectrum of international threats and requirements.

While some of the problems we face are unprecedented, such as international terror, as a global power our nation must continue to maintain its capabilities to act effectively across a broad range of more traditional obligations. These include the needs for robust conventional forces, and maintenance of our nuclear deterrent. It must also continue to perform a variety of missions in support of our alliances and diplomatic interests abroad. America's Army must support these obligations, and do so with constrained resources. For the United States and for America's Army, this will require greater flexibility and adaptability in an era of shifting alliances and evolving threats.

The transformation to more deployable and flexible units has improved the Army's ability to meet this requirement. To meet many others, the Army must seriously develop hedges for uncertain major contingencies that are difficult to meet with constrained resources. These include the capacity for fielding larger conventional forces than are currently available within manpower constraints, major domestic disasters, nuclear conflict and others. We address this issue in later chapters. In our view America's Army should undertake serious efforts in the areas of hedging and contingency to meet this need. We believe the Army Plan is seriously addressing the material and human needs for a new era.

In Chapter 2, we described the new threat of global jihadism. We stress that this evolving threat will demand more adaptive leaders, and continuous learning by individuals and the organization as a whole. An area requiring priority attention is the development of counter insurgency doctrine. The Army is making progress. But the continued evolution of the insurgency threat and the structure of terrorism are yet to be fully addressed in our doctrine. It must also continue efforts in the area of the mastering and exploiting of management and information technology as a means of countering this threat. These are ongoing efforts in America's army, and we devote several chapters to these later.

One of our primary goals is a far more effective implementation of security policy. We believe America's Army can offer both a model for this, and make key contributions to it. We discuss improving effectiveness through employing Teams of Leaders given appropriate support and authority to implement national policy at the local, national, and regional levels.

4

Sustaining Excellence: The Volunteer Force

THIS CHAPTER ADDRESSES the central issue of developing leaders for the all-volunteer Army. It will describe and suggest a number of programs and initiatives we believe are required for long-term success in this effort. But it must be fully understood that these are to be implemented within a unique institution with a unique culture. It involves far more than simply creating training programs and focusing on technical competence, although these are essential. We described the special characteristics of the components of America's Army in Chapter 3. Although the active components (ACs) and reserve components (RCs) have distinct organizational differences, they are bound together by and within a common set of values that unites them in purpose and a shared commitment to their institutions and service to the nation. These are not the province only of senior combat leaders but must pervade the force throughout all ranks and all elements of America's Army. The large and extended commitment of the RCs, particularly the National Guard, to operations in the Middle East has reinforced and accelerated common professional values throughout the total force. While the active Army must remain its heart and source of standards, the profession itself has been substantially enlarged.

This distinct culture is derived from the nature and purposes of the American military profession.[1] Samuel P. Huntington in *The Soldier and the State* identifies the core requirement of our profession as the "management of violence."[2] This is the service the profession provides to the American people. The nation, in pursuit of a democratic and secure society, rules out the use of violence save for those in which it places special trust and confidence. The United States confers on its military the authority to exercise violence on its behalf, including the taking of life and the inherent ferocity and suffering of combat. Soldiers of our country must be trained in and routinely must undertake actions that would be criminal if they were not sanctioned by society and civilian leadership.

This carries a heavy burden and enormous moral obligations. For as instruments of American democracy, our Soldiers must not only be effective in combat but must also conduct themselves and their actions in a manner that is consistent with deeply held American values. The Army must take ordinary citizens and convert them into highly effective warriors who are leaders, while conditioning them not only to the rigors of such service but also imbued with the deeply ingrained values that are the source of America's strength. This is an enormous leader development challenge that cannot be delegated by the Army to some other contract organization. The Army must train itself to be effective in the management of violence while ingraining common values in all elements of the force, including restraint in the face of life threatening dangers on the field of battle.

Aside from the United States Marine Corps, no other institution in America is faced with such a difficult leadership challenge. This imposes arduous moral choices on Soldiers, especially those in command. In his historical novel of the Civil War, Michael Shaara attributes to Robert E. Lee the view that generals must be "killer angels."[3] They must submit to death and destruction the very instruments that they create and lead in order to prevail in their missions. This is a terrifying but essential requirement of military leadership. It is a responsibility faced everyday by our military leaders of all ranks in the ongoing conflicts in the Middle East.

This unique requirement helps to explain much of the behavior of our Army and its emphasis on intangibles. Ceremonies, unit symbols, decorations, protocols, traditions, battle flags, attention to details of dress, and a host of other common elements of military life all serve to reinforce the culture of service, discipline, loyalty to unit, and commitment, whether this is consciously recognized or not. The all-enveloping culture must transcend individual traits that could weaken unit effectiveness.

America's Army reflects also the diversity of American society. It has been extraordinarily effective in accommodating persons of widely varying backgrounds and characteristics and incorporating them into a broader cultural milieu, making diversity a vital strength rather than a distracting weakness. Its diversity offers great promise, especially in our noncommissioned officer corps in interacting with other cultures in the Long War. The Army has a proud record for its successes in race relations, and expanding the participation of women are models for the nation as a whole.[4] This is made possible by the absolute primacy of organizational effectiveness for mission accomplishment, and by the disciplined and hierarchical nature of the military. These enable it to demand and enforce standards of behavior without challenging individual beliefs. Any behavior detrimental to unit performance and cohesion is unacceptable regardless of personal preferences. A Soldier's identity must be defined by the uniform itself. The Army has a distinct culture, but it evolves over time as American society undergoes changing attitudes. In the case of sexual preferences, for example, public attitudes have been undergoing substantial alteration. America's Army will accommodate itself to this as it has to other social developments. But it must do so in its own way, in a manner that preserves its integrity and effectiveness for mission accomplishment.

Earlier in this book, again in Chapter 3, we described the continuous emphasis on warrior values, such as the Ranger ethos. This is not necessarily an attempt to make the entire force elite, but is one of a host of efforts to make excellence the aspiration of every Soldier.

One of the most profound and beneficial changes for the Army has been the professionalization of the noncommissioned officer corps since Vietnam. It is a truism that NCOs are the backbone of the Army. They are the front-line leadership upon which all else depends. They are the principle trainers and role models for Army Soldiers. Yet we can recall the era when there was virtually no coherent career path for enlisted Soldiers. The highest formal rank was master sergeant; there were few professional education opportunities; and the position of Command Sergeant Major was not formally recognized. The professionalization of the NCO corps has in effect expanded America's military profession. This has taken place in all components of America's Army, to the great benefit of each component.

This professionalization applies not only to those now serving on continuing active duty. It has occurred equally in the RCs. It also applies to the many retired veterans. This has thus provided a core of competence and service to nation present throughout every American community. This is an enormous resource, one which is of special potential importance to homeland security.

Huntington concludes his book with the following: "Upon the soldiers, the defenders of order, rests a heavy responsibility. The greatest service they can render is to remain true to themselves, to serve with silence and courage in the military way. If they abjure the military spirit, they destroy themselves first and their nation ultimately."[5] One of the most painful consequences of the Vietnam War for military professionals was the threat to essential Army values by the potential erosion of discipline. It has been an historic achievement that America's Army has overcome that difficult past and today demonstrates to the American people and the world the highest qualities of service and commitment. We must ensure that our leaders of tomorrow can continue to keep America's Army equally strong for the difficult years ahead in the Long War.

We are convinced that these successes should be more broadly applied beyond the military establishment. We propose in our work that effective national security policy will require more extensive participation by other government departments and agencies. They also require highly professional leadership. The Army provides both a model for leader development that can be adapted by these other organizations, as well a pool of talent prepared to serve the nation. We see this of special relevance in the need to improve our responses to domestic disasters, which we address in Chapter 8.

Development of its leaders is arguably the most important single program of any army. Ground combat is the most complex of military endeavors. It is characterized by infinitely variable terrain, dominant influence of human interactions under great stress, and the complexity of missions often combining military, political, economic, social, and now religious elements. This is always an unpredictable combination in an uncertain environment often of kill or be killed.[6] The quality of leaders from the lowest to the highest echelons routinely determines the outcomes—winning or losing. Now as combat evolves to incorporate highly variable "mosaics" of land, sea and air power combined increasingly with special operations, moved from useful adjunct to essential partner, leaders assume even more dominant roles as complexity multiplies.[7]

Genuinely new leader competence requirements have arisen since 9/11.[8] President Bush put a broad global mark on the wall: "All nations that decide for aggression and terror will pay a price. We will not leave the safety of America and the peace of the planet at the mercy of a few mad terrorists and tyrants. We will lift this dark threat from our country and from the world."[9]

The spectrum of missions has expanded accordingly. The most current Department of Defense Quadrennial Defense Review identifies "defeating terrorist networks, defending the homeland in depth, shaping the choices of countries at strategic crossroads and preventing hostile states and non-state actors from acquiring or using WMD" as major military missions. "The Department is shifting its portfolio of capabilities to address irregular, catastrophic and disruptive challenges while sustaining capabilities to address traditional challenges."[10] More explicit Department of Defense direction established stability operations' priority comparable to combat operations "to help establish order that advances U.S. interests and values. The immediate goal often is to provide the local populace with security, restore essential services, and meet humanitarian needs. The long-term goal is to help develop indigenous capacity for securing essential services, a viable market economy, rule of law, democratic institutions, and a robust civil society.... U.S. military forces shall be prepared to perform all tasks necessary to establish or maintain order when civilians cannot do so."[11] This is a breathtaking mandate!

The challenge to leaders of all grades is explicit: expect the novel, the largely unpredictable—with a volunteer force. Each new mission, alone and in combination, places major new joint, interagency, intergovernmental, and multinational (JIIM) responsibilities squarely on the plate of Army leaders at every grade. This is not interesting theory but grim practice; not nested within the comfort of shared Army values but seriously joint and interagency in support of global offensive, defensive, and stability operations. And now, within the United States, it includes readiness for operations conducted in support of the Department of Homeland Security and Commander, Northern Command. In an Army of teams, execution with changing, often unpredicted cross-cultural teammates seem certain—more routine than exception. Preparing volunteer Soldiers to lead facing such variability across an extremely broad full spectrum of commitments is the decisive readiness challenge.

These circumstances place formidable requirements on leaders of all grades. They must have the ability to understand and then achieve harmony of the various Doctrine, Training, Leader, Organization, Material, Personnel, Facilities (DTLOMPF) imperatives from a perspective one or two echelons higher. This understanding is necessary to operate as leaders in JIIM teams.[12] This means company commanders who see and can act in combat across battlefield functions from the perspective of the battalion or perhaps even the brigade commander, or squad leaders who understand the cross-function perspectives of first sergeants or their JIIM equivalents. Increasingly the character of operations requires that JIIM competence and more, most recently with requirements to transition rapidly from combat in preemption to security, stabilization, transition and reconstruction operations (SSTR) in failed states or to emergency relief to civilian authority in homeland security.

A current example of the "JIIM imperative" is the leader shift to adviser responsibilities in security, stabilization, transition, and reconstruction (SSTR) operations in Iraq. Soldiers—leaders in small combat units in Iraq trained in their area of competence (Officer Speciality Code [SC] or enlisted Military Occupational Speciality [MOS]) for combat operations but not as advisers—find themselves placed into Iraqi units to train others as both the Iraqi unit and the U.S. small unit are in combat. This places enormous stress on the junior officer and NCO leader leading U.S. Soldiers and advising cross-culture Iraqi soldiers simultaneously. It would be difficult to imagine a more complex leadership requirement. Or, in execution, a stronger compliment that senior leaders could pay to assessment of the professional competence of subordinates.

Understanding and then skilful application of traditional landpower imperatives across normal battle functions is clearly necessary but increasingly insufficient. One must also add understanding of the combinations of the land-sea-air-Special Forces (SOF) mosaic that are available to leaders operating together in variable modular organizations composed to dominate immediate combat and stability operations requirements. Requirements that include "just in time" leader team building, including multinational leaders, to advise Iraqi soldiers or police inside a company or platoon that is operating likely at the squad level or below. This is tough to execute. It is equally difficult to develop competent multinational teams of leaders and trainers.

The current Army Plan clearly recognizes the new leader development requirements in identifying the need for Pentathletes: "we recognize that intellectual change precedes physical change. For this reason, we are developing qualities in our leaders, our people, and our forces to enable them to respond effectively to what they will face. We describe the leaders we are creating as 'pentathletes,' whose versatility and athleticism—qualities that reflect the essence of our Army—will enable them to learn and adapt in ambiguous situations in a constantly evolving environment. To ensure that our Soldiers are well led and supported, as they deal with complexity and uncertainty for the foreseeable future, we have undertaken a major review of how we train, educate, assign, and develop our military and civilian leaders."[13]

The Army Plan further describes the leader development requirement as a multiskilled leader who:

- Is a strategic and creative thinker
- Is a builder of leaders and teams
- Is a competent full-spectrum warfighter or accomplished professional who supports the Soldier
- Is effective in managing, leading, and changing large organizations
- Is skilled in governance, statesmanship, and diplomacy
- Understands cultural context and works effectively across it.[14]

Clearly, demands on leaders are changing. The excellent works of past Training and Leader Development Panels are embedded in current policies and programs of the Army Plan above, yet even they age in the face of accelerating Transformation stimulated by frequent combat operations in the Long War. New patterns of operations emerge to influence the wellsprings of leader development and their likely impact on leader preparation for America's Army as a volunteer force.[15] Several such wellsprings are outlined below.

WELLSPRINGS OF LEADER DEVELOPMENT

All Soldiers, Corporal and above, must be leaders. They should be recruited to be as diverse as is the citizenry of America and then prepared to lead others under stress, whatever their other Army competencies may be (Specialty Code for officers, Military Operational Specialties for enlisted Soldiers). Every Soldier, Corporal and above, needs to be prepared as a leader ready to adapt to excel facing unforeseen challenges or opportunities. First and foremost, they are warriors and they have been trained in basic combat skills to standard with Army warrior values inculcated in significantly toughened Basic Combat Training. Whatever their qualifications to join as volunteers, these warriors perform explicit tasks to standard and they are promoted or dismissed based upon ability to perform to or better than uniform standards across America's Army. As national samples of youth are recruited, so they, as young leaders, cause the expectations of new generations to be accommodated in the culture of the Army. Now with Generation Y, Soldiers are "digital natives," fully prepared to multitask in acquiring and then sharing multiple sources of data and information and then, provided the tools, to generate knowledge and actionable understanding—a national strategic advantage.[16] And America's Army is the full national population—men and women serving together to defend their country. Female Army warriors, including over 16,000 single mothers, are the majority of the more than 155,000 women of all military services who have served in Iraq and Afghanistan.[17] And they are as eligible for the combat badge as any male Soldier. This is not the Army of the past—volunteer Soldiers in America's Army share diversity across human characteristics unique among world landpower military establishments.

Volunteer recruiting is a center of gravity. A dominant issue for America's Army is accession and retention of volunteers that possess and continue to develop the skills, knowledge, and attributes required to serve. After a period of combat in the Middle East longer than World War II, the volunteer force has been sustained. The Army has done exceptionally well addressing this complex but vital requirement as it expands in size. The quantitative news for 2006 was excellent: Active Army 100 percent, ARNG 99 percent, USAR 92 percent. Quality is another issue, although quality today in the Long War may vary considerably from what it was when quality criteria were established decades ago. The Department of Defense standard is 90 percent with a high school diploma with 60 percent above average on armed forces aptitude tests. In 2006, only 82 percent had diplomas, and 61 percent met the aptitude test standard, down from 92 percent and 72 percent in 2004. Maximum enlistment age went from 35 to 42 with increasing personal conduct waivers. Enlistment bonus costs rose from $166 million in 2005 to $238 million in 2006; reenlistment from $120 million 2000–2004 to up to $650 million in 2006.[18] Is this increasingly costly success sustainable? Are there performance costs if quality in fact has been reduced? Just what is "quality"?

America's Army is uniformly competent. Across selected functions and echelons, at least to brigade echelon, active, Army National Guard and Army Reserve share competence. Never before in the military history of the United States have these remarkable common and high levels of citizen-Soldiers' competence occurred, including during total mobilization. These competent leaders—serving, retired, and veteran—are distributed throughout the nation and represent an enormous source of expert support for important national, state, and local programs. See the Appendix for an example of how pervasive this presence is in one state. Shared competence to defined standard created by enormous efforts to train to common tasks, conditions, and standards (TCS) is now combined with very high shared tempo of movement of personnel to service in common active and reserve forces combat operations. The result is greatly increased shared respect across active and reserves since the end of the Cold War. This shared respect is new and very important. It mandates a searching review of leader development policies and practices to advantage such shared competence and esteem.

All Soldiers share the fervor of patriotism, of dedication to national defense post-9/11, and to selfless service beyond self. Most have served in combat. Those experiences and values create a very potent combination of leader potential. Despite aggressive recruiting from U.S. industry and enduring repetitive assignments to combat, many active and reserve Soldiers want to continue to serve. Reenlistment rates are high running 101 percent active, 108 percent ARNG, and 92 percent USAR in September 2006. Traditional Selective Reenlistment bonuses are high, up to $150,000 for a senior Special Forces

NCO with lesser amounts dependent on skill requirements.[19] Active, reserve retention is clearly a well-supported, bipartisan Executive and Legislative priority.[20] How might these experienced quality leaders contribute more to national security including Homeland Defense?

Digitization of the battlefield vastly increases information flows both vertically by function and horizontally by echelon. No leader acts alone. He or she performs routinely as a member of larger teams, both vertical, generally hierarchical, and horizontal, generally peer. Preparation and sustainment of both peer and hierarchical leader teams is central to unit performance. The dominant team is the chain of command, although for the Long War, high performing JIIM leader teams become increasingly important. Preparation of leader teams is now as important, as is preparation of individual leaders.[21] How might this team preparation occur? It should be recognized that the enemy has a JIIM strategy too. By necessity they are opportunistic and rely upon cyber warfare to counter our overwhelming conventional power. The enemy is attempting to prepare the battlefield on his terms. We must adjust to this reality. Describing that adjustment is one of our primary goals in this book

Task migration from higher to lower echelon leaders continues to accelerate. Increasing "cascading excellence" of capabilities at each echelon places important new task competence requirements much lower in leader echelons than previously. How do we advantage "cascading excellence" while ensuring that certain quality of task performance is sustained at each grade?

The requirements for leader competence irrespective of source blur traditional concepts of service. A continuum of service that encourages lateral movement of leaders from active army to reserve to contract civilian to retiree appears increasingly likely. Traditional leader preparation has been vertical anticipating advancement to positions of higher responsibility. Now preparation should encompass horizontal task competency across domains of military service as well as support to responses to enemy employment of weapons of mass destruction (WMD) and probably natural disasters. Horizontal task proficiency has to extend also into JIIM teams of leaders. The most certain enhanced performance occurs when both individual and team proficiency are raised and sustained. These are central tasks for advisor teams and Provincial Reconstruction Teams (PRTs) in Afghanistan and Iraq.

Each of these wellsprings of leader development presages change to current leader development policies and programs. Combined, a significantly different model begins to emerge as is forecast in the current Army Plan reflecting accelerating Transformation. "The Objective Force is composed of *modular, scalable, flexible organizations* for prompt and sustained land operations."[22] The vision of deployment projected in 2015 essentially exists now. Highly competent leaders drawn from every source of competence—active military, reserves, contract civilians, retired—are brought together "just in time" hopefully to become very high performing teams to lead "modular, scalar" units, which may themselves morph in composition from army to joint to combined to interagency. Other than more prepared leaders per small unit, there is not much change for traditional rifle companies, tank companies, or artillery batteries—the enduring foundation of excellence in close combat. But for all else, significant change in leader preparation and expectations of performance seems imminent both for Soldiers in America's Army and in various JIIM combinations in teams, units, and organizations.

LEADERS ALL

"In a transformed Army culture, every soldier is trained and equipped to be a decision maker."[23] Expressed as vision for 2015, the Army approaches that level of preparation today, certainly for Corporals and above. The NCO Education System (NCOES) addresses leader responsibilities first in the Warrior Course for Corporals, which is essential learning to provide the young Soldier with the skills, knowledge, and attributes necessary for him or her to step out from among their peers and to assume the responsibilities of leading. At every step they are supported by senior NCOs who have been prepared themselves to regard development of their subordinate leaders as one of their most important responsibilities. Those courses are now being recast and improved for both grouped and distributed attendance in generating force schools and at various flagship installations in support of Army Force Generation (ARFORGEN) Road to Deployment.[24]

Then that new Corporal hopefully will have the opportunity to participate in the world's finest experiential leader preparation, attendance at a Combat Training Center (CTC). Here, intense job-related challenges are presented with each action of that leader mentored, coached, and trained by role model NCOs (Observers/Controllers), who in mentoring, coaching, and training prepare that young Corporal's seniors to be better mentors too. The combination of competent, confident, motivated young Soldiers who want to lead since their first exposure to a Drill Sergeant plus the Warrior Course plus CTC learning experiences produces superb young leaders in combat, combat support, and combat service support skills. Increasingly, these leaders are exposed to realistic JIIM situations during their CTC learning by experience. These are tough mission-related experiential learning environments with independent performance assessments to standard that apply to all Soldiers. Performance measures are not the somewhat academic accession standards developed for the volunteer force in the 1970s, but rather ultimate performance assessments reflecting competence, motivation under stress and will to serve our Nation under attack all while en route to combat service. So where do age or AFQT fit when discussing Army "quality"? What relevance has what accession quality measure in a service environment of continual learning and assessment frequently in combat?

But there is more from the CTCs; there is an unintended but welcome benefit. The After Action Review (AAR) process at the CTC exposes the

Soldier to the same experiential learning opportunities as are provided to their Squad Leaders, Platoon Sergeant, Platoon Leader, and often the fire supporter (FIST), medic, and logistics operator. Frequently, there is commentary on why what occurred when by the Company Commander and First Sergeant who may be sitting in on the AAR. All participate in such multi-echelon AARs. The young leader, attentive because of personal commitment to the mission, learns the tasks of "higher" like a sponge. In fact, he or she is encouraged to comment specifically on the performance of others—seniors, peers, and subordinates. This is a profound learning and teaching experience. Lastly, if they perform security, stabilization, transition, and reconstruction operations particularly counterinsurgency (SSTR COIN) missions as in the Middle East, those young leaders supplement their CTC learning by becoming leaders understanding that they are practically influencing events at the tactical, operational, and strategic levels in a world of saturation media coverage, and embedded reporters. This is extremely effective leader preparation that literally "trains up" Soldiers one or more echelons in likely operational environments! What a profoundly stimulating service environment to those who joined ARMY STRONG to defend the nation while drawn to personal improvement through challenge with significant financial reward. No wonder it is effective.

By a combination of programs, most intended, some unintended, the Army now has a leader train-up capability unequalled in modern times including the Reichswehr of interwar Germany—a former international military development model. By the time those former Corporals have served five to ten years, with multiple learning experiences in combat throughout the world whether they are in the active force or in the operational reserves, they are absolutely superb Soldiers not only in their competence but also in their ability to mentor subordinates and to influence others. Volunteer accession quality is simply not an issue. Rather the practical issue is what performance have you demonstrated to America's Army; what performance to standard are you demonstrating today? Competence is rewarded handsomely; incompetence departs.

These programs apply to the reserves as much as the active force. They apply in combat supporting rapid adaptation to new requirements as seen most recently in Operation Iraqi Freedom. Soon these young leaders with several years of growth under their belts will approach competency levels formerly associated with Special Forces at more junior or comparable grades. Leader proficiency itself has become a fine example of cascading excellence.

The young leaders—all Soldiers, Corporal, and above—have become strategic assets particularly when their competence and confidence are applied in interagency and multinational operations. Of evident value in active and reserve forces' service in the Balkans, Iraq and Afghanistan, the skills, knowledge, and attributes (SKA) practiced routinely today by young leaders will be of as dominant importance in rebuilding failed states as they have proven in combat operations and in relief of the massive destruction caused by Hurricane Katrina. These leaders, still serving and veterans, are a vitally important national resource fighting the Long War be it in overseas operations or supporting federal, state, or local governance in homeland security.

Leader task proficiency does not appear to be a problem. Of course, it is always a practical issue deserving of every leader's attention, but there is an effective system to ensure that increasing leader task proficiency requirements will be met. And a system that ensures that those who fail to perform to common standard are dismissed—"up or out." Should this proven leader development system apply to other federal and state agencies as they become more robust for the Long War?

ALL-VOLUNTEER RECRUITING

But is there likely to be a continuing supply of such competent, motivated American volunteers who can become the desired "Pentathletes" of the future? Is current apparent success sustainable? What may be the costs in the apparent current perceived lowering of standards governing enlistment? Are there alternatives?

Serious leaders have grave doubts about the current recruiting "success." "Generally speaking, we've quadrupled the number of lowest mental category recruits, we've quadrupled the number of non-high school graduates, and we're granting 6,000 to 8,000 more moral waivers," he said. "When you tell me that you think enlisting a 42-year-old grandmother is the right thing to do, you don't understand what we're doing. We need 19-year-old boys and girls in good health to carry guns and fight."[25] That is certainly an appropriate caution. America's Army exists primarily to fight and win our Nation's wars. However, entry criteria only open the door to service. All Soldiers must perform to standard the same common tasks and the tasks associated with their particular speciality. Competent performance is what counts.

There are several important issues to be considered in addressing All-Volunteer sustainability and accession standards. These issues are changing SKA requirements for Soldiers fighting the Long War that may not be reflected in current recruiting standards; increasingly sophisticated Soldier development policies and programs available for continuing development of the serving Soldier; embedded national consensus to provide financial incentives necessary to retain the volunteer force despite a declining demographic base; and serious continuing research to improve the performance predictability of accession standards and assessment measures.

Soldier skills, knowledge, and attribute requirements are changing rapidly. A minority grandmother who is competent in pediatric care—perhaps a midwife at one time—who speaks Arabic can be a more powerful multiplier to a Military Transition Team (MiTT) supporting an Iraqi unit than a Ranger

Corporal. Or the value of that same individual now more senior and assigned to a unit operating in an extremely rural, traditional Islamic area demonstrating what America stands for as she, both competent and confident, orders actions from subordinate white males.

There is currently considerable variation in mental requirements for accessions for 212 various MOSs. Combat Support and particularly Combat Service Support organizations (Sustainment Brigades) are changing dramatically. We doubt that there has been either money or time to establish new MOS requirements with appropriate ASVAB criteria (Armed Services Vocational Aptitude Battery). And when we do, do they include the cultural multiplier factor described above? How can they relate to subsequent individual performance to Army standard? That is what counts—MOS by MOS, individual by individual.

The Army is not a social welfare organization.[26] Yet there are increasing numbers of competent, motivated young people who come from challenging circumstances and who seek opportunity to serve and to improve their station in the United States. Perhaps, facing the cross-cultural requirements of the Long War, we want to recruit actively in certain countries where eventually American officers and NCOs can be important leaders in SSTR operations. There are some 750,000 undocumented youth of military age who might serve within specific conditions.[27] Or offspring of single parents who seek opportunity to advance. For families earning less than $15,000, only 20 percent of children live with two parents.[28] Or the offspring of families with few alternatives who are captured by the U.S. automobile industry in decline. Perhaps they are somewhat like the displaced "Okies" of the dust bowl Depression Thirties, brought into the Civilian Conservation Corps run by the Army and subsequently who became NCO cadre for mobilization in World War II. If they can perform including "reading, writing and arithmetic," and subsequently grow to standard, trained, coached, and mentored by caring NCOs, why should they not serve America's Army in the Long War?

There is more we don't know about new Soldier requirements for the Brigade-based Modular Force than we do know.

The Army has seriously toughened Basic Combat Training for all Soldiers. Combat skills are instructed largely by combat veterans. All Soldiers receive combatives training. Individual weapons are issued early and remain with the trainee—weapons immersion. There is engagement skills training of all individual and crew-served weapons. Training occurs in urban environments with Convoy Live Fire Exercises. Most tasks, all combat survival tasks, are trained in the field in task-demanding Situational Training Exercises (STXs). There is much greater use of live ammunition in various weapons.[29] As that volunteer grows as a Soldier to task, condition and standard, as they mature as individuals and as Soldiers, they experience arguably the best continuing education and training regime in the world—all competency based. They are promoted as boarded by the best NCO structure in the world that fully understands its charge to mentor subordinates. As the ARFORGEN Road to Deployment matures, all Brigades will be provided a CTC-like rigorous training experience. How might the presence of these continuing development gates ensure quality and influence accession standards? Perhaps accession standards can be modified more knowing that institutionalized in-service performance gates effectively screen out low performers?

The national manpower pool has receded on a percentage basis. The current accessioning prime market of Mental Category I-IIIA High School Graduates constitutes only 7.1 percent of the eligible population. That disregards significant variations in high school quality from state to state. Of the overall target Mental Category I-III A, 53 percent of the population being recruited for 212 MOSs, 90 percent spend 90 percent of their time indoors. Fourteen percent are obese, 25 percent overweight. Seventy-five percent do not have regular fitness classes in high school.[30] The Army accesses from a declining "best" of our population. Despite these constraints, all should feel justifiably proud that today's enlisted Soldiers in the active Army are the highest quality force in terms of education and aptitude testing for military service (ASVAB) in our nation's history. Fortunately, we are 300 million and growing as America's Army increases in size. But how relevant is the ASVAB?

There is a deeper issue concerning quality that may reduce desired diversity in the Army. Blacks make up about 23 percent of today's Active Duty Army, but the share of blacks in recruit classes of recent years has dropped, from 22.7 percent at the time of the Septebmer 11, 2001, terrorist attacks to 19.9 percent in 2002; 16.4 percent in 2003; and 15.9 percent in 2005. Of that total, there is a declining percentage of black males who are qualified, perhaps because they have single parents? The out-of-wedlock birth rate among women who drop out of high school among African-Americans is 67 percent.[31] The number of female recruits as a share of total Army enlistments has dropped 13 percent over the past five years.[32]

Fortunately, there has been broad national consensus to establish serious financial incentives. Incentive pay is being increased for multiple periods of service or tour extensions in a combat theater. Several increased enlistment and reenlistment bonuses have been discussed. Those increases remain significant and growing. Currently, the enlistment bonus for a two-year enlistee in 45 MOSs is up to $51,864 paid upon completion of basic combat training and advanced individual training.[33] These bonuses are accompanied by significant reenlistment bonuses "of up to $150,000 for senior special operations troops who agree to stay past the twenty-year minimum retirement mark."[34] Soldiers have defined benefit twenty-year retirement programs indexed to the cost of living—a benefit increasingly rare in American industry. These incentives are linked to an excellent health care program for those serving and retired (TRICARE for Life).[35] That too is increasingly rare. These clearly are powerful reenlistment incentives working today supporting career retention of officers and non commissioned officers.[36] Given endemic dislocations, turbulence in

American economic life, industry disruptions, the housing "bubble," success of financial incentives should not be surprising. The downside is the associated overall manpower cost now estimated at $120,000 to $180,000 per Soldier per year in pay, benefits, and training costs—a major consideration to those increasing the size of the active Army.[37]

Difficult policy choices remain. Clearly research and development of the kinds of accessioning issues raised above is necessary. Some is underway. For example in April 2005, the Army fielded a fresh look at pay. A Two Tier Attrition Screen (TTAS) is being reviewed as an improved screening tool. It combines a better motivation test with minimum score requirements on the math and word-knowledge portions of the military entrance exam. Finally, TTAS screens nondiploma recruits by using weight-to-height proportions also called a body mass index. Recruits who comply with the TTAS standard have a six-month attrition rate of 6.2 percent that is near to 5.6 percent reported for high school graduates. That is much better than 10.3 percent attrition after six months for non-high school graduates who failed the TTAS standard.[38] More such research conducted by Army Research Institute is better. Better in-service performance assessment seems likely to be even better.

TOTAL FORCE COMPETENCY

How might these experienced quality leaders contribute more to national security including Homeland Defense?

Current levels of competency of both active forces and reserves are remarkable and increasingly comparable. This has existed for several years in combat support and combat service support units as all Soldiers train to common task, condition and standard and as reserve units are activated more frequently for longer periods. Now parity is established for combat units particularly in execution of stability missions. Army National Guard (ARNG) units understand the dynamics of civilian political, economic and social power active in urban areas; they live this in their state. Repetitive assignments "in harms way" have developed fully competent, fully qualified, citizen-Soldiers at least to field grade officers and E8 non commissioned officers.[39] National Guard Divisions and Brigade Combat Teams serve with distinction in Iraq and Afghanistan.

The National Guard has responded aggressively post-9/11 to be responsive to both state and federal operational mission requirements. Newly formed Joint Combined State Strategic Plans (JCSSP) are designed to support the governor's need for capabilities in relation to the joint regional Combatant Command's requirements for forces. JCSSP closes the gap between a National Guard configured solely for the overseas warfight and a National Guard configured for both the overseas warfight and the homeland security/defense mission.

Improved readiness was proven to all during Hurricane Katrina. From a no-notice standing start, 50,000 Guardsmen were deployed in a matter of days, from every state and territory to save more than 17,000 American citizens from potential death and evacuated an additional 200,000 with Air Guard airlift operations rivaling the Berlin Airlift in 1948. Planning and readiness exercises addressing other national defense contingencies continue.[40] Recent important reserve force studies such as the Commission on the National Guard and Reserve (the Punero Report) address institutionalization of the increased roles of reserve forces.[41]

It now seems clear that in areas deemed important, sufficient military competence can be developed and sustained to make RC leaders interchangeable with AC, at least through field officer grades—and certainly including general officer or SES where the spectrum of service may be more political than military, such as supporting the local Governor or a subordinate major city Mayor in homeland security or supporting stability operations.[42]

But what should the areas be for shared competence and why? The opportunity (time) cost for preparation and subsequent active service for citizen-Soldiers is very high. How much competency and in what areas is appropriate? Time requirements to gain proficiency in traditional Army tasks mandated by Congress to train and equip land forces (Title 10 tasks) in generating force learning can be significant. Why train reserve leaders in combat development, training development or material development processes when such Title 10 support is provided routinely by the active army? The ARNG now has important competing requirements supporting state and also indirectly, the federal Department of Homeland Security. Many ARNG peacetime support tasks are state unique and thus not learned in the active army institutional training system. Time is consumed learning "just like" the active leader learns. Is this time diversion necessary for leaders in units focused on traditional hedging reserve missions, not on operating force missions, particularly when ARFORGEN Road to Deployment readiness training regimes will be provided predeployment?

The issue is the opportunity costs of developing leader competence for the reserve components. Time is limited, the most valuable resource in all units, particularly the Reserves. What cannot be done well if much of the preparation time is directed at one area of active force readiness such as administration or grouped higher unit training. Citizen-Soldiers have been conditioned to aspire to be "just like" the active army. "Just like" is a comforting goal that conceals tough issues on allocation of focus, and time, to develop competence comparable with the active army. The ARNG and U.S. Army Reserve (USAR) have now proven that can be done—a notable achievement that proves Emory Upton no longer relevant.[43] But at what cost in general unit retention and readiness? For America's Army, the nation wants highly competent, genuine citizen-Soldiers linked to their local communities absolutely prepared to support state authority in emergencies and, as appropriate, committed to ARFORGEN for operational deployment every five or six years. "Just like" must be approached with caution. That caution should also apply to preparation requirements should expanded departmental or federal agency "reserve corps" organizations be generated to support JIIM requirements overseas. Being "just like" the active department or agency may generate preparation time requirements that can be dysfunctional to attracting the "best and brightest." These folks have numerous other options for personal development and achievement.

In the Cold War, "just like" produced competent warfighting reserve forces' leaders. But now, how should this clear, very time-costly reserve leader competence be directed? Each component faces hard questions:

ARNG. How much unit leader preparation time for Homeland Security? How much focus on unit warfighting, on stability operations and support to the state in homeland defense? The Guard Bureau assumes that 25 percent of Guard units will be in intensive training for deployment, 25 percent mobilized and deployed, and 50 percent supporting Homeland Defense and Homeland Security National response plan support with an essential ten capabilities: Joint Force Headquarters (State), Civil Support Teams, Maintenance, Aviation, Engineer (Technical Search & Rescue), Medical (Mass Decontamination), Communications, Transportation, Security and Logistics.[44] The test of feasibility will be retention, currently running at 118 percent in 2006.

USAR. How much focus on traditional units to provide or fill out a typical Sustainment Command in contrast to developing very high tech leaders, teams, and units that are world class and able to serve as the organizational nucleus for detachments or units created from the national talent pool as the need arises? Much is there today. In many landpower competency domains, the USAR provides the national expertise.[45] Is it appropriate to expand the USAR as a talent pool of defense expertise? Could USAR in the future be forming the nucleus of national business functional capability to respond to domestic WMD organizing federal regional resource support? Or perhaps the USAR designed to provide the nucleus of very highly qualified Soldier support to the National Guard's State Partnership Program with fifty-four separate nations? "States and their partners participate in a broad range of strategic security cooperation activities to include homeland defense/security, disaster response/mitigation, consequence/crisis management, interagency cooperation, border/port/aviation security, combat medical exchanges, fellowship-style internships, and bilateral familiarization events. . . ."[46] Mormon language translator detachments have been a notable citizen-Soldier contribution in the past. Why not expand to detachments of former national immigrants now citizen-Soldiers regularly supporting State Partnerships for Peace and available to support SOCOM Plus deployments if required?[47] These reservists could provide enormous support to cross-cultural adaptation. Similar programs could apply to federal departments and agencies critical to the Long War.

Being "just like" all purpose active units that may sustain baseline proficiency in low intensity or mid intensity operations can become a cop out for hard decisions concerning locales of expertise for citizen-Soldiers in America's Army most likely to support SSTR operations. We suggest that national leaders really need to think through the manifest strengths of citizen-Soldier leaders and how to magnify those strengths through leader preparation focused to address new post–Cold War, post-9/11 challenges. But to do so seeking major savings in Soldier time so we have them for the long haul. Exactly that rationale needs to be applied to other federal departments and agencies that need to bulk up to respond to overseas Long War challenges.

LEADER TEAMS

One major effect of digitization, the explosion of the quality and quantity of information on the battlefield, has been to fuse leaders at all grades as teams with their leaders, their subordinates and their peers. No one wants to fight alone. Teams thrive everywhere, communicating continuously in person or by various electronic means as virtual teams. A vital team is the squad or the fighting vehicle crew; in each case fighting not to let their buddy down as they accomplish the mission. Every tank leader has a wingman just as does a fighter pilot. The company commander is a member of a team composed of the battalion commander (up) and subordinate platoon leaders (down). The company commander is also a member of the team of all of the other company commanders in the battalion cross-talking during the fight. So that company commander is a member of several teams—vertical and horizontal—simultaneously. The battalion operations officer is a member of a team of staff officers supporting the chain of command. And he or she is a member of a vertical team consisting of the operations officers at brigade and at division. All of these leader teams must be prepared. These teams are pervasive across offensive, defensive and the full range of stability operations.

Teams make a whole much greater than the sum of the parts. There can be no reduction of the individual authority and responsibility of the commander at any echelon, but teammates can provide solid counsel, shared intelligence, and information. If senior, that is, the hierarchical chain of command team, that senior team member provides both mission and intent, sage advice, and counsel while leaving as much initiative as possible to subordinate just as that subordinate is expected to provide to his or her subordinate leader. If a horizontal staff or crew team, each is expected to support the other, to provide for the benefit of the shared team. Collaboration to excel as professionals is reflected in the psychology of leadership of today's Army. While maintaining hierarchical structure and relationships, today's leaders are more open to listening and "conferring" with subordinates. It has become part of the culture. Incidentally and helpfully, such collaboration and teams is characteristic of Generation Y Soldiers as is being exploited in Teams of Leaders programs.[48]

Teams don't just happen. They need to be formed, nurtured, and reinforced when losses occur. In order to be high performing, all teams—hierarchical or peer, vertical or horizontal—must practice good teamwork, team decision-making, and team leadership. The latter consists of shared vision, shared trust, shared competence and shared confidence.[49] There are other requirements advocated as the literature of team building grows for both military and business applications. Suffice to comment that there is solid research and development yet to be done, particularly for hierarchical organizations performing under great stress but it seems clear that preparation of high-performing leader teams is an increasingly important Army learning requirement that extends to both joint and interagency operations.

The leader preparation challenge magnifies when teams become unstable. This could occur due to leader losses in combat or when task organizations change frequently as commanders reconfigure task forces or combat teams to dominate immediate tactical mission, enemy, terrain, troops available, time or civil considerations (METT-TC) or unanticipated domestic WMD emergencies. Emerging doctrine envisages frequent reconfiguration of modular units. The vision for the Objective Force now Army Modular Force is clear: "Teams form, change, relocate, expand and disperse without effect to battle command."[50] Hopefully recomposing leader teams will be as simple and as routine as is implied.

But, each reconfiguration brings new leader combinations that must gel into highly proficient teams. Now add leaders from other services, agencies (CIA, DHS, FBI), governments (U.S., state, or local) or nations—each developed as a leader in another operational culture as was experienced and observed with very mixed results after Hurricane Katrina. Leader team preparation would seem to become a complex challenge that should be addressed by each chain of command. For example, as team building facilitated by steadily improving information technologies is accelerated by the various tools of knowledge management (KM) such as Professional Forums and Knowledge Nets, there would seem to be a significant shift in task execution responsibilities down the various chains. Bottom-up data and information generating knowledge and understanding seem likely to shift the loci of responsibility for performance down. That is, competent performance of more complex tasks can be expected from more junior leaders.

Several years ago, we became concerned that traditional blue-collar (NCO)/white-collar (officer) distinctions were disappearing and that the Army had not begun to think through the implications. At the time, a new way was described to approach a traditional blue-white collar work force model:

> The old blue-collar-white-collar distinction seems dated. I believe that this traditional distinction is inadequate today, post–AirLand Battle. It is more useful to

> think in terms of iron-, blue-, white-, and gold-collar personnel requirements. Iron-collar requirements are robotic, computer driven.' Blue collar now includes disciplined execution of assigned individual and collective tasks by blue and iron collar. White collar refers to leading in the accomplishment of single battle function missions (maneuver, fire support, air defense, or combat-service support). Gold collar refers to the ability to integrate iron, blue, white, and other gold successfully, in a rapidly changing situation, under stress. More precisely, it is the ability to conceptualize and successfully execute the focusing of multiple BOS functions in time and space to achieve the intent of the higher chain of command.[51]

Gold collar could be the capability to accomplish innovative tasks that achieve tenfold to hundredfold increases in capability. They include the imaginative identification of new "solutions," exploiting existing capabilities as they have not been combined before, or conceptualizing and actualizing—by computer—new ways to fight.[52] Today, gold collar personnel are described as "Pentathletes" in the current Army Plan.

Subsequently, we suggested that Sergeants and below were blue collar, more senior NCOs were white collar, and that most officers, particularly Majors and above, were gold collar. The blue-white-gold distinction between tasks performed remains valid. However, as discussed earlier, white collar has moved from Sergeant to Corporal in terms of who should be prepared as leaders. Captains and above are gold collar.

In sum, all leaders are white collar or gold collar, both officers and NCOs. This has important implications in terms of requirements for continuous learning and in the need to reconfirm the most basic warrior relationships of trust and confidence between the officer and the NCO. And to reconfirm within the professional ethos too as it addresses both career and citizen-Soldiers where distinctions of service are becoming increasingly fuzzy. Perhaps the differences lay in the range of competence expected of the individual active or reserve leader in America's Army. The active force leader is responsible to develop and demonstrate competence across both the Warfighting Mission Areas and the Business Mission Areas, federal and global, across Long War and land war.[53] The reserve professional supports state and functional regional capabilities supporting homeland defense, homeland security and warfighting for either operating forces or reserve forces. Similar delineation of responsibilities seems essential for federal interagency organizations.

Whether white or gold collar, the pace of development of each aspect of DTLOMPF imperative across the full sphere of conflict mandates that continuous learning be provided to all leaders. It is even more important to advantage digital natives from the Millennium Generation. More is better to exploit white and gold drawing on the powerful combination of information management (IM) and KM. The Tactical Internet, and Land Warrior fielded in 2007 with an Infantry Battalion in an Stryker Brigade Combat Team (SBCT), provide each leader and leader team with capabilities to employ support across

JIIM. Soon each Platoon Leader or Fire Support Chief of Section will have capabilities to bring precision strategic support to tactical operations should events require much as Delta operatives were able to do in Afghanistan or more recently in Iraq now directed by Army or Marine or SF or CIA—a capability that comes partially to Al Qaeda with 3G cell phones. That was remarkable, flexible, very hard power that was available to small unit leaders.[54] The extraordinary competence of current leaders also provides tangible soft power. Young active and reserve state leaders "sold" Partnership for Peace to Eastern Europe and elsewhere. The sheer competence and confidence of similar white and gold collar leaders in combat in Iraqi Freedom co-opted the world media embedded in units in Iraq during OIF1.

This is downloading power to young leaders in a most profound sense. To be sustained, in fact increased as envisaged in current doctrine, leader learning opportunities need to be expanded both to remain current in what exist and to employ what is coming across the full spectrum. Whether in generating force, unit or self-development, new learning opportunities such as those provided by Army Knowledge OnLine (AKO) and the Battle Command Knowledge System (BCKS) need to be expanded to stimulate bottom up actionable understanding. Remarkable experiences from white and gold collar warriors in Iraq or disaster recovery leaders in Katrina need to be shared across the Army drawing on in-being or emerging Professional Forums or Knowledge Nets.[55] With such substantial task migration to younger leaders, leader preparation needs to be rethought. It should be continuous as is characteristic of great learning and teaching organizations.[56]

Those are applications for America's Army. Now think JIIM and ways to advantage the great strengths of the diversity within the NCO Corps able to influence across cultures represented in JIIM. Highly competent blue collar citizen-Soldiers have great credibility exercising their competence across cultures.

Some might see gold and white collar changing traditional relationships between officers and non commissioned officers.[57] That should not be the case. In fact, vital traditional relationships need to be reinforced. The basic relationship is expressed in the young officer shouting "follow me" to subordinates while leading in the fight by personal example. The sergeant prepared the Soldiers to fight while the officer planned then led the fight. Neither can accomplish the mission without the other—at least in America's Army. It is significant that important Army documents today are cosigned by the Secretary of the Army, the Chief of Staff, and by the Sergeant Major of the Army.

This cosignature is far more than pro forma courtesy. It represents one of the most important developments over the post-Vietnam era that has been the professionalization of the NCO corps. A formal recognition of the positions of Command Sergeant Major, for example, gave stature and a career path to enlisted Soldiers. This in turn has inspired the respect of the officer corps. Without this respect, team building is impossible across the profound range of national responsibilities associated with America's Army. Translated to state and local governance by the National Guard, it establishes essential sharing of blue collar-white collar-gold collar responsibilities central to organization of homeland security and homeland defense. Existence of this bond, nonexistent after Vietnam because the noncommissioned officer corps had been consumed, is a powerful safeguard against "breaking" America's Army today. Are there comparable bonds in service in other federal agencies supporting the Long War. Why not?

Former Sergeant Major of the Army Bill Gates has expressed this central relationship between officer and non commissioned officer exceedingly well:

> We trust and respect the young soldier, the young private. The officers trust and respect the non-commissioned officers. And the non-commissioned officers trust and respect the commissioned officers. And it takes that entire team in order for the Army to work. And it works better than any other Army in the world. And it's very difficult to explain that relationship....
>
> The introduction to a group about one or the other will go something like this. I know when I introduced my company commander, I would always introduce him as this is my company commander. My company commander. And when you say that, that carries a tremendous message. This is my commanding general or this is my chief of staff of the Army. So that carries a powerful message ... you ask the lieutenant, you know, whose soldiers are these? These are my soldiers. This is my Army and that's what soldiers say. This is my Army, not the Army. It is my Army, it is my unit. It is my lieutenant, my sergeant, my sergeant major. So people inspire to progress through the ranks of the non-commissioned officer corps because they can see how the NCO corps fits into the overall scheme of the Army.[58]

This vital relationship must be maintained, in fact, enhanced, as downward leader task migration continues. A similar positive mutually reinforcing relationship needs to prevail between active and reserve forces. Full-time engrossed overseas; reserves overseas when required as operational forces but also focused on homeland defense and security. In time, this combination of competence and service beyond self to Nation should apply to federal and state interagency organizations formed to address national security be it domestic or overseas.

CASCADING EXCELLENCE

The combination of an increasingly effective professional development program that provides continuing education and training combined with repetitive combat experience in a reflective Army increasingly seeking lessons learned is extremely powerful. Then add unique multi-echelon acceptance of After Action Reviews (AARs)—subordinate assessing senior discussing how to perform better—an important learning "best practice" that is effectively embedded in unit operating procedures. No wonder that America's Army is a, if not the, premier very large learning organization in the world, bar none.

And patterns of adaptive change are reinforced. AARs generate Lessons Learned, in turn stimulating adaptive behavior focused on adapting to new threats and requirements. As data and information are routinely converted to knowledge and actionable understanding to accomplish the unit mission, the understanding is increasingly shared rapidly across units increasingly decentralized "bottom up" by combinations of IM and KM.

Now expand the potential for broader applications of Army "best practice" as the diverse experience of citizen-Soldiers sharing the values and practices of the United States Army enter the unit-learning universe. Professional and citizen-Soldiers with diverse backgrounds bonding with pride as Soldiers—across diversity (ethnic, religious, gender, race), wholly competency-based, are performing complex tasks as bonded teams of extraordinarily diverse composition. Increasingly we regard Soldiers as leaders not solely within military context but also as "ambassadors" of what the United States stands for—the unique facets of America's Army. From such great diversity grounded in the values of America, America's Army can provide diversity "plug ins" whether ethnic, race, religion or sex. But all are first and foremost American—often (name the country)-American—proud to serve their Nation and Army in selfless service. It is precisely these unique characteristics of cascading excellence that are being drawn upon in assigning U.S. units to advise Iraqi units. JIIM applications of "cascading excellence" have barely been scratched for domestic or foreign use.

CONTINUUM OF SERVICE

The Objective Force 2015 Concept Paper proposed striking change to existing personnel accession policies and programs. It advocates establishing a "continuum of service ... from new recruit, to AC, to RC to retiree or contractor. This allows trained and experienced soldiers and leaders to continuously serve. In effect a soldier is able to move from active to reserve status and back throughout his career."[59]

Application is best explained by one of the Department of the Army G1 advocates of continuum of service:

> The only way to get an Active Component Lt Colonel today is to grow a 2d Lieutenant, which takes about 16 years. Add the retirement package, and you're looking at a big investment in time and money, and a pretty static, linear process. In order to rapidly increase or decrease a unit, we need the ability to bring skilled Soldiers in and out of active duty. Before a build-up, we'd search the database of properly acculturated people (AC and RC) looking for the needed skills and grades. Skills could be acquired via military or civilian schools. Grade would be acquired much as it is now. But instead of growing a Lt Colonel, we could take

> one off the shelf. During a draw-down after the mission, some members would move back to RC status, seamlessly. All members called up to AC status would retain any benefits earned during their AC stint.... That is the continuum of service concept: Moving seamlessly in and out of Active Duty over a lifetime of service.[60]

Such a continuum of service would certainly seem to apply to federal and state departments and agencies. Continuum of service could apply experienced competence to support national, state, and local priorities. Extend vested defined pension benefits for years of service in support of response to domestic WMD. Distribute functional expertise through Knowledge Nets and Professional Forums to provide regional, functional WMD support. Continuum of service could be reinforced by opportunities for virtual contributions and teaming so experience can be drawn upon without physical presence through drawing on "participatory media" such as YouTube or use of avatars.

Think of continuum of service as continuity of service—competence plus a culture of service in America's Army applied to public service in other agencies of federal, state or local governance to continue to draw on the competence and experience of former Soldiers or former experienced civil servants. An incentive could be continued retirement benefit accrual perhaps with some cost sharing with federal, state or local governance. Programs such as these would reinforce institutionalized preparation of public officials such as the proposed U.S. Public Service Academy comparable to the military service academies.[61]

The devil may be in the detail if concept were to become practice in a strongly competence-based America's Army. There are challenging leader issues that will likely require research. For example, there would seem to be three broad issues in lateral movement of personnel of all grades:

- Establishing then maintaining task proficiency to perform tasks to standard. Required task proficiency for leaders as individuals and members of teams grows vertically appropriate to position and translates horizontally. How much task proficiency preparation can be (must be) done prior to reentry; how much upon reentry? Is preparation the responsibility of the unit or institution or self-development by the individual? What are skills, knowledge and attributes where there is absolute civil equivalence and thus no problems in ensuring competency? What are appropriate ground rules to determine level of lateral grade equivalence to be permitted when there has not been recent service? Increasingly, proficiency sustainment could be supported by conducting continuous mentoring/coaching programs drawing on KM that could interface active to reserve and vice versa as well as senior to subordinate. This is a potential application of Teams of Leaders discussed in Chapter 7.

- Assimilation then practical demonstration of understanding of Army values and cultures appropriate to the position to be occupied. Once core Army values are established, do they endure? For example, if Initial Entry Training (IET) was ever experienced (USMC, USN, USAF?), does that suffice? What if no prior IET learning experience? Alternatives if the individual has never served? Internet-based inculcation of Army values desirable? Feasible? Valuable insights should be developing as America's Army accesses serving Air Force and Navy leaders to meet Long War personnel requirements.
- Incentives required to retain availability of desired personnel (quality/quantity) in all categories?

These are not intended to be negative comments. Establishing a continuum of service is long overdue in America's Army clearly requiring the best in leaders from whatever the source. If highly competent warriors want to serve, they should. But the implications of these novel and important new policies that permit the personnel system to seek then access the finest leader talent available wherever in the United States will be equivalent in cultural impact to the movement to an all volunteer Army. All volunteer brought quality leaders from the bottom up, grown over time. Continuum of service brings quality leaders laterally, from whatever source, practically immediately. Similar policies need to be thought through for interagency applications.

CONSCRIPTION HEDGE

Now, the wild card. Various hedges have failed; the United States faces serious military manpower shortages. There is total mobilization and conscription must be reinstated. A drafted Army returns.

There would be immediate policy implications for America's Army:

- Much higher percentage of lower mental category Soldiers below the fiftieth percentile of the population. Soldiers in very poor physical condition.
- Transition to a mobilization production base which would likely compete for higher mental category Soldiers—the strength of the volunteer force.
- Activation of a mobilization training base.

Most of the leaders for the expanding Army would be from those present at the start of hostilities. Hopefully, premobilization leader preparation policies will have prepared leaders to occupy positions several echelons higher. Battle casualty replacements and leaders for immediate expansion units could be provided by these officer and non commissioned officer leaders. New leaders would be selected and trained from draftees by Officer Candidate Schools and various institutions of a residual NCOES. Hopefully, the rigorous competency-based standards of NCOES could be maintained although that seems doubtful if the mental category quality of the draftees declines. Experiential training practices should continue and likely be expanded to accelerate new leader training.

A major leader source would be those retired and contract personnel who have participated in past continuum of service programs. They should be able to support sustainment of the training base as experienced leaders are diverted to become replacements to combat operations.

Thanks to improved learning capabilities (training and education) available both grouped and distributed by the internet, rigorous training requirements descriptions by task, condition and standard, and flexible leader accession and preparation precedents, leader preparation should be adequate in a drafted America's Army.

We sense that a potential problem would be cultural differences between the volunteer Army Soldiers and the draftees. Motivation to join would certainly be different, which may carry over into performance. We would need to avoid significant differences in attitudes and acceptance of discipline. Shared performance required to common task, condition, standard should mitigate the differences as all team to meet the national challenge that precipitated the total mobilization.

Advance planning to ensure DTLOMPF synchronization will be essential. There are likely to be severe shortages of facilities.

Realistically, the return of conscription would require major adjustments. There would also be significant time lags between a decision to mobilize and results. Are these acceptable when we are facing a major crisis? How do we reduce them? We have to be serious about a hedge of this type. Major contingency planning and standby plans must be made. In Chapter 9, we will discuss the importance of anticipating and preparing for this and other major contingencies.

A NEW MODEL

Iraqi Freedom has demonstrated startling increases in the capabilities of Army units fighting fully integrated with joint, interagency, and multinational formations. New organizations have been created to address new problems such as WMD detection—"an unusual group pulled together for the current campaign. It includes members of all branches of the U.S. armed forces, as well as the British military and a host of civilian U.S. agencies."[62] Startling but not surprising. They are the most recent evolutions in spiral development across each element of DTLOMPF beginning after Vietnam. Combat in Panama and Iraq/Kuwait were performance checks as were Partnership for Peace, Balkans, 9/11, Afghanistan, and most recently Iraq. Doctrinal visions have become reality with the concerted support of Executive and Legislative leadership. Most heartening has been the accelerating progress in the vital area of leader competence. Adaptive self-aware leaders—gold and white collar, Corporal and above—thrive.

Now continuum of service should spread this competence and confidence across a much broader leader pool including interagency competencies. Precise expertise could be enabled through lateral entry. Leaders' individual and team competence seems certain to accelerate "cascading excellence" across a spectrum of conflict which has been broadly redefined since 9/11. Special Forces' individual and team competence is an excellent example as it spreads across a much broader America's Army.

The next steps will provide supporting DTLOMPF, particularly leaders and leader teams, accustomed to be grouped just in time to become very high-performing teams to lead modular, scalar units which may themselves morph from army to joint to interagency to combined to dominate execution of new missions much as was created to detect WMD in Iraq. Precise expertise was required and developed in an ad hoc hybrid unit created for explicit mission accomplishment. That is the future, today. This seems increasingly understood as leader teams are prepared in the ARFORGEN Road to Deployment for unit employment and now in the Transition Team Road to Deployment for advisers.

Other than more prepared leaders per small unit, there has not been much change for traditional rifle companies, tank companies or artillery batteries even as the latter were employed as Infantry in Iraq—companies, the enduring foundation of excellence in close combat. But for all else, significant change in leader performance and preparation seems imminent.

CONCLUSION

America's Army has now been through two recent crises requiring significant change in human development. The first was individual leader development post-Vietnam involving improved quality through volunteers, creation of the officer and NCOES, and leader development through the development and institutionalization of the CTC paradigm.

Now, post-9/11, comes sustained all-volunteer accessioning for the Long War, with the enormous support of Executive and Legislative, generating high-performing leader teams, institutionalization of Internet-based KM, creation of stabilized units and lifecycle personnel management, and now growing application to JIIM in the Long War context. All was accomplished while continuing to develop outstanding adaptive leaders.

Clearly, this has been a very successful institutional adaptation of leader development.[63] Now in a domestic WMD support context and to generate effective interagency organizations across federal agencies deployed overseas, is it time to apply Lessons Learned through local, state, national perspectives and the root values and competence of America's Army to broader U.S. citizenry?

All is likely, if the wellsprings discussed earlier are nurtured and thoughtful preparatory research and development is conducted to transfer best practices. As a superb learning organization, America's Army has proofed then institutionalized most of the leader development policies and programs that will be required to increase significantly the quantity and quality of federal and State departments and agencies support to winning the Long War. Who will draw upon this national treasure of implementation experience?

5

Improved Responsiveness as a Learning Organization

DURING THE PAST decade, Army leaders were interviewed about the rebuilding of the Army from Vietnam to Operation Desert Storm. We discussed all DTLOMS aspects of rebuilding.[1] While most agreed that Army general change during this period was evolutionary, all believed that the changes in training were revolutionary. There was striking agreement that either the training changes or the improved quality of personnel in the all-volunteer force were the dominant influences in that very successful transformation after Vietnam. There has been ample focus on both practice and potential of quality personnel leading to the individual competence associated routinely with Special Operating Forces (SOF)—and now spread across both active and reserve forces. There has been less discussion on the training side, yet it is the training of Soldiers, increasingly as leaders, that realizes the national investment in quality Soldiers. After Vietnam, America's Army reinvented itself as a premier learning organization permeating both full service and citizen-Soldiers. The latter—citizen-Soldier transformation—is remarkable, reflective of the enormous power of the current training system drawing from and multiplying experiential learning from prolonged combat service in Iraq and Afghanistan.[2]

How did this all occur? The initial revolution immediately after Vietnam institutionalized performance-oriented training to task, condition and standard. That was embedded in a Combat Training Center (CTC) training model that generated the most effective major learning organization in the United States. Then varying forms of simulation drawing on laser-based simulation of direct fire weapons, virtual simulation, and computer-based modeling were introduced, and then institutionalized across the force as a second revolution in training exercises structured to ensure effective task training to standard.

Deliberate, paced, change in training has accelerated since the end of the Cold War and Desert Storm. America's Army is now embarked in a continuing revolution since 9/11 that will be an order of magnitude more important at every level—strategic, operational, and tactical—than the preceding two revolutions. This continuing revolution expanded emerging institutionalization of learning drawing on tactical engagement simulation both grouped and distributed but now assembled then distributed globally by the Internet.

Exploitation of the Internet is providing enormous new learning capabilities to a globally disposed force culturally prepared to learn.

The Internet has stimulated multiple major learning system improvements since 9/11. They include design of learning, both grouped and distributed; drawing on the Internet supporting simulation; design of individual, team, and unit learning; and most recently, training of Army Force Generation (ARFORGEN) programs now institutionalized in support of the Army Plan.

Simultaneously, there has been growing focus on preparation for full spectrum operations, routinely joint, interagency, intergovernmental, and multinational (JIIM). These operations address irregular, catastrophic, disruptive, and traditional military challenges as described in the most current Quadrennial Defense Review.[3] Beginning with operations in the Balkans in 1995, increasing emphasis was directed at preparing individuals, leader teams, and units for both kinetic combat operations and nonkinetic stability operations. This emphasis builds both requirements and practices for generating very high-performing teams of leaders across the range of likely commitment of America's Army—JIIM.[4] Interagency application of Army-initiated leader team development programs and processes to support domestic and international Long War applications may be the next learning revolution.

That is the good news. The bad news is current inability to institutionalize broadly these beneficial changes because of the intensity of commitment to fighting in Iraq and Afghanistan. This has been a rocky path as an overextended Army currently struggles to support extended commitment with too-few Soldiers. Reduced time to rebuild and refit units in the United States, training equipment shortages, and instability of personnel particularly in reserve units all contribute to reduced individual, team, and unit readiness today. Although enormously frustrating, these stresses will pass; the Army is poised to rebuild as training tools and opportunities multiply for a highly responsive learning organization.

In rebuilding, America's Army will be molded by continuing evolution of the training and learning revolutions past, present, and future that we now describe.[5]

PAST—THE INITIAL REVOLUTION

The revolution began in the early 1970s with several propositions advanced by the then-emerging TRADOC.[6] They were deceptively simple:

- Soldiers train best by doing. Conduct Performance-Oriented Training.
- Train to Task, Condition, and Standard (TCS)—the systems approach to training.
- All training is evaluation (that is, includes performance evaluation or assessment and informative feedback); all evaluation is training.

These propositions spawned an enormous effort to define individual and collective tasks and then to provide Soldier training and evaluation support products ranging from Soldiers Manuals to Army Training and Evaluation Programs (ARTEP) for both unit and generating force (school) use. In the early 1980s, the successful Navy Top Gun fighter training program from Vietnam combat inspired creation of the National Training Center (NTC) as the first of the CTCs. A novel individual and collective training model was developed. And, throughout the period, ways were sought to better distribute the training support to Soldiers in units. Each of these efforts was successful well beyond the original expectations of the inventors of TRADOC. Each in turn had revolutionary effects on Army readiness. And now they need to be applied to joint and interagency operations that are essential for security, stabilization, transition, and reconstruction operations (SSTR) for the Long War.[7]

Train to TCS

Rigorous, well-defined common training requirements converged the active and reserve forces by establishing uniform training requirements and assessment across active and reserve forces. The requirements were then institutionalized in common prescribed processes: design of a Mission Essential Task List and command training reviews (Quarterly Training Briefings). Individual replacements were uniformly prepared in their Soldier Military Occupational Specialty or officer Specialty Code across most grades—an enormous benefit to unit leaders in a globally disposed force. This rigorous standardization permitted fair, unbiased assessment of individual task proficiency. This was of great value in implementing equal opportunity programs. Either you performed to standard or you didn't. If you did, you were rewarded. If not, you were out, whether you were active or reserve, male or female, black or white. Without such accepted assessment tools, it is unlikely that the Army would have been able to institutionalize equal opportunity so rapidly in our litigious society. Now the uniformity of training stimulated by the rigor of training to common task, condition, and standard can be applied to developing and sustaining competency across enormously diverse multinational, multiethnic organizations created for Long War offensive, defensive, and stability operations.

The CTC Model

The component parts are now well known—Observer-Controllers (OCs), an Opposition Force (OPFOR), the After Action Review (AAR), and a reliable Instrumentation System (IS). There is much more here than meets the eye. The original concept was for preparation of leaders for a unit combat environment. Improved unit mission readiness was of course highly desirable, but it was secondary to leader preparation. This has succeeded beyond expectation. Now the CTC experience, fighting a tough enemy with unrelenting combat requirements and observed by highly credible mentors/coaches/trainers who have "been there," has been shared by all of the current Corps Commanders and higher. Each has experienced the "combat crucible" of CTC training and assessment as battalion, brigade, and division commanders. The Army now possesses the equivalent of General George Marshall's "black book" listing highly competent leaders from which assignments were made at the start of World War II. Today, CTC-revealed "combat producers" whether combat, combat support, or combat service support (C, CS, or CSS) are known and assigned with care when combat looms.

The credibility of the CTC process and associated combat-based performance standards was established when the NTC would not certify several National Guard units for deployment to Desert Storm. That experience was a clarion call to citizen-Soldiers that there is one standard for America's Army. National Guard Brigades now train to standard and deploy regularly as operating forces expecting deployment to combat on a predictable ARFORGEN schedule—once every five or six years. Now these highly effective proven learning processes are applied to stability (SSTR) operations.

The learning model was modified to prepare units for employment into Bosnia in the 1990s. A particularly noteworthy accomplishment was developing then institutionalizing training center learning processes to transition units rapidly from kinetic combat operations to non-kinetic stability operations. In preparation for NATO operations in Bosnia, a two-week training center rotation was divided about in half. Sequences could vary dependent upon command priorities but generally during the first several days, the unit had to demonstrate proficiency in intense mid-intensity fights. Then, a Zone of Separation had to be set up almost overnight, and stability operations begun requiring effective peacekeeping and peace enforcement operations. The unit "personality" had to be changed very rapidly from "kill them" to "kiss them." Then various performance requirements were presented, at increasing pace: practice in negotiations, aggressive patrolling to demonstrate benign presence, preparation of junior leaders for advisory responsibilities, and support of UN or other multilateral entities with inappropriate unit actions immediately met with increasingly negative consequences. The learning model was fine-tuned at the Joint Readiness Training Center at Ft. Polk or the Combat Maneuver Training Center at Hohenfels, Germany, while executing Partnership for Peace Operations well before 9/11. The model works exceedingly well, and it is very adaptive to changing unit focus to offensive, defensive, or stability operations.[8]

A second aspect, perhaps more important, is the abiding effect on leaders of the After Action Review (AAR) process itself whether operations are kinetic or nonkinetic. The United States Army is the only U.S. military service (or Army in the world, bar none) that permits commanders to be openly assessed in front of their subordinates. This has created a vitally important openness in working through success or failure on the battlefield that has been inculcated across the force. This openness creates a strong chain of command mutual team building culture in the unit during the rotation. All work through issues together, learning from and teaching each other to "beat the Opposition Force (OPFOR)."[9] Add to this candor and focus the expectation that the OPFOR will fight "no holds barred" just as an enemy will, and the Army has a superb practical vehicle to introduce change. If "it" works at the CTC against the OPFOR, recognized in the street language among leaders in units, accelerated troop acceptance is certain.[10] This is a practical vehicle to accelerate assimilation of ongoing Transformations as has been done expertly with mounted forces digitization.

The combined effect of these Army-unique learning processes and the pace of commitment in the Long War has made the active force and the reserve forces about equal in proficiency at least battalion and below, and at Brigade level for those deployed. That is a noteworthy precedent in the volunteer Army, a precedent recognized by assigning operational deployment missions to highly receptive reserve forces wanting to defend America actively post-9/11. That significant improvement of capability of reserve forces enabled by abiding patriotism plus a superb, fully institutionalized learning system is an important strategic advantage. Highly competent Guardsmen linked to state political authorities are a ready hedge against domestic weapons of mass destruction (WMD) and natural disaster. Now the successful processes generating citizen-Soldier competence need to be translated to other state and local civil servants and to federal agencies. No more inept Katrinas![11] "A way" ahead seems clearly evident in broader federal and state application of highly successful Army practice.

Distributed-Training Support

Continuous training must take place throughout the force, not only at the CTC. Fortunately, TRADOC invested heavily to provide training support (training aids, devices, substitution, and simulation) to enable individual and collective training in school and unit locations. While there were occasional failures, excellent material has been developed to support distributed training as funding has been available. Stimulated by the high costs of training mounted force units to requisite proficiency, distributed virtual simulation (originally Simulation Networking [SIMNET]) was invented by the Defense Advanced Research Projects Agency with Army collaboration and then proliferated. Subsequently expanded then linked with constructive and live simulations in a larger Tactical Engagement Simulation (TES) program, the Army established both requirements and capabilities for excellent distributed training. Aside from expanding training opportunities, particularly for reserve units routinely separated from their actual equipment, the great power of TES was, and remains, the capability to train repetitively on all the combat tasks, even those tasks too costly, too dangerous, or too ecologically proscribed (such as depleted uranium) for training on the ground in peacetime.[12] TES enabled iterative experiential training for individuals, teams, and units. That repetitive training is critical path for attaining then sustaining very high levels of individual, team and collective task proficiency.

When the first revolution culminated with complex joint operations in Panama (Just Cause), force preparation for deployment into the Balkans and the superb performance in Desert Storm, the ingredients for a global "leap-ahead" in training were present—and had been assessed favorably during Desert Shield/Desert Storm. All that was required to exploit fully emerging training opportunities across function and echelon was the Internet. The task is now to apply the individual and team learning opportunities enabled by emerging web-based social networking—text messaging, wikis, blogging and podcasting, rapidly becoming visual as well as aural-based. These learning opportunities should apply with equal effectiveness to joint and interagency operations—domestic and overseas.

There had been profound improvement in Army training in the 1970s and 1980s. Equally important, a paradigm (DTLOMPF) had been broadly confirmed ensuring that training and leader development were embedded in balanced force development—*D*octrine, *T*raining, *L*eader development, *O*rganization, *M*aterial, *P*ersonnel, and *F*acilities—the "imperatives" or DTLOMPF. This mandated balanced development across multiple areas—important recognition of the need for responsive, interrelated, and coordinated programs responsive to the nature of the particular military challenge being faced.[13] Now the combination of political, economic, social, cultural requirements for effective stability operations (SSTR) and domestic defense mandate application across federal and state agencies. "A way" to institutionalize effective responsive learning within America's Army had been proven for potential application by other departments and agencies of federal and state governance.

As one result of the focus on interrelated coordinated programs, not only was training highlighted but also leader development was given important, separate, and equal status. Leader development became a major Army program.[14] The Army Training and Leader Development Panel charted the course:

> Our Army must be a learning organization. Our leaders must commit to lifelong learning through a balance of educational and operational experiences, complemented by self-development, to fill knowledge gaps educational and operational experiences do not provide. To be a learning organization that supports this lifelong learning, the panel recommends that the Army provide the training and educational standards and products that are the foundation for standards-based training and leader development. Needed are the doctrine, tools and support to foster lifelong learning.[15]

The performance records of Desert Storm, Enduring Freedom, and initial Iraqi Freedom operations demonstrated success to all. But that was not to be a ceiling; it was a very substantial floor supporting accelerated expansion from training to learning (training and education) and teaching in the next decades.

THE PRESENT: A REVOLUTION GROWS

The next steps, now well institutionalized, were to draw upon the power of the Internet; to expand the focus from training to education (grouped together here as learning); to include leaders and self-development in the domains where learning had to be provided; to better focus learning through structuring of the learning experience; and finally to increase significantly the intensity of learning experiences. But, as in any organization, the essential support was command support from Army leaders.

Command Emphasis

Support in the current Army Plan reflects the continuing focus on development of warriors and adaptive leaders.

> The Army has undertaken a major review of how we train, educate, assign, and develop our military and civilian leaders. At installations around the world, at our Combat Training Centers, and across our institutional training base, we are enhancing our education and training programs. We are leveraging lessons learned from combat to counter insurgents, promote stability, and support reconstruction. We are expanding our military education programs to emphasize cultural awareness and foreign language training.[16]

Advantaging the Internet

Effective distributed learning to standard was an Army objective for years. Print and video were the first media used for classroom instruction tailored to be exported to be distributed classrooms and to units. After an unsuccessful early 1970s start with video disc, content was distributed through CD-ROM. Various combinations of synchronous and asynchronous instruction were developed drawing on telephone-linked computers or satellite-distributed courses using techniques of video teleconferencing. In every case, learning was to be caused by exporting both course and classroom instruction practices from the proponent school responsible for doctrine and instructional content to the student in the school or unit. Modification of content for effective distributed, not grouped, learning has been difficult and costly. And there are lingering reservations about the effectiveness of preparing known teams—such as unit staff teams—when they are separated virtual teams using past course content oriented to individual not team instruction. Performance has not yet matched clear potential.

From Training to Learning

The combination of the power of the new training system with its associated tools such as AAR methodology and TES ability to create any warfighting cues required to train individuals and units, all added to the emerging capabilities of the Internet, gradually expanded the training revolution to a learning and teaching revolution. Particularly as more and more officer professional education content employed TES, such as the Command and General Staff Officer Course at Ft. Leavenworth, the distinctions between training and education blurred. Then, as the evolving spectrum of conflict broadened from near-exclusive focus on mid-intensity conflict to stability and support operations, then counterterrorism then counterinsurgency and now security, stabilization, transition and reconstruction operations (SSTR), the need grows to prepare officers to be adaptive and self-aware. Leaders must be able to transition rapidly and effectively from kinetic combat operations to various non-kinetic stability operations and back. This central conclusion of a recent Training and Leader Development Panel increased both officer and non commissioned officer preparation in "how to think" as well as "what to think."[17] Stimulated by cross-cultural learning requirements for leaders in operations in Afghanistan and Iraq, advanced postgraduate learning opportunities are being expanded. Language training is in. The blurring between education and training particularly for leaders of all grades has been intensified as JIIM considerations influence more operations. Now, it is no longer a training revolution. It has become a fully learning and teaching revolution. Both "trainers" and "educators" expect increasing improvements in learning. This is an important change in the Army frame of reference and development expectations for the brigade-based modular force and beyond—a vital enabler for the next learning revolutions to come.

Expansion of the Domains for Learning and Teaching

From the very beginnings in the 1970s, the focusing domains were individual and collective training in the generating force (school) and the unit. These have proven necessary but not sufficient. Clearly, there are requirements for professional self-development that need to be acknowledged. There is nothing new in that. Professional reading has been encouraged for years. Now, however, more and more content can be distributed to office or home, and the requirements for serious continuing education grow as the intensity and variety of force deployments increases. Formal recognition of the requirement for self-initiating development programs was required. The second expansion was much increased attention to the leader as a focal point of learning preparation.[18] Self-evident in an organization that professes to be leader-dominant, this was nevertheless an important defining action to explicitly focus development on preparation of warrior leaders. Lead not manage. All other DTLOMPF "imperatives," particularly material development and organization, had to address leaders formally. That is, leader development was reemphasized as an obligatory check bloc in the bureaucracy of continuing force development. Both expansions could apply to improved interagency training.

Focus Learning and Teaching Through Structuring of the Learning Experience

A vital ingredient in solid learning is the presentation of the proper cue to the learning audience.[19] A stimulus, or cue, triggers learning according to cognitive learning theory. The cue sets the stage for a self-initiated response. Correct, timely cues stimulate good experiential learning. Good night training obviously requires night. Training target acquisition requires correct target representation under the varying conditions of combat, such as battle obscuration or chemical warfare. Cues may be complex human interactions such as those required for learning how to dominate tough negotiations with a difficult Serbian Mayor—a challenge in preparing leaders for service in the Balkans in the late 1990s.

The answer has been structuring of the learning. As described in 1993: "the combination of the training requirements [mandated by doctrine and civil restrictions] can be attained only by deliberate design or 'structuring' of the training process to ensure that specific training events occur in the manner and sequence desired to achieve specific task training purposes."[20] Lane training applied structured learning to live simulation (Multiple Integrated Laser Engagement System or MILES) on the terrain. The Close Combat Tactical Trainer (CCTT) provided structuring capability for virtual simulation, with carefully prepared training exercises providing the essential catalyst (e.g., the SIMNET/CCTT then Force XXI Training Program training programs designed by the Army Research Institute, initially for National Guard training, but later adopted by the active Army).

The best continuing structuring is at the CTCs. The Mission Rehearsal Exercise (MRE) that preceded unit deployment to the Balkans in the late 1990s are excellent examples of structuring to emerging mission purpose. MREs were adapted substantially for Bosnia as described previously. These operations were seen in advance of commitment as what are now recognized as likely offensive, defense, and stability operations. Leaders prepared for combat then transitioned to stability operations supporting a Zone of Separation. A full operations spectrum was presented to units in CTC rotations leading to successful operations in Bosnia then Kosovo. In sum, there is a proven structured learning process to transition leaders and teams of leaders from kinetic to nonkinetic patterns of operations. This is an important building block in refocusing units for hedge contingencies.[21]

Structuring is costly. It is complex to sustain because it requires absolute verisimilitude of learning cue to actual operations in the objective area when the goal is seamless transfer from training to operations. Cues change as operations progress so updating has to be continuous based on detailed feedback from combat operations. But it causes exceptional learning to occur when the structured learning situations can be used repetitively by leaders.[22]

Increasing Significantly the Intensity of the Learning Experience

The last building block of the continuing revolution has been thoughtful varying of the structuring of the learning to intensify the learning and teaching processes themselves. Much of this came from increasingly experienced OCs at the CTCs, the font of learning and teaching. The "best" from units training at the "dirt" CTCs were invited to become OCs. The best OCs were invited back again in more senior positions at the CTCs. This excellence in understanding of practical learning and teaching in a tactical environment is reflected in the experience base of the most senior leadership at the CTCs.[23] This remarkable learning experience base matured over thirty years now could be a national treasure if focused on developing joint and interagency teams of leaders conducting homeland defense and overseas stability operations. There are literally hundreds of highly CTC-experienced retired officers and noncommissioned officers (NCOs) available to support translation of these learning practices across federal and state agencies. This valuable trained-leader resource base, possessing inculcated values of service to nation, is well distributed geographically to support state and local governments. See the Appendix for a representative example in one state.

Several examples from the NTC in California reflect the levels of intensification of individual, leader, and operational unit learning that have been achieved recently. Two caveats to these examples are in order. First and foremost, the infrastructure of the NTC exists to support the unit in its preparation for combat. All actions described below are taken after detailed consultation between the General Officer present from the Division in NTC rotation and the Commanding General NTC and Commander, Operations Group (OCs). The Brigade in rotation is not informed. They are fighting "for their lives" against a very tough enemy. Second, the OPFOR is not scripted. It is "free play" responding to its orders—designed to cause the OPFOR to execute operations required for requisite learning to occur in the unit in rotation. These OPFOR counter-tasks create the cues necessary to cause visiting unit learning to occur as the OPFOR fights. While the examples pertain to midintensity conflict, they have been applied with equal effectiveness to counter-terrorist (CT) and counterinsurgency (COIN) Contemporary Operating Environments (CoEs) within the framework of the doctrine, tactics, techniques, and procedures being taught at the CTCs.[24] Exactly the same processes were applied to transition units from kinetic combat operations to nonkinetic stability operations in the Balkans.

- There is manipulation of the resources provided to the OPFOR. Dependent on progress by the unit in rotation, "battlefield enablers," such as attack helicopters or chemical attacks (persistent or non-persistent) or actions of role players reflecting interpersonal and cultural interactions, are metered to the OPFOR daily. The normal guidance is to enable what the unit in training appears competent to handle, "then some."

- If a unit has not received desired learning from a particular mission—assessed by each of the OC teams assigned to subordinate organizations—the unit "recocks" and executes the same mission or a similar combination of human interactions again.
- As the unit deploys to and occupies a military city portrayed at the NTC, the number, frequency, and level of complexity of the tactical situations presented to the unit are metered by relevant function in the Contemporary Operational Environment. As each battlefield function becomes operational, it is stressed. OCs determine how challenging the actions will be that cues will stimulate and how many functions will be stressed simultaneously. Complexity presented to the unit in training can be varied enormously.

The results are truly memorable learning and teaching experiences tailored to the capabilities of individuals, leaders, and operational units. Intensity is varied to generate then sustain the most effective learning and teaching environment. Having observed many "fights" conducted at over one hundred CTC rotations since the original NTC opened in the early 1980s, we are witness to remarkable improvements in both effectiveness and efficiency of tactical learning during both "revolutions." The effects of the several sequential revolutions multiply as in a geometric progression. There is substantial reason to expect this growth to accelerate as the ingredients of a continuing revolution appear. That acceleration would be the extension of successful institutionalization of an adaptive learning system into joint and interagency organizations focused on national security. Now being exported nationally for active and reserve Army Force Generation (ARFORGEN), CTC-like learning programs exported to multiple locations could become valuable cross-cultural interagency learning facilities.

The strategic effects of this institutionalization of America's Army as a learning organization are profound. The National Guard and the Army Reserve are direct and powerful evidence of the growing effects of what America's Army has achieved. The Army Guard currently maintains Guard/U.S. State partnerships with fifty-four countries. Under these various Partnership for Peace programs initiated by Gen. George Joulwan as Supreme Commander in Europe, the Russian glacis was moved significantly to the east after the Cold War. This was a major national strategic success. Army Reserve forces possess national and regional functional competencies immediately available to support America's Army as a first responder to domestic WMD. Could these learning organization successes be expanded more broadly to national WMD or improving interagency competencies for the Long War?

Can the rest of the executive branch copy such clear success to prepare their equivalent officers and NCOs?

Several ingredients of emerging acceleration as a learning organization for both domestic defense and overseas offensive, defensive and security (SSTR) operations are present now. The Army possesses many exceptionally experienced, competent leaders, serving and retired, who know how to draw on current learning tools to structure and intensify learning and teaching to develop high-performing individuals, leaders and operational units. They have learned as OCs and in combat.

Combat Training Center Opposition Forces (CTC OPFORs) (including numerous role players and those of the Battle Command Training Program [BCTP] preparing larger Corps and Divisions) are proud and confident in their demonstrated capabilities to replicate any potential enemy or JIIM interpersonal interactions across the full spectrum of operations. OPFORs can make units fight the "worst case" enemy, kinetic or nonkinetic, as determined by national intelligence agencies. These CTC fights can be linked to the Center of Army Lessons Learned (CALL) to provide timely feedback from on-going combat operations so that learning cues are current and so that decentralized doctrine, tactics, techniques and procedures (DocTTP) development is stimulated. The Army Training and Leader Development Panel (TLDP) recommends increased use of CTC expertise for doctrine development—closing the loop to very responsive adjustment of DocTTP to ongoing operations.[25] Now digital manuals linking operational lessons learned to doctrine developers emerge to provide highly flexible tactics techniques and procedures development and subsequent leader training. FM 7.1 Battle Focused Training (in preparation) will be the first Army digital manual.

IS continue to improve for the documentation of operations—more detail from lighter, smaller, data-linked collectors tied to much-improved simulations are able to represent more complex battlefield interactions including joint (the Emerging Digital Battle Staff Trainer [DBST]). These instrumentation systems are equally applicable to security, stabilization, transition reconstruction (SSTR) operations.

There is absolute acceptance of the AAR process. By its accepted practices—candid, mentored, discussion of tactical strengths and weaknesses up and down the chain of command including introspective review of battle command style (seeing oneself)—the chain of command is developed as a vertical team of leaders. These are leaders learning and teaching others, through AAR processes, as they learn. The product is shared competence and frequently shared vision, trust, and confidence as the chain of command proceeds through the CTC rotation. The door opens to explicit preparation of *very high-performing teams of leaders—a new domain of leader preparation*. These teams can be Army or JIIM in organization.

Iterations of successful Mission Rehearsal Exercises with confirmed success in "seamless" unit handovers in Balkan then Mid East deployments prove the application of the various learning processes in preparing individual leaders, teams of leaders and operational units for highly successful operations, kinetic or non-kinetic. It is effective as the appropriate DocTTP are being taught. The nation needs now to make it more efficient and apply to JIIM teams SSTR—grouped or distributed.

Last, these solid improvements are being institutionalized effectively in the Army Force Generation (ARFORGEN) Road to Deployment. The practical application of a highly structured process to prepare combat, combat support and combat service support units for deployment is best explained by Lt. Gen. David Petraeus, in his words as Commander, Combined Arms Center Ft. Leavenworth. He was the designer and executer of the ARFORGEN Road to Deployment for TRADOC. Note the orientation to nonkinetic operations. This explanation could be a model for routine interagency preparation if agencies were provided access to the "treasury" of experienced Army mentors, coaches, and observers developed over three decades and personnel authorization overhead for training and operational training opportunities in support of Country Teams:

> Heard there (at Camp Atterbury IN) of a aviation bn/TF that came from six or so different states. Its leaders were brought together for pre-mob(ilization) gatherings (initial team building) at Atterbury, then were mobilized with their units, then went through a variety of training events, including CPXs that start at low level to build the teams and then culminated in a BCT-level CPX (Command Post Exercise) (as always, with an SRO (Senior Retired Officer) ... as the unit is preparing for Kosovo). Next they will deploy to JMTC (Joint Multinational Training Command) at Hohenfels (Germany), do additional leader/staff/individual training, go through an MRE, (Mission Readiness Exercise) and deploy into the Balkans. As always, huge amount of team building of all types—leaders, leaders with staffs, staffs with counterparts up/down the chain, NCO chain, and so on ... full of team building—and full of objectives developed by the leaders in coordination with the organizations that guide them through post-mob activities (nearly three months), pre-MRE CPXs/exercises, and then actual MREs. And then ... the right seat ride process links them with any additional JIIM partners that haven't been part of the prep. Throughout it, by the way ... they are virtually linked with the unit they'll replace and virtually looking "over their shoulder." There is also use of web-sites, VTCs, and both functional and, often, unit virtual communities.[26]

Figure 1 portrays this complex comprehensive process as a thoughtful sequence of learning events.

Again leaving the description of the process to the responsible commander:

> We've been conducting the COIN (Counterinsurgency) seminars for about 5–6 months ... all leaders from CPT to COL, plus staffs and NCO counterparts at each level. Ret'd 4-star SROs (Senior Retired Officers), BCTP (Battle Command Training Program) facilitators, recently returned Battalion/Brigade Commanders,

Figure 1

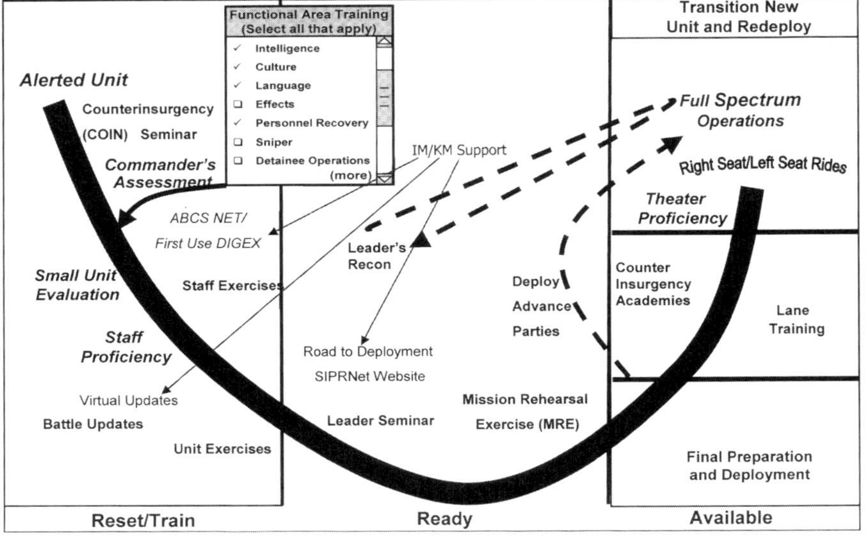

and functional area experts (as well as BCKS[Battle Command Knowledge System]) all participate. Same continues a few months later when the same team of leaders/staff/NCOs gathers for the pre-CTC (Combat Training Center) MRE (Mission Rehearsal Exercise) seminar. And then, of course, all reinforced by the CTC MRE.... Once in theater, there's an additional seminar, by the way, and then the units link up with their true interagency/multinational partners and operate.[27]

The ARFORGEN Road to Deployment is important institutionalization of adjustment of Army training and leader learning to the force projection training requirements of the Modular Force.[28] It groups, resources, and explains to individuals, teams, and units the various responsibilities of preparation for all units in America's Army. As a required learning program, it establishes the rigor of embedded assessment as well as justifies the resources necessary for execution. Now the quality training and learning of the Road to Deployment is being exported from CTC to home-based Brigade Combat Teams (BCTs)—active and reserve. That quality is being extended further to combat support and combat service support brigades as an important extension of proven learning practices to tasks associated with stability operations. Can the next step be institutionalization of interagency leader team preparation supportive of SSTR operations? Focus next on interagency preparation as a stepping stone to intergovernmental and multinational operations?

There is certain application of these proven, fully institutionalized learning capabilities to sustainment of America's Army capabilities for full spectrum operations. The Army Plan discussed in Chapter 3 generates highly material-intensive Heavy, Light and Stryker BCTs designed organizationally for low and midintensity operations. That is the Army Plan fully in execution. The leader time requirements to gain and sustain unit effectiveness employing the various technologies—today, then more with Future Combat Systems (FCS)—is consuming. As a practical issue, baseline proficiency for these units must be immediate readiness for kinetic low and midintensity operations.[29] However, the unit learning system advances described earlier combined with intensification of grouped or virtual officer and NCO continuing education can maintain proficiency to lead nonkinetic stability operations when required. The Bosnia precedent in preparing units to transition rapidly to a situation of extraordinary ethnic cleansing in a civil war is both highly relevant and very important for Long War and hedge readiness for America's Army. With prestocked individual, leader team, and unit learning programs and appropriate support content, rapid conversion from kinetic to nonkinetic—and the reverse—is desirable and feasible.

This is a vitally important, powerful, assembling of best past training and learning practices linked to proven evaluation "best practices." As they are understood, and are provided sufficient resources to be proactive not reactive, these new technologies offer the promise of substantial distribution of the learning best practices nationally across federal and state jurisdictions if not globally. Those are the next steps.

THE FUTURE: EMERGING ACCELERATION OF TRAINING AND LEARNING EFFECTIVENESS

New ingredients emerge to accelerate and expand the effects of accelerating learning best practices. These ingredients are substantial downward leader task migration; the opening of important new learning and teaching domains; the development of a model to focus leader team and team leadership preparation; emergence of powerful World Wide Web (WWW)-based military-oriented Professional Forums supported by Army establishment of internet-based policies and programs of Army Knowledge Management (AKM), Army Knowledge Online (AKO); and new forms of participatory media, such as avatars that offer promise of effective, very efficient, global team leader building. All can be applied to provide a highly adaptive new multidomain training/learning national defense resource.[30]

Substantial Downward Leader Task Migration

The combination of highly competent, motivated, volunteer Soldiers and increasingly distributed tactical data and information are driving task performance responsibilities lower and lower in the chain of command. The leading edge of "power down" to ever-lower echelons is likely present in Special Forces individual Soldiers directing B52-delivered fire support in Afghanistan. Land Warrior brought these capabilities to the Infantry Squad in 2007.[31] Corporals are expected to master tasks formerly expected of much more senior NCOs who in turn have assumed many responsibilities formerly expected of officers.[32] So, in thinking of learning futures, we consider leaders to be Corporal (E4) and above. That is ALL Corporals and above should be prepared as adaptive, self-aware leaders—certainly for combat arms MOS and probably for all MOS. *Inter alia* that infers preparation not just for performance in their own grade but also to perform competently one to two grades higher in the face of casualties. Although this change is occurring gradually, it is nonetheless profound as it modifies substantially both preparation and performance in America's Army. New domains of Soldier preparation emerge addressing offensive, defensive and stability operations.[33] Increased depth of leader preparation supports timely readiness for both kinetic combat operations and nonkinetic stability operations.

The Opening of Important New Learning and Teaching Domains

The first training revolution addressed individual and collective training in institution and unit. That is, individual training had to be prepared for execution by Soldiers in the generating force (school) and in units. In addition, collective training had to be provided to institution and unit, with the vast majority of the collective training occurring in the unit. That collective training established a total of four domains for which effective and reasonably efficient training programs had to be prepared.

FM 7.0 Army Training, stimulated to increase focus on leader development and to acknowledge the importance of self-learning, added an additional two learning venues: self-development and leader, creating a total of nine potential domains—a three by three matrix. That formulation seems overly complex. It aims too low in terms of the objectives and the capabilities of America's Army. The Army should consider replacing the leader venue of FM 7.0 with teams since JIIM teams are the lifeblood of stability operations. With the advent of vastly expanded data and information exchanges associated with Army digitization, no one acts alone. At every echelon across all battle functions, individuals perform as members of teams. Soldiers are always part of vertical teams because the Army is a hierarchical organization with subordinates following the direction of superiors. Normally, all Soldiers are members of horizontal teams with buddies, wingmen, or peers at the same echelon (commanders or staff officers and NCOs). So it is necessary to prepare teams—primarily the many existent in the operational unit or organization but also to develop DocTTP for "how to team," prepared and perhaps learned by individuals in the generating force so that they are prepared to build and sustain hierarchical and peer teams in operating forces.

Focus on self-development—that is, continuing development initiated by the individual, team, or unit for its own improvement—is vitally important in an institution facing continuous change. Self-development of the individual is clear. Requisite skills, knowledge, and attributes (SKA) have been described in doctrine and the requirements for supportive supervision, mentoring, assessment, and feedback of individuals are understood if sometimes neglected. Such is not the case for teams. An abiding challenge is how to develop the team skills knowledge and attitudes to being productive team members through developing together in the actual team environment, be it grouped or virtual. Every young commander striving to "go out to the back forty" to prepare his or her unit as they deem necessary, understands unit-initiated learning. Doctrine and training processes abound for unit preparation. Both teams and units are in hierarchical environments with available supervision, mentoring, assessment and feedback. Apply unit development goodness to teams.

New domains seem vitally important as they represent the initiative characteristic of America's Army. Clearly, more learning research and development of appropriate supervision, mentoring, assessment and feedback is required for these domains. This research and development should be structured to support joint and interagency team-building initially and then intergovernmental and multinational leader team building.

A second and more profound change to current doctrine is the explicit expansion of all domains from training to leader learning and teaching. America's Army prepares high-performing leaders—leaders as individuals (Corporal and above), performing together as leading teams (crews, sections, staffs, commanders) and elite leading units or organizations. The Ranger Regiment is an excellent unit example. Obviously, lesser proficiencies have to be tolerated but the objective of all individuals, teams, and units or organizations is dominating excellence—to lead as the world class. Neither training nor education is adequate in the current environment creating adaptive, self-aware leaders. Some of each is always necessary, Corporal and above. Combining the two as learning and teaching is essential. Therefore, there are the leader learning and teaching domains proposed as indicated earlier. The merit of D*TL*OMPF created during the early Revolution remains, but Lead is now the goal of all activities of individuals, teams and units in America's Army and in JIIM stability operations fighting the Long War.

There are SKA or their equivalent for each of these various domains. For example, the SKA for team preparation are separate and distinct from those agreed to be essential for individual leader preparation. They are stated well for America's Army in the new FM 6.22 Army Leadership. It is also necessary to develop team leadership consisting of shared vision or purpose, shared trust, shared competence, and shared confidence.[34] Note the repetitive requirement for sharing of SKA. In each case, the suggested skill, knowledge, or attitude of a team is not the same as the SKA possessed by each individual. Think of the shared skills, knowledge, and attitudes as the overlap area in a Venn diagram. Development of those team overlap skills, knowledge, and attitudes—shared vision, shared trust, shared competence, and shared confidence—are essential to preparing and sustaining very high-performing teams. Similar SKA become collective tasks for units and organizations to acquire to become high performing. For tactical units, these are developed in the alchemy of superior unit performance created at the CTCs drawing on the learning model discussed previously. They seem more broadly applicable to organizations in general.[35]

Development of a Model to Focus Leader Team and Team Leadership Preparation

One way to think about leader teams is indicated in Figure 2. The horizontal bars represent echelons of command from platoon to division. The vertical bars represent tactical battle functions. At every intersection of every bar is at least one leader, more often several leaders, who are in near-continuous communication vertically with seniors and subordinates and horizontally with peers making decisions. All vertical and horizontal combinations of leaders become teams of commanders and leaders. A horizontal staff team is shown

Figure 2

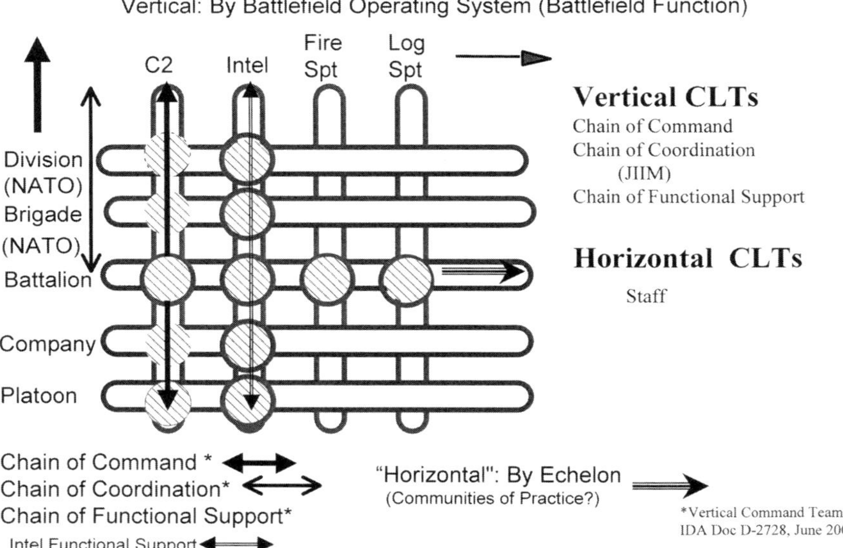

above at battalion consisting of intelligence staff officer, fire support staff officer and logistics staff officer. The chain of command, a vertical, hierarchical team of leaders, is represented by the solid arrow from Platoon to Division within the command and control function (C2). Next to it, with multi-striped arrow, is a chain of coordination introduced with the NATO Division. Note that in intelligence (IEW), the leader team is a combination of commanders and staff officers—intelligence staff officers (S2s) and Military Intelligence unit commanders. These are chains of functional support. They may consist of officers or non commissioned officers, within one function or cross functions.

Clearly the chain of command is the most important team of leaders but there are many other teams that need preparation if this organization is to be competent, much less really high performing. And what if joint or multinational operations are involved? Or what if functional support is to be provided to civil authorities during domestic WMD attack? Or if various other important Departments such as State, Treasury, or Justice, or nongovernmental organizations such as Doctors without Borders are members of the teams? In every case the decision authorities rest in chains of functional support or chains of coordination not in a chain of command. Something more than direction is required to get results. There must be shared SKA, particularly shared vision and shared trust if there is to be high performance among leaders from disparate organizations.

Figure 3 addresses that situation in a Stability operations environment for high-performing CLTs in complex JIIM organizations. Notice that the vertical areas now represent vertical teams responsible for Stability Operations' functional areas such as force protection operations and negotiations. Comparable adjustments could be made for counter terrorist (CT) or counterinsurgency (COIN) operations. A multinational unit has been interjected reflecting Afghan operations. Alternatively a level could be Department of State, Department of Justice or Northern Command or an Air National Guard command for homeland defense. No longer is it an Army chain of command with well-understood responsibilities and authorities. This is a chain of command up to the point of multinational or interagency presence. Above that, it becomes a chain of coordination. More complex teams exist here collaborating across often diverse cultures sharing Address Books or Rolodexes. In fact post-9/11, all teams are likely to be increasingly Joint, Interagency, Intergovernmental, and Multinational (JIIM) striving to become high performing as they develop team leadership.

JIIM will be the area of greatest application of the leader team preparation model. There will be little shared knowledge of DocTTP acquired in common institutional preparation such as that which exists within the Army. No common battle functions that can frame acting (and learning/teaching) as occurs in chains of command or chains of functional support. DocTTP for chains of coordination in JIIM evolves today through practice in various multinational counter terrorism operations or domestic WMD response exercises. For now, the model may support best by indicating where within the organizational structure the

Figure 3

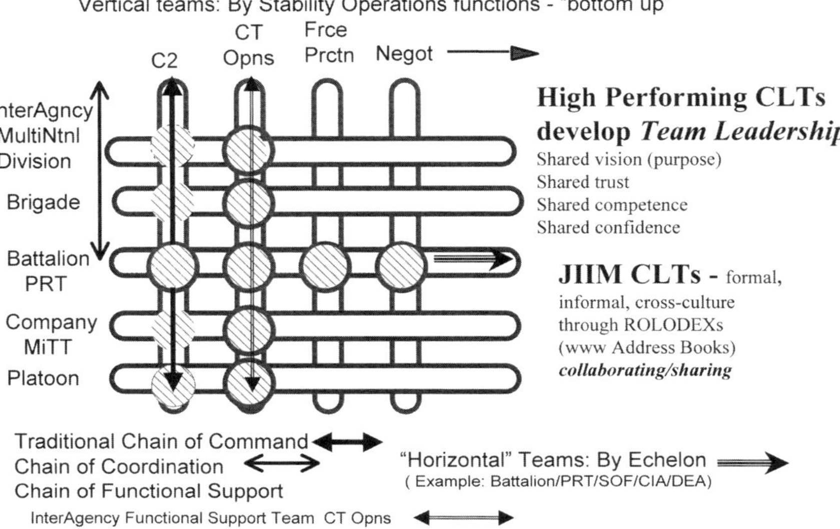

various leader teams are to be sought, prioritized, then prepared. Today in a period of rapidly expanding participatory media (YouTube, Facebook, Instant Messaging) there are multiple paths to use to access supporting expertise such as friends—friends of friends or professional expertise associates. Each leader has a Rolodex from which to tap informal support.

Suffice to comment that there would certainly appear to be lots of individual leaders, leader teams, and units that need to be prepared. Most of the learning tools appear to have been developed in past revolutions, but they have yet to be applied to the various learning audiences mentioned above. In fact, the Army doctrinal larder seems sparse in these areas. Lots of room here for exploitation as the ARFORGEN Road to Deployment matures. There is even more when emerging Internet capabilities are included to link individuals, teams, and units globally or nationally for homeland defense.

Emergence of Powerful WWW-Based, Military-Oriented Professional Forums and Army Establishment of Army Knowledge Management (AKM), Army Knowledge Online (AKO), and the Battle Command Knowledge System (BCKS)

The potential of digitization is increasingly evident.[36] Effective communication encourages routine exchange of data and information both vertical for the exercise of command and horizontal for command or staff coordination. Less appreciated is the recent emergence of Internet means to share knowledge such as volunteer discussion groups (Professional Forums) addressing important professional issues.

The Army has several knowledge management tools embedded in the current Battle Command Knowledge System (BCKS).

- Structured Professional Forums (SPF). These are groups of Soldier leaders drawing on the Internet and informed mentors (forum leaders) to voluntarily share counsel about improved job performance in America's Army. "Passionate professionals" seeking to improve their units, their leader teams, and themselves to win the Long War. They are the "engine" of BCKS. An outstanding current example of the vibrant power of SPFs is Companycommand.army.mil, linking company commanders globally.
- Knowledge Nets (KN). Networks of readily available and timely data, information, expertise, and applications supporting individual, team, or unit performance. A recent unit-oriented combat example was CAVNET, providing combat information and most current tactics, techniques, and procedures between Soldiers and small unit leaders in the First Cavalry Division in Operation Iraqi Freedom.[37] Other functionally oriented KN have been fielded usually under the tutelage of the TRADOC Proponent. Examples are Fires Knowledge Net (FKN) from the Chief of Joint Fires at Ft. Sill and Logistics Net (LOGNET) established by Department of the Army G4 but now under the governance of the logistics integrating Proponent at Ft. Lee.
- Action Teams (ATs). Army ATs, potentially Joint Action Teams (JATs), Intergovernmental Action Teams (IATs), and Multinational Action Teams (MATs) are quick response temporary teams formed, if necessary, globally across JIIM, to assemble the best expertise available to support the accomplishment of specific tasks. ATs are teams that build things or advise those who run or recommend things. ATs come into being when you need to innovate, whether in solving a problem, making a decision, or in building new knowledge or expertise. They work hard and fast to enable action, but do not run or formally recommend actions. Commander leader teams act. An important example is telemedicine, providing the most competent medical specialists expertise from CONUS to combat medics in Southwest Asia.

Important professional issues discussed on AKO expand rapidly as young leaders, digital natives, discover opportunities to engage in professional collaboration.[38] There are already families of Communities of Practice (CoPs) and Professional Forums where concerned professionals can share data, information, and knowledge. These CoPs exist across job position (First Sergeants) and battle function such as Fire Support or those colocated in a particular theater of operations (Balkans) or in a particular mission such as SSTR or COIN operations. Users data, information, or knowledge needs determine knowledge management tool requirements.

Knowledge management can stimulate effective learning responsive to the explicit requirements of participants who are essentially concerned peers working together to address shared command problems by each drawing on counsel from experiences of the other. Frequently, the merits of alternative "best practices" are discussed. Mentors channel the discussion to subjects of mutual interest. Recently, there has been extended discussion on Company-command.mil of the implications of Transformation and concerning the challenges of combat in Afghanistan and Iraq. Clearly both learning and teaching occur.

Now add to these voluntary peer relationships similar data, information or knowledge-sharing practices by virtual teams of leaders, both vertical and horizontal. These teams may be either grouped or distributed. Whether a distributed chain of command likely to assemble together only after deployment, if at all; a chain of functional support; or an interagency chain of coordination, there would be seem to be many opportunities to stimulate leader team acquisition of the known skills, knowledge, and attitudes of high-performing teams. Products may be enhanced tactical battle command or improved interagency stability operations or really high-performing teams of federal, state and local leaders addressing domestic WMD.

Then add horizontal peer Communities of Practice (aka Structured Professional Forums) directly supporting vertical virtual teams of leaders (Corporal and above) in execution of their responsibilities. This interwoven interaction of vibrant vertical and horizontal exchanges of data, information, and knowledge to generate "actionable" understanding is termed double knit.[39] Double knit can occur in a tactical unit with horizontal CoPs at each leader level supporting the vertical chain of command or functional support. Land Warrior-equipped Soldiers will identify these quickly.

Such is the vision of the emerging BCKS, as it can reinforce America's Army as a learning organization. It offers exciting new transmission vehicles for knowledge transfers such as timely access to data, information, and knowledge linked to the TRADOC generating force. These vehicles can also provide ready support to individuals and commander leader teams in units that in turn support important joint or interagency teams of leaders.

Army acceleration as a learning organization will "cut its teeth" bringing these kinds of new ingredients to bear to create and sustain very high performing leaders as individuals, as leader teams and perhaps as leader "Lehr" units, elite modular force formations of leaders (Corporal and above) performing at unprecedented levels of unit proficiency. Double knit has the potential to further accelerate the Army as a vibrant learning and teaching organization with the majority of both occurring in most units and organizations. That prospect alone promises to change dramatically the role of the generating force or the institution in training and educating as the loci of learning and teaching moves to practitioners in units.

Double knit can be extended also to support sequential, structured, ARFORGEN Road to Deployment training by using avatars to support leader team preparation particularly when the leader teams are distributed, nationally or overseas.[40] Avatars supporting distributed CTC role-playing seem likely to magnify the value of existing CTC and CCTT investments. Role players in the flesh at the CTC could, as avatars, be available to support continuing post-CTC Mission Readiness Exercise (MRE) training at the unit home station. This support could be particularly useful preparing leaders and leader teams for nonkinetic stability operations. After all, the Army investment in virtual simulation embedded in the CCTT and supporting digital functional exercises for other combat systems such as aviation seems likely to be the most extensive digital world in existence with structured training and learning exercises already built in. So there is a ready digital world at Battle Simulation Centers where role players or OCs could continue to support individual or leader team training. And in fact if leader teams can be assembled from various locations solely for the CTC MRX, perhaps their avatars could meet and continue to train as a leader team in the digitized CCTT world at a local Battle Simulation Center.

Avatars seem a very important supplement to the current Combat Training Center model of OC, OPFOR, AAR, and IS. Perhaps avatars are equal in potential value to the OPFOR or the Instrumentation System in supporting learning. Matched to requirements of Lifelong Learning and ARFORGEN Road to Deployment, now adding requirements for joint task training/competency learning (Joint Fires, and so on) shared learning could be enabled by avatar Professional Forums or Knowledge Nets "meeting" around a digital table in a digital world. Or the meeting could be a joint and inter agency staff team discussing support of a pending operation? Given current Army assimilation of digital training worlds and the wealth of Soldiers who are digital natives, avatar possibilities appear near endless.

There also may be important opportunities to draw on the current TRADOC analytical infrastructure for improved Army learning—Battle Command Training Program (BCTP), School of Advanced Military Studies (SAMS), TRADOC Analysis Center (TRAC), Center of Army Lessons Learned (CALL), Combat Training Centers (CTCs])—to generate new individual and leader team learning exercises to be used in Life Long experiential learning with the student performing "on the ground" through his/her avatar. Learning exercises addressing the application of new doctrine, training, leader development (DTL) could used by leader teams in units including JIIM in any operating environment to implement new DTL. Learn "how to" in exercises requiring knowledge and understanding of the new DTL. This is an important capability when "fielding" new DTL combinations responsive to a new or evolving tactical challenge—such as low intensity conflict to counterinsurgency to unrestrained civil war. Cr perhaps addressing team learning requirements across agencies and federal, state and local jurisdictions in homeland defense.

Other Potential Applications

There would seem to be practically unlimited opportunities to apply all the above in varying combinations to current and likely future operational challenges. First and foremost, the continuing learning revolution would support the preparation and sustainment of very high-performing individuals, leader teams, and units of the active and reserve forces. Additional opportunities abound: applications to create high-performing teams oriented to specific kinetic or nonkinetic patterns of operations in units composed of late additions to the task organization—including joint forces—en route to the objective area; teams in units anticipating lateral entry of highly qualified individuals from reserve forces or DA civilians (DAC), contractors, or retirees advantaging any "continuum of service" personnel sources;[41] or teams of personnel drawn from interagency or multinational organizations grouped for overseas counterterrorism operations or teams hastily assembled for Homeland Defense under a state governor. Each operational application suggested above could spawn a family of learning policies and programs with most drawing on connectivity through the Internet. As each application adopts better learning practices, evolution to both learning and teaching should occur.

Whatever the contingency, the important envelope of new learning and teaching capabilities likely to emerge will focus current intensified learning practices to emerging distributed learning, teaching, and team building. Both could be provided to important teams facing substantial leader personnel turbulence or turnover. These are potentially debilitating personnel additions or losses as they may occur to very high-performing leader teams across most operational units or organizations.

Even as the Army establishes a unit replacement system, there will still be changing combinations of functional support as organizations morph to apply exactly the right mix of combat, combat support, and combat service support assets to dominate various Common Operating Environments. Individual leaders need to become very high-performing leader teams in lead units, rapidly. These requirements and new capabilities seem certain to expand across the full spectrum of JIIM organizations.

Last, there appears to be a notable opportunity to increase significantly the overall contribution of digitization to improved combat effectiveness in all units—combat, combat support, and combat service support. To date, digitization impacts have been largely confined to improved command and control—essentially the science of war. Even greater payoffs may come in improved battle command—excellence in the art of war in both kinetic and nonkinetic operations. High-performing commander leader teams demonstrating extraordinary team leadership, teamwork, and team decision-making developed through expanding double knit seem certain to result in major improvements in battle command.

Thus, the acknowledged advances of earlier revolutions and Army acceleration as a learning organization proceed. This promises a future of vastly improved unit effectiveness as the tools of digitization are applied to both art and science of war to increase the effectiveness of the Army as a learning organization.

Why stop there? America's Army is a national institution pervasive across various jurisdictions with a wholly assimilated world-class learning infrastructure in being. Likely the Army is the global "best practice" for a very large distributed white- and blue-collar organization. How can this asset be better advantaged nationally?

After 9/11 then Katrina, there seems to be general agreement that interagency collaboration among and between both federal and state departments and agencies is poor. The spectacle of FEMA in Katrina is dismaying. Katrina provided warning. We would not have the luxury of advance notice of a dirty bomb in a metropolitan area. But more than improved collaboration seems required. Most federal and state agencies need to become more responsive learning organizations, perhaps following the Army model.

The United States needs to have initial and continuing learning policies and programs comparable to those provided the military but now applied to the professional development of federal, state, and local public servants for both domestic and overseas operations. A U.S. Public Service Academy has been proposed to "offer an all-expenses-paid education to 5,000 undergraduates. Its liberal arts curriculum would emphasize leadership development, analytical thinking and service to others, with requirements for summer service internships and a year of study abroad. Graduates would be required to work for five years in public service. They could choose from jobs in state, local or federal government, law enforcement, public health, education or nonprofit organizations."[42] That would be quite a start. Such an academy could provide institutional focus on training national security professionals in a common culture. But what about continuing development of these professionals as individuals and as members of interagency teams deployed domestically as in Katrina or overseas as in Provincial Reconstruction Teams (PRTs) in Iraq or Afghanistan?

We can't be team players if there is no team. Could various existing agency schools share processes developing synergies and collaboration bottom up supporting continuing education for public servants? There are the Foreign Service Institute and the FBI Academy. The military services all have institutional school systems. Might they be expanded? Perhaps establish interagency schools supported by creating school accounts within federal agencies to support school development? Perhaps an expanded National Defense University system could provide institutional focus on continuing education of national security professionals in a common culture?

Why stop with America's Army as a premier learning organization? How might the "best practice" embedded in America's Army support grouped and distributed interagency team development? Draw upon Army best practice policies and procedures to improve professional development across the U.S. government, both federal and state. Establish Interagency Team Training Centers comparable to Army Combat Training Centers? Draw on that institutionalized experiential learning model? More is likely to be required but that would come in time. There need to be common shared standardized administrative processes. These were implemented as standardization agreements (STANAGs) in NATO. Similarly common decision-making processes were developed successfully across NATO and across the military services. Why not across federal and state jurisdictions in the United States? Lots of highly experienced veterans of America's Army are available routinely but now they are particularly available to defend America post-9/11.

Once these capabilities are established, it then becomes both desirable and feasible to expect that senior political appointees in all federal departments have prepared in a learning environment appropriate to the skills knowledge and attributes expected of professional civil servants in that particular department.[43] It is absolutely feasible to establish minimum task-based learning experiences for patronage appointees "on the ground" in the basic area of responsibility envisaged for their public service. In time perhaps develop political party "back benchers" serving and learning with political party think tanks but including nationally subsidized "grounding" experience within the federal bureaucracy as part of "back bencher" development for subsequent nomination to high federal position? Preparation could be grouped or virtual, gradual or intense—all variations proofed by America's Army as a learning organization.

Competency-based high-performing interagency teams composed of competent civil servants and their political leadership become a reasonable public expectation rather than the uncoordinated incompetence expected and all too often seen today. This need not continue. We are greatly encouraged by the recent bipartisan, executive and legislative call for a volunteer Civilian Reserve Corps and by the presidential mandate to develop a national strategy providing "security professionals access to integrated education, training, and professional experience opportunities for the purpose of enhancing their mission-related knowledge, skills, and experience and thereby improv[ing] their capability to safeguard the security of the Nation. Such opportunities shall be provided across organizations, levels of government, and incident management disciplines, as appropriate."[44] The proof will be the quality of execution. We encourage national authorities to examine the existing institutional resources and practices of America's Army as a basis for moving on a broad front to achieve the goals of this new initiative.

6

Imperatives for Tomorrow: Organizational Adaptation to Continuing Change

> We will experience the same level of technological change in the first decade of the 21st century that we experienced in all of the 20th century.
>
> Col. Kip Nygren, "Emerging Technologies and Exponential Change," 2002

QUITE A PROSPECT, even if it is only half correct because that level of technological change would stimulate a tsunami of social and economic if not political change crashing upon human institutions. America's Army endures as an enormous institution undergoing change routinely, much externally directed, but is now about to encounter tsunami-equivalents? America's Army always seeks relative stability, predictability, and certainty, but seldom finds either as perpetual transitions occur, frequently unpredictably. The Army is uniquely reshaped in the processes of transition but often at significant institutional physical and spiritual cost. But if the Army is to succeed in defense of Nation, change, even of tsunami magnitude, must be accepted then fashioned to build not erode capability.

The challenge grows, as acceleration of the magnitude of sudden change does appear to be occurring. Global stability seems on a knife-edge. Overnight, successful assassinations of Pakistani leadership could produce a radical Islamic nation armed with nuclear weapons. The military challenge suddenly would become not competency in conducting nonkinetic stability operations; it would be deterring or defending against a well-armed hostile nuclear power requiring solid U.S. capability to fight and win highly kinetic mid- or high intensity conflict. An Israeli nuclear attack on Iran resulting in closure of the Persian Gulf would have immediate global economic impact, perhaps requiring early midintensity joint forced entry operations.

These are external changes; internal change can be equally influential. Today, the Army Plan that executes transformation results in substantial near-simultaneous change in almost every aspect of Army operations—arguably greater concentrated change than occurred in World War I or II. In departing remarks as Secretary of Defense, Donald Rumsfeld commented recently that now the Department of Defense is undergoing greater change than at any other time in its sixty-three year history.

America's Army needs more than solid adaptive leaders. It must be a wholly adaptive organization prepared not just to endure but also to thrive and grow with endemic change not only expected but also welcome. This is a tall order but not wholly unprecedented.

The Army has been constantly in transition. We served in five distinctly varied armies from 1952 to 1989. They were: post-Korea/Cold War, Vietnam early, Vietnam late, all volunteer, and Reagan rearming. And more recently as interested observers: end Cold War-Operations Just Cause and Desert Storm, Peace Dividend of Nineties (commitments up/resources down), Transformation and 9/11, and now the Long War. Nine distinct phases in sixty years with increases and declines in size often greater than entire strength of the Marine Corps. Now the Army is adapting to unexpected change in the Long War such as Explosively Formed Projectiles (EFP).[1] Some changes are global and increasingly ambiguous, such as nonstate enemies, domestic weapons of mass destruction (WMD) use, or expanding reliance on proxy forces. Some changes are highly transitory, such as significant increases in operations intensity exacerbated by resource shortfalls. Even more different America's Armies have existed if parallel periods of change in reserve forces and the civilian force, a sizeable proportion of One Army, are considered. Due to the global nature of U.S. interests, probably the broadest range of change experienced by any state's land force today has occurred with those serving today in the United States Army—with every prospect that the pace of change will increase in fighting the Long War as decentralized "open source" warfare grows.[2]

The Army today is fully engaged in transforming, in scale considerably beyond what was accomplished so successfully by the Army in rebuilding from Vietnam to Desert Storm. Now very substantial change occurs in the midst of full and likely continuing commitment to the Long War. After Vietnam, the essential challenge was forcing the pace of change while retaining, in fact rebuilding, readiness to defeat the Warsaw Pact. And the change was fundamentally linear. There were no basic surprises in doctrine, organization, or material. Essentially, there were substantial improvements to what had won in World War II.

That general continuity of practice is not the situation today. This second, more substantial and essentially unending Transformation proceeds in addressing the challenge of responding to evolving conventional threats as well as novel asymmetric attacks, domestic and foreign, all the while transforming to conduct substantially different joint and combined operations in the future. Long War success in the second continuing Transformation poses several interrelated requirements, which will need to be mastered simultaneously. Each is a significant challenge for U.S. landpower. Together, they are formidable, well beyond those present in the earlier Transformation. These new requirements stimulated by the Long War are:

- Adjust the ethos of the Army. The Chief of Staffs have been changing the culture of the Army. A translation of the Special Forces culture proceeds across combat, combat support, and combat service support functions. Facilitated by the nature of conflict in Operation Iraqi Freedom (OIF)—support functions have been under direct attack since OIF 1—it was imperative to prepare the entire force as warriors. Make active and reserve, combat support, and combat service support into ground combat fighters as well as supporters. The warrior ethos has been inculcated in much more demanding Basic Combat Training and reinforced in the officer and noncommissioned officer (NCO) education systems. Traditional Ranger maxims increasingly become Army maxims—such as "I will never leave a fallen comrade." This inculcation of the warrior quality/spirit is likely as important post-9/11 as is the full current Transformation prescribed in the Army Plan for it represents a sea shift in organizational perception. It is the absolute renunciation of the Euro-centric postmodern nonfighting Army model presented in the 1990s as representative of future landpower. Unfortunately, that post–Cold War ethos resides in some NATO forces currently physically present but provided an uncertain national mandate to actually engage in ground combat for NATO in Afghanistan as requested by local commanders.

- Regenerate the quality of America's Army, impaired by a decade of intensive commitment in the Balkans then Afghanistan and Iraq. There is an abiding need to "repair" a decade of consumption of capability with scant regeneration prior to initiation of combat operations after 9/11. The accumulated material reset requirement is in the range of $45 to 60 billion, as well as an authorized personnel strength shortfall in responding to multiple contingency requirements. Significant seed corn has been consumed. As commented by recent Army Chief of Staff General Peter Schoomaker: "In the last seven years, we have retrenched in the Army to pay our bills and terminated $86 billion worth of modernization. If [the] Future Combat Systems in some form or fashion does not go forward we will not have, for over 40 years, a new start at the modernization of the U.S. Army."[3] To put this in relative terms: "In 1969 the Army was one and a half million. Despite the fact that we're engaged in combat in Iraq, in Afghanistan, in the Philippines, and committed to peacekeeping missions in Bosnia, Kosovo, and the Sinai, and on operational deployments in over 70 countries, our Army is now less than one third that size. We had more soldiers in Saudi Arabia in the first Gulf war than we have in the entire Army today. In fact, Wal-Mart has three times as many employees as the American Army has soldiers."[4] The cumulative effect was summed in 2006 by LTG Douglas Lute then-J3 OJCS: "This nation can field and deserves the world's best Army and the world's best Army has to be more than one fight deep."[5]
- Adapt rapidly, practically continuously, to defeat terrorism globally in a campaign promising to be years if not decades in duration.[6] Support other federal and state agencies' adaptation to Long War support requirements.

- Sustain and probably accelerate the current Transformation programs envisaged in the Army Plan (Modular Army, ARFORGEN, Future Combat Systems [FCS], Resetting the Force) if and as Long War funding is available; hopefully not withdrawn mid effort. Continuation of resource support to reset and rebuild a severely depleted Army is the critical path to future U.S. landpower capability.
- Support national responses to natural disasters such as Hurricane Katrina.
- Maintain a very substantial general conventional mobilization capability to shift from a small quality force to a considerably larger quantity force should mid- or high intensity conflict be initiated by a peer competitor.

None of these requirements is a showstopper, but each needs to be weighed in combination and incorporated in adjusting Transformation—post–Cold War, post-9/11, and post-Katrina.

All that the Army accomplishes is achieved as America's Army—landpower molded by a unique combination of requirements in the United States as a democracy, a nation, a state, a federal republic, and a continent.[7] These requirements generate developmental imperatives normally mandated by legislative oversight should executive governance be uncertain. They are prescriptive in channeling the energies of continuing transformation.

And Transformation must overcome the burdens caused by almost two decades of chronic resource anemia recalled by the Chief of Staff. As a result of the training revolution of the first transformation—proficiency defined by task condition, standard, and "proofed" in quasi-combat at the CTC complexes and combat for over four years—no Army has ever known in such detail what is required to be combat-ready. Soldiers in units can contrast known quality requirements with what is actually occurring in many units stressed by intense, repetitive combat commitment amid enormous beneficial disruption caused by a greater magnitude of change today than the Army faced gearing up for World War II. Absent sufficient equipment, small unit leaders in Brigade Combat Teams (BCTs) regularly attempt to train to return to the Middle East, often without appropriate equipment making training to combat task, condition, and standard extremely difficult—shades of Soldiers training with wooden rifles at the onset of World War II because the real weapons did not exist. But this is a training deficiency made far more serious today in an Army of Excellence expecting to train to standard on the equipment with which they will fight.

Observers justifiably concerned by stresses on the Army today tend to forget that this current level of intense commitment began at the end of the so-called "Peace dividend" of the Clinton Administration. As Chief of Staff in the mid-1990s, Gen. Dennis Reimer warned for years that inadequate resources were causing the Army to have to "put the horse away wet" repetitively. This was well before operations began in Iraq or Afghanistan. The intensity of commitments reflected in the activities of the First Infantry Division in Germany in the late 1990s was typical:

> On my watch, the 1st Infantry Div conducted accelerated reintegration training following Bosnia; aggressively trained for combat according to its war plans; prepared for a peace-support operation in Kosovo; had units already deployed and operating in the Balkans; underwent a transition to a new division design that required standing up new formations and reducing others; fielded a robust assortment of modernized equipment that required additional training at all echelons; received and trained soldiers from attached active-duty and reserve component units from the United States and other non-US-based locations; and integrated NATO and other allied organizations for deployment.[8]

A psychology of decades of "drawdown" endures—aging of legacy forces as major systems have been terminated, disturbing junior leader attrition, "cliff-hangar" volunteer recruiting success—all which combined to moderate responsiveness of the institution at the turn of the century.[9] The Army has been there before, most recently in the early 1970s when pundits moped that the Army was on an inevitable decline represented by contraction from thirteen to ten or fewer divisions. Then CSA Creighton Abrams successfully reversed the psychological gloom by mandating Army expansion to sixteen divisions.

Today, post-9/11, America's Army remains severely stressed but far from "broken" due to the extraordinary depth of experienced officer and NCO leaders throughout the force united in selfless service to nation fighting the Long War. America's Army endures.

Countering reactive dismay is not an insurmountable problem, but it merits continuing attention in a force that should rightfully consider itself to be the premier quality Army in the world.

Fortunately, there is a fully assimilated comprehensive rebuilding framework developed during rebuilding after Vietnam and practiced since. This response, further modified, suits the future of change. The response is considering the Army as a system of interior management systems that constitute the imperatives of Army Transformation or adjustment to change. This methodology may be equally applicable to federal and state agencies as they adjust to foreign and domestic challenges of the Long War.

Doctrine, training, leader development, organization, material, Soldiers (personnel), facilities—or DTLOMPF. These "Six Imperatives," now becoming seven with the addition of facilities, provided integrating focus during the rebuilding of the Army post-Vietnam.[10] The model served as a translation vehicle from the general Army mission mandated by Congress in Title 10 U.S. Code into specific foci for the practical policies and programs of rebuilding. Just as they served as a compass for rebuilding post-Vietnam, they now undergird ongoing Transformation. A leader of the first Transformation, Gen. Carl Vuono, CSA, commented: "I've always used the six imperatives as a way to describe how the Army internally reshaped itself."[11] And the six imperatives served as timely operating guidance for the various branch proponents in TRADOC charged with guiding the actual rebuilding. They really provided the practical framing foundation for a concept-based requirements system that guided overall Army development. Employment doctrine drives requirements.

Soldier focus has been subsequently enlarged to Personnel to include the variety of human support, both uniformed and nonuniformed, that is today's Army. Now the addition of Facilities signifies realization of facilities importance projecting deployments of a largely U.S.-based Army. And that focus also addresses the importance of facilities provided to support a largely family Army.

What should be necessary and appropriate evolution of the original six DTLOMS into DTLOMPF for continuing future Transformation?[12] While unfamiliar to most outside the defense establishment, this acronym "DTLOMPF" is widely used and understood within the military as a shorthand expression of the comprehensive array of core functional areas, all of which are vital to the effectiveness of the institution.

Our proposition is that as future forces evolve, it is essential that balance among these imperatives be created and sustained in preparation for and the conduct of Long War operations. This must be a dynamic balance tailored and readjusted frequently as necessary in preparation and execution of any mission. And it is a dynamic balance that must be responsive to joint, interagency, intergovernmental, and multinational requirements stimulated by the Long War. This is not new. FM 1.0, *The Army*, prescribes balance. "The Army, balanced across the six imperatives, can achieve sustained land force dominance throughout the range of military operations and across the spectrum of conflict."[13] Furthermore, we suggest that this assessment then building process seems absolutely applicable to federal and state agencies as they become more robust to provide enduring nonkinetic support for conducting the Long War. The approach combined successfully top-down guidance with decentralized bottom-up execution. Fortunately, there is a core of former practitioners who rebuilt America's Army available to support broader national purpose.[14] There millions of veterans experienced in balanced institutional development available to support federal or state agencies "bulking up" to fight the Long War.

Balance means that each imperative is in harmony with the other imperatives. That is, each element of DTLOMPF supports each other element and it is positioned for rapid adaptation to advantage opportunity or to reduce adversity, hopefully across Joint, Interagency, Intergovernmental, and Multinational environments, usually summarized as JIIM. What should harmony be in the context of full-spectrum kinetic and nonkinetic operations in a broader sphere of Long War conflict? Harmony means mutual reinforcement, infectious collaboration, each imperative in near-continuous modification improving, adapting more rapidly than the comparable imperative serving actual or potential enemies. Also, harmony means that changes in one imperative are routinely translated into complementary reinforcing change in the other imperatives. For example, leader development changes initiated to prepare for implementation of new doctrine or training are likely to also change training requirements of associated new equipment. Such cross-DTLOMPF harmony that reinforces change by extending it horizontally across other imperatives is necessary but not sufficient. This harmony should extend routinely across agencies of federal and state governance.

There must also be longitudinal harmony; that is, compatibility with previous DTLOMPF imperatives that may be used by legacy or hedge forces or that may have been provided "reach down" to various allies or less robust agencies unable to afford state of the art.[15] New radios should talk to old. New ammunition should be usable in older weapons. New tactics, techniques, and procedures (TTP) should accommodate prior TTP whenever possible. "Reach down" means that within each DTLOMPF program, an umbilical cord is sustained back to forces of friends/allies joining in revolving coalitions and who may be accustomed to prior United States Army or agency DTLOMPF.

Notice that we no longer address each imperative separately. Rather, they become one long unpronounceable acronym that, as one term, reflects the new and vitally important paradigm that all must occur in absolutely interrelated policies and programs—balanced, each harmonious and reinforcing of the other. The term DTLOMPF expresses that essential essentially bottom-up synergy.

Nor can the imperatives be addressed in isolation from the evolving requirements of the Long War. TRADOC routinely addresses future requirements, most currently "the strategic, operational and tactical challenges that might lie ahead" in 2015 in projecting the Contemporary Operational Environment that is the foundation for DTLOMPF.[16] This is a valuable recurring requirements review process that serves as a lodestone for concept-based requirements for each warfighting functional area such as maneuver, fire support, command and control. and logistical support.

As new requirements arise to fight and win the Long War, the dynamic DTLOMPF balance must adjust quickly and responsively as the nature of the campaign changes. For example, as new patterns of operations emerge such as transition from midintensity conflict to counterinsurgency (COIN), the appropriate new or modified old doctrine tactics, techniques, and procedures need to be established then quickly embedded in the training and leader development imperatives. This is far easier commented than done as has been recent experience adjusting TTP in Iraq.

DTLOMPF should be configured to support balance on two axes—in harmony to reinforce continuing adjustments or advances in other imperatives and in harmony to retain continuity in operations with JIIM capabilities prepared in earlier versions of the imperatives.

Balance increases in relative importance in the fighting concepts of recent writings particularly "Conceptual Foundations of a Transformed U.S. Army"[17] and *Concept Paper for the Objective Force*[18] and more recently the *'06 Army Plan*, which are exceedingly well done. Note the issue of balance: "At base, the challenges confronting the Army today have less to do with materiel than with organization, doctrine, education, and training. As in the past, victory on future battlefields will not result from technology alone, but rather from the creativity with which it is employed."[19]

The objective then is a continuously evolving harmony of imperatives that is challenging to sustain within landpower itself much less with other Services and federal and state agencies in Long War operations. Creating then sustaining synergy with armies of other nations and with the various jurisdictions in JIIM operations will be difficult. It seems likely to be a responsibility of some forces to maintain "backward compatibility" to less well-supported agencies or allies across the seven imperatives somewhat similar to responsibilities to support hedge forces.[20] In this case, the goal is not just the harmony that creates a whole much greater than the sum of the parts looking forward, but it is also the sustainment of a compatibility which permits basic interoperability across past generations of DTLOMPF. Shared SOPs and Standardization Agreements (STANAGS) can help, but there needs to be a broader effort extending across each imperative singly and in high potential combinations such as doctrine, training, and leader development (DTL). "A way" to do this is suggested in Chapter 7.

America's Army challenge grows as flexible, modular fighting organizations become common. This is occurring now as the conversion to modular brigade-based forces proceeds. Harmonious balance of DTLOMPF appears a precondition to "adaptive force packaging" permitting the ability to "rapidly tailor the force." Without thoughtful, sustained DTLOMPF balance across the AC/RC/Civilian force "just in time" organization en route to combat can create unacceptable national risk. The balance must be dynamic, as recognized in FM 1.0: "These imperatives are interconnected, and constantly evolving; this cycle is a continuous process. In every period of change we must carefully balance The Army imperatives."[21]

Balance must include agency representation. Particularly for Stability, Security, Transition, and Reconstruction (SSTR) nonkinetic stability operations overseas in the Long War, robust presence of leaders from the various Departments of State/USAID, Treasury, and Justice can be more important to national success than is the Army presence. Imperatives, adjusted to requirements and cultures of each agency, simply must be mutually supporting across JIIM teams such as Provincial Reconstruction Teams if there are to be effective high-performing JIIM teams of leaders.

Preeminence of quality not quantity poses another problem. Potential major power competitors are out there with sizeable and improving armies. Prudence dictates that expansion capability to build a significantly larger

Army is maintained. That is, capability permitting the Army to shift from focus on quality to reliance on quantity forces achieved through a World War II-like mobilization. Credible expansion hedges across each imperative of DTLOMPF are required.[22]

An overarching strategic issue is composing the Army philosophically and practically "to turn on a dime" with respect to continuing readiness for various conventional conflicts requiring offensive, defensive and stability operations. These operations range from global "World War" to COIN while fighting asymmetric counter terrorists—akin to maintaining robust health while containing a dangerous very long-term infection effecting both domestic security and international security interests.

The Army has been slow to "turn on a dime" recently. COIN operations were too slow in coming to Operation Iraqi Freedom. There is a clear need to improve the responsiveness of DTLOMPF. The Army—TRADOC as a force generator—has to put a timely doctrinal "mark on the wall" then guide, mentor and assess efforts to match the doctrine with capabilities across each aspect of DTLOMPF. An excellent example of this role has been recent remedial correction of a slow Army response to one manifestation of the Clash of Civilizations—removal of highly repressive regimes suppressing national, ethnic or religious violence that then became civil wars when the repressive leadership is removed—the Balkans and Iraq. Exactly that occurred in the Balkans, an important reason for U.S. involvement. Subsequent debrief of Iraqi senior leadership after the invasion of Iraq revealed that Saddam's primary fear was civil war between Shia, Kurd. and Sunni not U.S. invasion.[23] Yet the U.S. national security establishment appeared surprised as this occurred for the second time in a decade and was slow to respond to adjust doctrine, training, or leader development (DTL) to insurgency then to emerging civil war. There has now been appropriate DTL catch up—innovative training and leader learning in COIN seminars and in the ARFORGEN Road to Deployment as described in Chapter 5. But these were catch-up actions when in retrospect and given the prior civil war issue in Balkans, there had been failure to learn and to institutionalize appropriate COIN in DTL for Army, Joint, or Interagency drawing on either COIN RVN experience or the civil war in the Balkans. There was clearly inadequate responsiveness to a central sphere of conflict of the Long War.[24]

Implicit in successful implementation and responsiveness of DTLOMPF is the sustainment of TRADOC with sufficient resources to have sufficient if not excess capability to investigate opportunities—not an impoverished, hungry organization struggling to accomplish the most basic missions as has been the situation for almost two decades now.

The accumulating effects of neglecting support of DTLOMPF can be severe. The hidden costs of such institutionalized organizational penury is in JIIM force multipliers that are not developed, or basic tasks that are not accomplished. And the substantial cost of events such as Abu Ghraib when among other failures, the Military Police docTTP necessary for the training of Military Police (MP) for such prison custodial missions and the associated training packages were not available. The TAGUBA Report with respect to Abu Ghraib is a compelling indictment of TRADOC DTLOMPF failure:

> 4.(U) ... I find that the 800th MP Brigade was not adequately trained for a mission that included operating a prison or penal institution at Abu Ghraib Prison Complex. As the Ryder Assessment found, I also concur that units of the 800th MP Brigade did not receive corrections-specific training during their mobilization period. MP units did not receive pinpoint assignments prior to mobilization and during the postmobilization training, and thus could not train for specific missions. The training that was accomplished at the mobilization sites were developed and implemented at the company level with little or no direction or supervision at the Battalion and Brigade levels, and consisted primarily of common tasks and law enforcement training....
>
> 5.(U) I find that without adequate training for a civilian internee detention mission, Brigade personnel relied heavily on individuals within the Brigade who had civilian corrections experience, including many who worked as prison guards or corrections officials in their civilian jobs. Almost every witness we interviewed had no familiarity with the provisions of AR 190–8 or FM 3–19.40. It does not appear that a Mission Essential Task List (METL) based on in-theater missions was ever developed nor was a training plan implemented throughout the Brigade.[25]

There were certainly other more important contributing factors, but lack of doctrine and related Soldier training and leader development indicate a breakdown of operations. TRADOC and the subordinate Chief of the Military Police Corps bear partial responsibility for what appears to have been at best passive not proactive functional support of deployed MP forces. While performance depends on the chain of command of the operational unit, aggressive adaptation across DTLOMPF requires a proactive TRADOC.

We have been critical of the breakdown in leadership associated with the Abu Ghraib scandal, and that judgment remains unchanged. But there were other factors that contributed to the disaster. The Office of the Secretary of Defense halted reliance on the Time Phased Force Deployment List (TPFDL) as the system for identifying and issuing orders to units for assignment to Iraq.[26] This decision interfered with the ability of senior officials to determine troop assignments and manage the process in detail. "After the fall of Baghdad, an independent commission chaired by former Defense Secretary James R. Schlesinger concluded that the decision to do away with the TPFDL had played a role in the Abu Ghraib prison scandal. Without that system, military police units had been deployed pell mell. Units had arrived in no clear sequence. Units had arrived without their equipment and often in no clear sequence. 'The flow of equipment and personnel was not coordinated." the report noted. "The unit could neither train at its stateside mobilization site without its equipment nor upon arrival overseas, as two or three weeks could go by before joining with its equipment.... MP brigade commander did not know who would be deployed next."[27] As a result, a proven system for timely selection, preparation, and deployment of units was ignored. Abu Ghraib may have happened anyway, but overriding the TPFDL contributed to assigning individuals and units to Iraq without proper screening and preparation. It is widely agreed that the individuals and units assigned to guard duty should never have been selected for that critical job.

The system failed, as did leadership to and including the Secretary of Defense. The results were devastating. This underscores the interrelated nature of the imperatives we have been discussing. A failure of one element can affect the proper working of the others. This should be borne in mind as we consider the importance of ARFORGEN and Life Cycle Management to the proper exercise of leadership and discipline. Predictable "quality control" and management systems are essential to the ability of leaders in the field to perform leadership tasks to required standards. Failure to ensure balance between imperatives, and ensuring that these imperatives are being fully supported, can have a direct impact on success or failure in missions.[28]

There needs to be conceptual acknowledgment that a requirement for "war reserves" exists as much for every element of DTLOMPF, particularly DTL as there is for M (material) to replace battle-damaged equipment. To extend the COIN example above, there should have been a DTL "war reserve" upgrade of COIN DTL energized by Balkan experience and ready for Afghanistan or Iraq implementation as a hedge if not as an expected requirement. That DTL should have been interagency too.

Apply this requirement for a DTL "war reserve" to another potential operational requirement—a reintroduction of tactical nuclear weapons to the battlefield. An astute leader observed recently "There is little institutional memory of battlefield nukes in the Army today, and it is fast decaying among the retired. New doctrine and training publications make no mention of the subject and certainly all of the material assets have long been recycled or passed into junk piles." Referring to the possibility of an existent low yield North Korea nuclear weapon, he added, "The threat is there and contemplating the plight of conventional forces attempting to stall an enemy employing tactical nukes in a blitzkrieg offensive is not just an intellectual challenge-it may well be an operational necessity in the not distant future."[29]

Doctrine, unit training, and leader preparation today are wholly inadequate for a tactical nuclear battlefield. Where is training for individual protection, for individual and equipment decontamination? Where is staff leader preparation for estimating nuclear effects (past Prefix Five training for leaders)? Where are doctrine, tactics, techniques, and procedures for tactical dispersion—the genesis for Pentomic unit reorganization in the 1950s? What about tactical dispersion reaction procedures? Whether tactical nuclear weapon use in Korea or perhaps a dirty bomb in a major Middle Eastern population center, DTLOMPF for necessary responses are lacking today. To be sure there is an Army resource crisis now a decade in duration but that cannot be a credible excuse when the consequences of neglect can be so profound.

One's abiding perspective about change within the Army or the larger interagency community sets the nature of the response. Is change seen as threats to be minimized or beneficial reinforcements to be accelerated? We suggest an essential perspective must be that change is normal! It is the "steady state." And it can be clearly beneficial if the Army can assimilate change and sustain conflict readiness more rapidly than other armies.

Acknowledging that, it is useful to think through how to advantage the many transitions that are generated by the various processes of change.[30] The interrelationships of transition are genuinely complex. How to channel perpetual transitions to advantage the inevitable change to support the purposes of the Army? It seems useful to compare to nature. To stretch a metaphor: if the daily operations of the Army may be compared to the onrushing flow of a turbulent mountain stream, that is, "whitewater"; there are swirling eddies, pools, and cross currents constantly influencing the overall flow of the current. For the stream, those are comparable to the various forces mentioned above, changing continuously. But assuming constant water flow rates, each eddy, pool or cross current is influenced greatly by two major influences: the "fall" in the terrain and the width of the stream. Of course both may occasionally occur simultaneously.

For the Army too, there are really just two overarching conditions that influence all transitions: the Army is growing (building); it is consuming (diminishing); or it may be transitioning from one to the other. For simplicity, we discuss the steady states. That is, the Army is building or it is diminishing.

Leader knowledge of both the prevailing condition and the odds of transitioning soon to another state are essential to success in an institution facing perpetual transitions. The practices and implications of each (growing/building and consuming/diminishing) evoke varying combinations on a policy/practice continuum! *Givens* are unlikely to change. A *long-term* trend might be changed. A *cycle* seems certain to be influenced, whatever the period. The point is that policies associated with rational growing are likely not the same as those associated with declining and probably not even those appropriate for the difficulties associated with "changing over" when that occurs.[31]

The leader effecting change first needs to assess the overall environment. How stressed is the Army? Is this the proverbial straw that may break the camel's back? How much is already undergoing comparable change—to the extent that the effect of some new change may or may not be detectable. To what extent is there shared officer or NCO consensus that the time is right for such change? Is there a background of shared doctrine or practices that will support the change? For example, the very effective Army training system has a bias to train kinetic operations to task, condition, standard. That bias impedes shifting to nonkinetic stability operations. This latter bias does not appear to have been realized in adjusting to COIN for the Long War.

The leader needs to assess where he or she is with respect to a particular transitional force or "current" flowing, then tailor their actions accordingly. By their intended policies and programs would they be responding to a mere *cycle* that might be "ridden out" or "suddenly improve" with no action having been taken anyway; fighting a *given* with low prospect of success whatever they do; or perhaps bucking or reinforcing a *long term* trend which just might be doable—over time? Dependent upon the prevailing condition, and the nature of action required, the prospects of success will vary significantly.

Therefore, prudent leaders should conduct routinely an informal estimate of where the Army or their federal or state agency is in their areas of responsibility in its odyssey of perpetual transitions. Then, they should think through the probabilities of success and the likely next steps as the forces or "currents" play out. For example, consider the *cycle* of centralization–decentralization. If the "current" is strongly pro decentralization, it is probably an inopportune time to make a major change to centralize. Or take current operations in the Long War. Is the Long War a cycle that will wax and wane, or is it a long-term structural change as Sam Huntington would suggest describing a continuing global clash of civilizations?[32] The answer, whatever, influences many of your hedge policies and programs.

We suggest such an analytical process should:

- First: identify the transition forces underlying the policy issue being analyzed. Where are we today, a new issue realized recently or still fighting the last war? Operation Iraqi Freedom seems about to become the "last war."
- Second: determine where current policy/programs are within the flow over time of the particular transition. Army or agency building or diminishing? *Given, long-term change* or *cycle involved?* Are the forces or "currents" waxing or waning? Near a limit established from past practice?
- Third: seek leading indicators of future developments within the particular transition element be it *given, long-term* trend, or *cycle*. Sometimes the indicators are clearly there if one can look at events through a lens of understanding of the dynamics of transitions. For example, support of the current Professional Forum Companycommand.mil in the Battle Command Knowledge System combined with Army Knowledge OnLine are a clear leading indicator of decentralization necessary in the Long War.

These three steps should provide a start in thinking through how to analyze then advantage perpetual transitions.

Institutionalization of the DTLOMPF paradigm has provided an important foundation for the Army to thrive on perpetual transitions by addressing several *givens*. The 50 percent of us all who are "below average" in normal distributions are assured that tried and true processes proven as the Army rebuilt after Vietnam and then again in the current transformation will be sustained.

We are much more likely to "buy in." And DTLOMPF reassures that when the Army fights "come as you are," always at unexpected locations and times, the force will have balanced capabilities.[33] Now the focus can go more readily to support of balanced JIIM force combinations.

Continued focus on sustainment of the finest NCO corps in the world has been exceedingly important in addressing *long-term* task migration down the enlisted grades. It has epitomized the meaning of improved individual development—probably the high point in a *cycle* of individual versus unit development. It has created a vastly better and still improving NCO corps for the reserves—a *long-term* change that promises to be critical in addressing homeland security.

To thrive, any organization must have a vision of transition to an improved future state or a range of improved capabilities to perform its mission as it evolves. For the Army, that vision is landpower furtherance of national interests. The vision is the evolving Brigade-centric Modular Force. This effort addresses vital *givens*—the abiding purposes of landpower and reinforcement of public support—what the "crabgrass Jacksonian" majority of the citizenry ("Joe and Mary Sixpack") expect and deserve.[34] The Brigade-based Modular Force may suffer as it is marketed widely as the solution to whatever ails the Army in the view of the beholder—a typical high point in a "dominant answer" *cycle* but probably unavoidable as the Army "circles the wagons" to field the capabilities in a highly competitive national security environment and fighting the Long War. All occurring as America's Army strives to rebuild with now over a $100 billion cost to recapitalize equipment, reorganize, and relocate the force.

Synchronization of the seven imperatives is assumed in Army implementation of Title 10 expressing fundamental Army responsibilities to provide forces ready to fight in joint and combined operations, often with very little notice. TRADOC was created just to ensure this synchronization as the Army rebuilt after Vietnam. But are the current Army force management mandates implied from Title 10 adequate for the Long War future? Is enough expected of Army development of forces in current interpretations of the requirements of Title 10?

The congressional charge is broad. Section 3062, Title 10, U.S. Code provides:

> It is the intent of Congress to provide an Army that is capable, in conjunction with the other armed forces, of
>
> - preserving the peace and security, and providing for the defense of the United States, the Territories, Commonwealths, and possessions, and any areas occupied by the United States;
> - supporting the national policies;
> - implementing the national objectives; and
> - overcoming any nations responsible for aggressive acts that imperil the peace and security of the United States.

> In general, the Army, within the Department of the Army, includes land combat and service forces and such aviation and water transport as may be organic therein. It shall be organized, trained and equipped primarily for prompt and sustained combat incident to operations on land. It is responsible for the preparation of land forces necessary for the effective prosecution of war, except as otherwise assigned and, in accordance with integrated mobilization plans, for the expansion of the peacetime components of the Army to meet the needs of war. [35]

We suggest that more should be expected. Forces provided to the operating geographic Combatant Commands (COCOMs) need expanded capabilities. The mandate of the current Title 10 is certainly to generate capable land-power force—organizing, training, and equipping—all traditional requirements in force management. That formulation seems necessary but not sufficient. Additional Title 10 implementation management categories seem necessary to enable a promise of consistent, reliable harmonization of the seven imperatives in sustaining DTLOMPF balance as forces are provided to operating forces that are increasingly joint. Additional Title 10 management responsibilities should include teaming and adapting that would be regarded of equal importance to accessing, manning, training and equipping. That is, responsibility to prepare all Army Soldiers and units to operate as very high-performing teams which not only are prepared to handle uncertain change but also to seek, welcome and positively thrive upon change, more rapidly than any potential opponent faced in joint, interagency, intergovernmental, and multinational operations. Army experience should then support joint and interagency teaming.

TEAMING

It is simply insufficient to have harmony across DTLOMPF if the resultant unit or organizational capabilities are uncoordinated. If leaders fail to act to common purpose, the best "new," however capable, will not produce results in the fight. The product must be teamed capabilities where, for example, leaders at all echelons realize the necessity of developing effective team leadership—shared vision, shared trust, shared competence, and shared confidence—despite inevitable personnel turbulence.

Army management guidance should mandate that the Army determine then provide to operating forces those DTLOMPF characteristics that are required to provide Army forces routinely capable of very rapidly building and regenerating very high-performing teams to execute operations. Because the Army always teams to fight and because of the likelihood that team composition will be highly flexible to dominate local Mission, Enemy, Troops, Terrain—Time and Civil considerations (METT-TC), teaming needs to be specifically recognized and supported. Examples of specific recognition of the dominancy of teaming—often at the last minute due to "just in time" modular force composition—could be increased Liaison Officers embedded in organizations, use of common standardization agreements with frequent JIIM partners (STANAGS) including development of common decision-making processes or creation of standard combined and joint organizational and interagency "plug-ins" that train routinely teamed with Army units. Army Knowledge Management (AKM) can encourage Professional Forums and Knowledge Nets oriented to support the formation and sustainment of leader teams both grouped and virtual. These leader teams could be applicable to both overseas operations and for Homeland Defense, Homeland Security—the latter likely determined by the National Guard given their close associations with States' executive and legislative leadership.

An immediate objective could be to shape DTLOMPF to support teams. This is difficult but not impossible. Such is already done exceedingly well across active and reserves with common task, condition, and standard that have made hybrid AC, ARNG, USAR organizations routinely successful. Operations in Panama in the early 1990s saw remarkable teaming across light infantry, mounted, airborne, and Special Forces. Different combinations evolved in Afghanistan and Iraq. Quite an achievement! What of these new practices should be acknowledged and provided resources through codification in force management practices drawn from Title 10 requirements and then perhaps extended across major federal agencies?

ADAPTING

Adapting is providing DTLOMPF such that Army forces routinely change responsive to success or failure faster than any enemy. The Title 10 implied task would be to create infrastructure to magnify the existing American proclivity to innovate—consistently "finding the better way." Army imperatives would be designed not just to permit but rather to accelerate institutionalization of innovation across DTLOMPF. For example, innovation to better, more rapidly transition between kinetic combat operations and nonkinetic stability operations. This would be done initially for Army and joint forces but eventually for federal and state agencies or coalition partners, however great their need. TRADOC is structured to do just this top down as the architect of the Army. But, currently it is inadequately and inconsistently resourced to support this vital Long War mission.

But for most Americans, particularly Soldiers in America's Army, the best innovation is clearly bottom up. An example of programs supporting adaptation could be a protected local command "good idea" fund—funds and authority to procure in order to establish locally generated improved practices. The shared discipline of common task, condition, and standard and shared doctrine, tactics, techniques, and procedures executed by prepared leaders would ensure that startling local adaptations would fit a broader framework of incessant unit innovation across landpower particularly as disseminated as "best practices" by AKM Knowledge Nets. Cross-organizational "fit" of continuous innovation would be supported by emerging AKM practices such as the sharing of "good ideas" on Companycommand.mil or Platoonleader.org. Army Knowledge Online (AKO) offers powerful teaming opportunities. Hundreds if not thousands of these Communities of Practice seem likely as AKM expands.[36] These practices extend now to joint organizations. They should expand to include federal and state agencies.

The practical impact of such Title 10 insistence on adaptation should be extraordinary emphasis on developing modularity of capability—combat, combat support, and combat service support across DTLOMPF, as well as plug-in, plug-out across DTLOMPF. Quality Soldiers and shared rigor of task, condition, and standard permit high unit proficiency today despite very flexible individual Soldier assignment policies. Plug-in, plug-out of material emerges as a family of fighting vehicles in Future Combat Systems of the Objective Force; a thirty-year development trail.[37] Unit cohesion remains vitally important to unit performance. That aspect is addressed in Title 10 teaming above.

Such modularity would clearly be advantageous across federal and state agencies, but that seems likely to be slow coming. It is a reward of decades of balanced DTLOMPF preparation started as a largely bottom up concept-based requirements system.

Assessment must be built into all activities. Accelerating spiral development, a quicker decision loop, encouraged local innovation—all potentially could lead to disparate, fragmenting loss of unity of purpose across the Army. A risk? Yes. But assessment to ensure necessary uniformity now can be far more comprehensive in forcing modular commonality to compensate for increasing local variations likely stimulated by encouraged adaptation. The unifying presence of common Combat Training Center (CTC) rotations is a powerful assessment cross-leveler—a "hamburger helper" extension of self-awareness development support as that has been sought recently in various Army training and leader development studies.

The future presages extensive Professional Forums sharing information and data to generate knowledge and actionable understanding to enhance individual and leader team awareness. A far higher level of sensitivity to external events will evolve that will be shared within various peer and hierarchical leader teams.[38] The explosive development of the Battle Command Knowledge System with tens of professional forums demonstrates the remarkable unifying potential of AKM in ensuring that extraordinary local adaptation does not erode the desirable balanced harmony of DTLOMPF across One Army. This capability can be extended locally as part of the ARFORGEN Road to Deployment discussed addressing America's Army as a learning organization. There are clearly opportunities for interagency collaboration in the Road to Deployment.

Now, apply teaming and adapting to existing DTLOMPF. How might these imperatives change, influenced by the guiding hand of enlarged Title 10 direction—all to increase Army adaptability to rapidly changing conflict environments?

DOCTRINE, TACTICS, TECHNIQUES, AND PROCEDURES (DocTTP)

DocTTP link doctrine to TTP of "a way" acquired in shared experimental learning provided by AKM. Knowledge "mining" by the Center of Army Lessons Learned (CALL) of strong Professional Forums such as Company-commander.com and applied in the Road to Deployment of ARFORGEN may provide a way to short cut development of doctrine absolutely responsive to new requirements of evolving conflicts. A stimulating sharing of current and emergent practices between doctrine writers and practicing leaders in operating forces could speed the creation then institutionalization of new DocTTP. Members of an appropriate Professional Forum stationed at a combat training center could observe and confirm unit DocTTP adaptation to new requirements during a training rotation—and then spread the gospel of new tactical practices through the DTLOMPF mandate provided to the responsible TRADOC Proponent. That would certainly serve to encourage innovative adaptation then sharing of evolving "best practice" and "good ideas."

This innovation has been pursued aggressively in a Lessons Learned Initiative as the CALL was substantially reorganized in 2004. CALL is the focal point for collecting and analyzing observations, identifying or developing Army lessons learned data and materials, and submitting these products through command channels to the Army's leadership for review, approval, and integration into ongoing Army combat operations as well as readiness training, generating "new core operating capabilities necessary to support the accomplishment of joint/operational level lessons learned."[39]

But the doctrine has to be maintained complete and current across the great variety of types of units to support the range of operations included within the full spectrum of offensive, defensive and stability operations. Common, timely, doctrine supported by doctrinally based TTPs responsive to extraordinarily diverse, ever-changing operational environments and shared among like units and supporting interagency organizations seems essential to winning the Long War. The TTP should include common Standard Operating Procedures applicable across all of the units and agency representation that may join a deploying force "just in time." This quick response commonality could be based on hierarchical and peer teams of leaders sharing TTP data and information regularly to develop and sustain shared knowledge and then shared understanding-employing knowledge management (KM).

Such KM practices would co-opt more diverse leader development in actually developing doctrine thereby encouraging more rapid understanding and application of emerging DocTTP bottom up across the Army. More unit leaders would have participated in doctrinal development. So more than the typical fifty percent who quickly understand, accept and execute new DocTTP should emerge because more leaders in units have been co-opted practically, routinely, into DocTTP development.

Growing AKM through Defense Knowledge Online (DKO) information technologies seems to provide emerging capabilities to reshape and inform with respect to DocTTP. Just as standard "boilerplate" orders and reporting formats are provided today on Companycommand.mil, TTP could be similarly disseminated from the TRADOC Proponent through Knowledge Nets to the force and perhaps migrated to federal and state agencies' leader development institutions. The ubiquitous nature of influence of DocTTP will ensure that these advances are shared across the other imperatives.

Link DocTTP formulation to attache's schooled to seek out local national military adaptations. "Steal" ideas globally then scrub to refine in Structured Professional Forums or Knowledge Nets networked on Defense Knowledge Online (DKO) and linked to various forms of simulation. TRADOC Proponents could overwatch informal on line "trials" either unclassified or "classified" in chat rooms with very closely controlled access. Use the coming power of DKO to permit much more detailed acquisition and analysis of foreign tactical practices.

Tactics, techniques, and procedures (TTP) could be developed for various hi-low DTLOMPF mixes or cross cultural assimilation. These should be provided routinely in legacy forces with their built-in bridge to less DTLOMPF-balanced armies. "Reach back" from projected forces is necessary to readiness of a deployed force but it is not enough. There is an abiding need to "reach down" to militarily less advanced coalition partners with DocTTP adjustments focused in advance for the particular user. "Reach forward" is practiced routinely in "right seat rides"—new leaders learning from their predecessors in combat—as part of the Road to Deployment of ARFORGEN. Similar logic and practices could be applied across interagency partners in the Long War.

In sum, the key to balanced harmony in DocTTP development adjusting to increased emphasis on teaming and adapting is not just a fountain of U.S. innovation but also it is explosive dissemination of DocTTP responsive to changing operational environments plus "a way" to execute to very high performing leader teams certain that their adaptation to advantage U.S. innovation will be rewarded. This is both desirable and feasible in America's Army in months not years. In fact much is being done today with listening and adapting "bottom up" under the umbrella on the Battle Command Knowledge System.

TRAINING

Most training changes necessary to adjust to increased focus on teaming and adapting to change are underway, as resources permit, in execution of various panels and studies provoked by Operation Iraqi Freedom. There is clear understanding of both purpose and institutionalization of self-awareness and adapting. America's Army accelerates as a learning organization. New training practices and implementing programs such as the ARFORGEN Road to Deployment are being provided resources. Institutional leader professional development is facing significant beneficial improvement. The CTCs are both assimilated and modernized. Army KM opens new opportunities for distributed individual, team, and unit learning.

But, as always, more can be done. First, establish several common learning practices. Common means neither training nor education but rather both—learning. Common also means that as practicable the policies and practices suggested below should apply joint and interagency. The natural breadth of learning ensures increased understanding across multiple imperatives. As more Soldiers become leaders down to and certainly including squad, crew, or section leaders, the focus on learning not just training becomes more important. By tradition, Soldiers learn as individuals but now with much greater attention to preparation of hierarchical and peer teams of leaders thriving on change. New practices may be required, such as:

- Unit learning is experiential requiring task performance to standard where unexpected change requiring team adaptability for success is routine.[40] Learning occurs in basic skills, knowledge, and attributes (SKA) plus actual fighting team SKA resulting in near-continuous learning of critical tasks due to need to adapt to ever-present change. Team learning also needs to become near continuous due to inevitable turnover of team membership caused by turbulence or attrition, although that turbulence should be reduced due to stabilization of Soldiers, teams and units as well as life-cycle unit personnel management.
- Advanced training is intensive and totally team-based—linked to new DocTTP—training combinations of "plays" in packages of virtual, constructive or live simulation which have been deliberately designed to draw on balanced DTLOMPF.[41] Training becomes absolutely execution-based as has been recent practice in multi-echelon, multi-grade leader training at the Armor School in Gauntlet exercises. This is the future of institutional training, literally "learning by doing" drawing on new and emerging forms of participatory media provided across the generating force by the Battle Command Knowledge System.
- Plays (combination of battlefield tasks integrated by function) become appropriate TTP for BCTs and below. Train for both kinetic and non-kinetic operations as quick response "audibles" consistent with execution-based

decision-making described in recent guidance.[42] That is, build integrated multi-function tasks as Army Battle Command Systems (ABCS) macro programs executed by trained leader teams. Examples could be Joint Suppression of Air Defense (JSEAD) or Hasty Breach of Obstacles. Then introduce new capabilities in leader team packages as a part of New Equipment Training. Fighting teams exist and train routinely in cross-reinforced joint/combined organizations engaged in offensive, defensive or stability operations. So that is where training must occur, after the individual has been provided initial entry training to standard. Very rapid team learning to mastery of the tasks, conditions and standards of a specific capability needing to be mastered to dominate the local situation is the critical path that should be a focal point of learning R&D. Similar processes should apply to vastly more complex cross-cultural teambuilding particularly in nonkinetic Stability, Security, Transition, and Reconstruction (SSTR) operations. In sum, design TTP to be easily learned by teams of leaders. Start with Army teams, but the major payoff will be routinely through success in the JIIM area.

Learning R&D should also address improved evaluation of learning. All learning—training and education, individual and team—is assessed routinely at all echelons. Demonstration of proficiency in actual combat task organizations and commander leader teams becomes routine. Where the team can't be grouped, distributed demonstration of actual team proficiency is supported. This is increasingly feasible as Distance Learning and reach back/reach forward unit learning occurs drawing on Army KM. An important, precedent, "good news" story is in the family of Stryker Brigade Combat Teams (SBCTs) supported by I Corps at Ft. Lewis. All of the SBCTs have been effectively brought together to share Lessons Learned and both developmental and combat experiences. These practices are now being extended across all heavy and light brigades by Forces Command.

LEADER

Support of the leader imperative to increase adaptiveness and teaming is a "no brainer." Solid leaders are the lifeblood of tactical success. And leaders today are generally adaptive. If they weren't, they would have survived neither the personnel attrition of the past decades nor the incredible diversity of assignment experiences in complex force projection operations attendant to an overstressed Army. Approach any ten leaders (E4 or above) in line in a Burger King at Ft. Hood, Texas, or Ft. Bragg, North Carolina, and ask where they have served during the past five years. The geographical and mission diversity of service described by young leaders is remarkable. "Been there, done that" in tough situations. The Balkans, Afghanistan, and Iraq have now become "old hat" with increased leader learning occurring routinely due to multiple tours into new environments each time they deploy. That escalating experience occurs for both active and reserve Soldiers. What a virtuous circle of leader experience and competence! Repeated training center tours reinforce a bank of combat lore in young leaders. Repetitive stability operations tours develop complementary background lore in complex civil-military, joint, and combined operations. That is the good news.

The bad news is that there is a growing deficit in midintensity combat operations as small unit leaders are prepared for stability operations not midintensity operations. Increasing numbers of small unit mounted force leaders have never "fought" midintensity operations in training or in combat. "War reserve" remedial training processes and products are clearly required to sustain baseline hedge leader proficiencies.[43]

A current leader imperative challenge is to advantage this very diverse experiential lore resident in Army young leaders today and then apply it to interagency leaders whose participation is central to many nonkinetic stability operations. Clearly, there is an abiding case for increased authority and responsibility down to these highly experienced young leaders. This situation is analogous to the World War II intensive combat experience that created very competent leaders, very young. Subsequently, they led the Army for decades. There is justifiable pride of accomplishment in young adaptive leaders today gained from clear operational successes in spite of increased complexity of the changing operational environment into which leaders are committed.[44] How to further hone and exploit this bank of valuable experience?

Good news here. The School of Command Preparation at Ft. Leavenworth has highly effective new learning tools that are in the process of full adaptation to online learning. The tools capitalize on student experience to create powerful learning "how to think" more than "what to think." These techniques could be extended throughout generating force leader development programs and into Agency leader preparation. Now new KM capabilities encourage near continuous voluntary mentoring of senior to junior in a school environment or expectations that a leader preparing for deployment "reaches forward" learning current TTP and lore of the operational environment from the leader he or she will replace.

All leader development in preparation for Brigade-based Modular Force operations requires additional cross functional familiarity so that future tactical leaders can more easily combine—to grow at every echelon into new teams of new compositions. Leaders anticipate continuously evolving, changing organizations as well as changing TTP ahead of any enemy. Each leader will need to understand the enduring application of the seven imperatives so that the balanced harmony is sustained. Then add interagency understanding for stability operations.

So we believe that even deeper understanding will be required of leaders. Leaders will need to understand the interrelationships of the imperatives applied at their level of responsibility plus the implications of those interrelationships as they interact one or two echelons higher—perhaps best described as a "super harmony"? The challenge is to possess the SKA and motivation to adapt (adjust) the balance within the seven imperatives to retain battlespace dominance in offensive, defensive and stability operations. This is the essence of a knowledge-based force. Routinely, leaders will need to be prepared to assume responsibilities one or two levels higher.

The benefits will be ubiquitous. Active force to active force, across active and reserve operating forces in America's Army deployed in overseas operations. Also from the National Guard to the leadership of the various States in execution of Home Land Defense or Homeland Security operations to address domestic Long War requirements.

So there is not much to be done to sensitize the leader imperative to adapting and to teaming. This imperative is recognized now for America's Army. It needs to extend now to JIIM leaders and teams of leaders.[45]

ORGANIZATION

The imperative of organization is there also. Adaptive force packaging and routine preparation of modular mission packages provide a DocTTP prescription of design requirements for organizations to be highly adaptive. What was exceptional ad hoc niche force design years ago now becomes routine expectation with the Brigade centric Modular Force supporting the Integrated Global Presence and Basing Strategy.[46]

Plug-in capability becomes routine in the current Modular Force strategy. It is not just "reach back" within the various operating functions but also plug-in of joint, combined, and civilian resources—increasingly these are interagency post-9/11 in Joint Inter-Agency Task Forces (JIATFs). Organizations are designed to facilitate adaptation, often on short notice. Common characteristics are coming to ensure organizational adaptability such as maximum commonality of support functions, and organizational design to facilitate easy plug-in of any functional capability.

Organization can also be configured to support new teaming. For example, increase authority and organizational flexibility to team with industry—not just to use commercial equipment or establish dual use agreements such as the civil reserve air fleet (CRAF) but authority to establish long term teaming with industry. Why not AOL-Time-Warner, Citicorp, Bechtel, United, or WalMart depending on full-conflict spectrum requirements to form new civil–military combinations particularly in support of homeland security? Team with certain foreign organizations or multinational corporations to ensure support when deployed? Precedents abound in contract support of equipment or installation support (Brown-Root in the Balkans and Middle East).[47] Certainly increased civil–military association is essential in urban warfare, and more recently in homeland security. Associations such as these with appropriate governance and accountability could be sustained out of the active or reserve forces.

New information management (IM) and KM capabilities could support new forms of distributed liaison capabilities ready to be assembled when the appropriate regional contingency occurs.[48] There could be Iraqi-American or Turkish-American or Croatian-American expanded liaison capabilities consisting of reserve but operating force cadre advisors—all warriors, sharing rigorous socialization, prepared as leader teams by IM "participative media" exploiting KM tools and associated with other capabilities required across the spectrum such as Individual Ready Reserve (IRR) multi-purpose warriors? The diversity of America represented by America's Army permits highly competent foreign-American liaison or advisory teams from most everywhere. The National Guard maintains teams in Partnership for Peace-like associations with fifty-four countries today—a substantial start particularly for global stability operations.

The Army Reserve may be the best organizational structure for generating national expertise available as functional plug-ins. Create organizational frameworks (shadow organizations) in being to be filled out and rapidly "teamed" when "world class" capability is required that is not sustainable in the normal Army force structure. This is exactly what was done as AT&T migrated to the Army Signal Corps in World War II. Such stand by functional organizations could have been very helpful responding to Hurricane Katrina in New Orleans in 2005.

There would appear to be numerous paths available to make organization both more adaptive and more supportive of teaming particularly as the exceptional collaboration capabilities of KM come on line.

MATERIAL

The ability to adapt material rapidly to advantage battlefield opportunities has been sought for years:

> The Future Close Combat Vehicle (FCCV) is really a family of vehicles with very specific characteristics. The goal is to employ a single common chassis that meets the needs of the future force, both light and heavy. This single FCCV chassis will be fully integrated with the principles of Vetronics and will be capable of performing various functions through the addition of various mixes of capability modules. The FCCV can be viewed as nothing more than a mobile, variable protected space, which can be left as is or fitted out-tailored–with one or more capability modules which have been optimized for specific battlefield functions.... In the final outcome, the design and construction of all modular capabilities must permit the close combat force the inherent flexibility to tailor itself at the subunit level—a level as low as is technically, economically and practically feasible.[49]

The vision of 1983 continues to fruition in the Future Combat System (FCS). "Mobile, variable protected space" evolved through the M1A2 Abrams with design optics in the Commander's Independent Thermal Viewer (CITV) to a hoped-for drop in laser or other killing mechanisms selectively replacing the CITV thermal viewer. A plate was placed in the roof of the M1A1 to permit selective retrofit of advanced technologies from the M1A2. However, it is fielded in affordable segments, FCS will supplant all of this as the logical product of decades of material development. Adaptive is "old hat" to the material community.

There are really fine examples of cross-imperative collaboration in FCS development. The program developer prepared a multi-player game Future Force Company Commander (F2C2) as a leader "training tool demonstrating the networked battle programs that are part of the Future Combat Systems."[50] Over 25,000 copies have been distributed as free downloads for gamers—Army or otherwise. With one endeavor, the program is confirming technical Battle Command capability requirements with serving leaders, conducting leader development as players exercise the capabilities in combat operations and training potential mounted force Soldiers in capabilities—perhaps encouraging them to volunteer as does the America's Army game—one of the most popular games in the United States. Of course, major power competitors are playing and learning too!

The FCS in concept and in evolving practice is important material development for Soldiers, leaders, commander leader teams and for BCT organizations—Light, Heavy, or Stryker. Current planning to spin out modular FCS capability inserts as they become available—whether retrofitted on heavy armored vehicles (Abrams/Bradley) or Stryker wheeled vehicles until a future platform becomes feasible is a brilliant strategy. F2C2 makes it even better as "digital native" leaders learn capabilities in advance—and figure out better ways to employ—bottom up—shared with their peers through KM collaboration among "passionate professionals"! F2C2 is an astute precedent in linking doctrine, training and leader development (DTL) to the material acquisition process.

The imperative material is fully supporting both adapting and teaming.

PERSONNEL—SOLDIER

The sixth imperative is arguably the most important. That is, the provision of the competent, confident, disciplined young Soldier proud to serve his or her country.[51] Each of the other imperatives defers to the Soldier as the ultimate arbiter of that imperative's adequacy. But while the Soldier, the dominant Army capability, is important, he or she is part of a larger human team. Department of the Army Civilians (DAC), numerous contract personnel, retired Soldiers and thousands of volunteers all fill out America's Army. In recognition of those essential contributions, the sixth imperative was broadened from Soldier to Personnel.

The new Soldier learns both adapting and teaming from first exposure to basic training or comparable initial Army experience. What is vitally important is that they learn in the context or environment of selfless service to nation. They acquire the values, attitudes, and skills associated with service—service beyond self. Disciplined performance to standard. It is retention, in fact augmentation, of this training and education that must characterize emphasis on the Soldier imperative in the future.[52]

Soldierization of the new Soldier must be even better than it is today. Young Soldiers face increasing responsibilities in unexpected situations often under great stress. With the advent of increased distance learning, face-to-face "regreening" to the values, attributes, skills, and actions of more responsible positions during professional development in the institutional setting is becoming less frequent. Less must become better as KM becomes a de factor surrogate for traditional branch school bonding and values reinforcement.

Recent Army Chief of Staff emphasis on Army values and the Warrior ethos has been superb:

> I will always place the mission first.
> I will never accept defeat.
> I will never quit.
> I will never leave a fallen comrade.

Application of the Warrior ethos to all Soldiers—combat, combat support and combat service support in Basic Combat Training has been a major, very important adaptation post-9/11.

Soldiers have in fact become national strategic assets, placed in complex situations often requiring personal actions of near instantaneous tactical, operational, and strategic importance. They must have a more solid foundation in duty, honor, and selfless service to nation. Therein lies the challenge to this imperative—sustain then reinforce intensive early soldierization to prepare that young volunteer for a career of professional service despite inevitable cycles of serious resource shortages. And to bond them to all of the other folks included in personnel who are so vital to performance of America's Army.

Hopefully, that competence in service to Nation demonstrated in JIIM operations will influence "soldiers" in other U.S. agencies, such as the Department of State and Department of Homeland Security. Absent that broader public service competence, America's Army will be called upon to provide support—a significant but potentially distracting compliment to Soldier competence required to be fully adaptive to fluid and changing operational environments.

FACILITIES

Facilities are a new addition to the imperatives acknowledging the importance of the physical infrastructure from which America's Army launches trained

ARFORGEN units overseas and in support of domestic emergencies. Facilities set the practical stage for the integration of generating forces and operating forces. Improved facilities are essential for family support. Family units are stressed seriously by repetitive deployments. The commitment to family support has grown, with senior leaders establishing an Army Family Covenant expressing explicit command support and funding to improve family readiness.[53] The best deserve the best.

The new Installation Management Command orchestrates such diverse major Army transformation programs as Base Realignment and Closure, Rebalancing and Redistributing Forces and the Integrated Global Presence and Basing Strategy. But in fact during a period of phenomenal Army change, facilities are often the critical path in about every Army program. Sometimes by default, facilities programs are integrated in every other Army imperative for better or worse, reflecting undeniable requirements.

The seven imperatives look as applicable for the future as they have been for the past quarter century. The practices are present to ensure balance; balance in that each imperative is in harmony with the other imperatives. Harmony that means mutually reinforcing. Each imperative is in near-continuous modification, improving, adapting more rapidly than is the comparable element serving actual or potential enemies. Also harmony means that changes in one imperative are routinely translated into complementary reinforcing change in the other imperatives.

However, now, post-9/11, DTLOMPF may be an incomplete guiding formulation. The Long War is a war fought globally with diverse individuals and organizations focused to common purpose. No single imperative will prevail unless it can draw successfully on JIIM components of that particular imperative. Aggressive, robust federal and state interagency support is absolutely essential. In fact, post-9/11 with a credible threat of enemy employment of WMD, such as nuclear or chemical weapons within the United States, it may be appropriate also to add P (Private Industry). That connotes a necessary new relationship with U.S. industry in order to be able to respond rapidly, effectively, decisively across a sphere of conflict—broader and more diffuse than a linear full spectrum of conflict.[54]

It cannot be assumed that there will be an orderly progression of distinct phases or types of warfare. As we see in the Middle East today, conventional, counter-insurgency, and nation-building operations are occurring simultaneously and must be conducted in large part by the same Soldiers and units of both active and reserve components. Extensive transformation of Army enterprise business practices—lean Six Sigma—increasingly apply proven business best practices to Army management. As practices converge including increasing use of commercially available resources, contract support expands, and a massive orchestrated response to WMD or major natural emergencies may be perhaps required. There should be far greater inclusion of business assets across support and service support in emergency planning.

Organizational adaptation to continuing change is clearly alive and well albeit currently under-resourced. Army rebuilding post-Iraq must continue to acknowledge the essential balance and harmonization of DTLOMPF that must be supported if America's Army is to be fully adaptive. And the "architect of the future" TRADOC—the repository of Army adaptation—must be fully, in fact generously, provided resources to "think about the unthinkable" in adapting DTLOMPF to change—both that change forecast and that change that is wholly unpredicted—hedged or not!

7

Teams of Leaders: An Implementation Force Multiplier

EFFECTIVE COMMUNICATIONS HAVE been a critical component of command and control throughout the ages of armed conflict. Most recently, there was national focus on ensuring the ability to communicate among and between complex systems across all Department of Defense operations—the Defense Enterprise.

The central military vision has been the enabling of joint net-centric operations as an important part of the U.S. Revolution in Military Affairs—"force transformation." Confirming tactical success across systems was demonstrated early post-9/11 in operations in Afghanistan—the horse-mounted Special Forces soldier employing successfully strategic airpower.

There has been an enormous and generally successful effort to extend this capability across the various functional areas of both generating and operating forces of America's Army. Top down, ubiquitous Information Technology in both classified and unclassified domains extends from Combined Joint Task Force (CJTF) and above down to the squad level in emerging Land Warrior, globally. This correct and successful focus has been to provide leaders at all echelons with both data and shared information with appropriate security.

But data and its conversion to usable information, the staple of information management (IM), is necessary but not sufficient to prevail across an inordinately complex spectrum of conflict including offense, defense, and stability operations as coequal operational requirements. Data and usable information need to be converted into knowledge (information analyzed for meaning and value or evaluated for implications) and hopefully then into actionable understanding (synthesized knowledge with judgment applied in a specific situation to understand situation's inner relationships).[1] That is, conversion to knowledge and then actionable understanding that accomplishes the mission at hand for highly competent leaders—the multiple peer and hierarchical teams of leaders who execute operations or the larger organizations these leaders serve.

The purpose of evolving knowledge management (KM) is to complement IM to cause the conversion to occur effectively and efficiently from data and information to knowledge and understanding. The challenge is stimulating a social process of learning much more than merely supporting an important technical process of communication. In fact, KM developed to generate intense human collaboration to build and sustain battle-effective teams of leaders (commander leader teams [CLTs]) multiplied by effective global communications that is enabled by IM seem likely to serve to define the processes of command and control for battle command of the future. In that context, KM supporting leader teams completes the larger command and control vision associated for years with IM programs.[2]

Battle command seems likely to become "IM times KM," not "IM plus KM." A multiplier effect of increasing social sharing or collaboration among leaders expands the impact of shared actionable understanding achieved through net-centric operations. With expanded collaboration comes intensified development of CLTs, many of whom become high performing. CLTs themselves become another performance multiplier. The interacting combination of IM, KM, and high-performing commander leader teams (HP CLTs) is what we describe as Teams of Leaders (ToL). ToL is a three-legged stool—IM, KM, and CLTs—with the combination becoming most effective when the teams of leaders are high performing.

Such social as well as technical transformation is vitally important to success in each of the four strategies of the Army Plan because understanding permits second- and third-order insights and implementation initiatives that capitalize on the quality of deeply experienced Soldiers.

When CLTs supported by IM and KM are added, opportunities for exponential improvement in America's Army and national programs emerge, both domestic and overseas. The combination seems sufficiently powerful that ToL can be considered a new force multiplier across the full range of national security operations. We will discuss each in turn then describe several likely domestic and foreign applications.[3]

INFORMATION MANAGEMENT

Effective information technology is the lifeblood of IM. Tools range from telephone to television, the Internet, and top-down net-centric Battle Command command and control systems. IT provides the capabilities of Army Knowledge OnLine (AKO), now with almost two million users across the Army family. AKO provides the practices and tools that generate shared usable information. But more than the essential tools of IT are required; data and information characteristic of IM need to be created. Then, from the shared information of IM, again with supporting practices and tools, comes the knowledge and understanding characteristic of KM. Global KM will be only as good as the supporting IM.

The impact of IM is even deeper. With omnipresent communications at every level, rarely, if ever, are decisions taken alone by individuals. Teams make decisions. Teams of peers—and in a military organization, hierarchical teams such as the chain of command and peer teams (staff or cross-talking commanders)—decide. Satisfaction of individual IM needs is rarely sufficient. Teams decide.

IT has also developed tools that reinforce expectations of and capabilities for sharing data, information, knowledge, and understanding applied to team building. More and more social networking practices and tools appear. Blogging, wikis, visual blogging, Second Life (avatars living in a digital virtual world), Blackberries, even iPods and now iPhones with expectations of ubiquitous handheld visual (movies) or oral (podcasts) communication.[4] IT tools for social networking multiply.

The avalanche of social networking tools experienced almost from birth has created youth accustomed to incessant communication. Youth—Generation Y Soldiers and other young adults below the age of 30—can multitask, monitoring and acquiring information, knowledge and understanding from multiple sources simultaneously and at will. A recent article in Business Week says it all about social networking in business: "the water cooler is now on the Web."[5] This ability is a considerable national advantage. However, there is a substantial difference between these young people ("digital natives") born in the age of IT and their elders ("digital immigrants") who may be resistant to, if not suspicious of, IT multitasking.

There is another, more complex relationship. IT (AKO) is to KM as *yin* is to *yang*. Top-down IT (net-centric) interfaces uneasily with bottom-up KM. Neither can be fully successful without the other. With mutually complementary support, each becomes better, stimulated by inevitable tensions of top-down "science" supporting and competing with bottom-up "art" expressed by highly experienced young leaders. All too often, however, there can be competition, not cooperation, when top-down IT meets bottom-up KM. The need for effective collaboration grows. IM supplies both complex advantages and challenges to KM. But it is KM that provides the Long War support essential to addressing the decentralization and "open source" warfare practiced by al Qaeda.

KNOWLEDGE MANAGEMENT

We need first to review both the present and immediate KM future and then to discuss what seems achievable through KM enabling high-performing teams of leaders (HP ToL).

America's Army KM today is grounded in the Army Knowledge Management (AKM) Plan. The AKM vision is "A transformed Army, with agile capabilities and adaptive processes, powered by world-class, secure, network-centric access to knowledge, systems, and services, interoperable with the Joint environment."[6] There are five subordinate goals that extend across the

Army Enterprise and include among others: Governance (Enterprise Portfolio Management), Best Practices (The Battle Command Knowledge System [BCKS]), Infrastructure (LandWarNet), Army Knowledge OnLine (AKO), and Human Capital (E-Learning).

While attaining each of these goals is central to achieving the Army vision, the Army Battle Command Knowledge System (BCKS) enabled by Army Knowledge Online (AKO—IT supporting almost two million Army users "inside the OPSEC wire") seems to be most important in reshaping America's Army because BCKS performs the multiplier function in acquisition of knowledge and understanding. BCKS, established in 2004, already consists of tens now growing to hundreds of Army Professional Forums, functionally oriented Knowledge Nets, and ad hoc ToL. All are expanding as leaders discover better ways to share information and generate shared knowledge and shared actionable understanding by mission function, such as logistics or fires or by echelon of command or some combination of the two.[7] Practically, the intensive sharing of data and information characteristic of KM/BCKS is the lubricant facilitating the balancing of the imperatives of DTLOMPF in building the modular brigade based force.[8] KM directly supports leader and leader team preparation. Actionable understanding enabled by KM also provides vital support to rapid effective transitions from kinetic combat operations to nonkinetic stability operations. "The Battle Command Knowledge System (BCKS) supports the online *generation*, *application*, *management* and *exploitation* of Army knowledge to *foster* collaboration among Soldiers and Units in order to share expertise and experience; *facilitate* leader development and intuitive decision making; and *support* the development of organizations and teams. BCKS enhances professional education, facilitates exchange of knowledge, fosters leader development, supports doctrine development, supports lessons learned, supports training, and enhances battle command."[9]

While each of these missions is clearly important, each develops at a unique pace largely determined by the perceived degree of immediate support to existing missions. That is of relevance to better, faster, current mission accomplishment. Thus, with the Army at war, enhanced battle command is the current major KM/BCKS focus. But there are more far-reaching purposes now recognized as the operating forces become more familiar with and confident of the value of the BCKS. In a seminal presentation to the Commanding General Forces Command, major purposes of BCKS knowledge networks were to "transfer cultures of compliance to cultures of innovation" and "develop and apply 'weapons of mass collaboration.'"[10] Potentials of KM and command realization grow at an increasing rate.

To accomplish these various missions, BCKS connects Soldiers supporting their conversations developing professional content in a mission context. It connects individuals, ToL, and organizations within the larger Army team based on expertise, interest, location, and assignment. BCKS facilitates, asynchronous, online, and facilitated discussions designed to help Soldiers share ideas and seek solutions. These discussions often result in improved shared knowledge for all members. It manages content. The Warrior Knowledge Base (WKB) is the knowledge repository for all knowledge created within BCKS. The WKB also links throughout the Department of Defense Knowledge nodes. BCKS works to put knowledge within context so that common solutions can be applied to a common problem. Various Unit Networks such as CAVNET (1st Cavalry Division) and IRONHORSE net (4th Infantry Division) developed in Operation Iraqi Freedom are excellent examples.

The centerpieces of BCKS are the various Professional Forums. They exist for various groups of leaders such as Command Net, S3-XO Net, Company Command, Platoon Leader, Warrant Officer Net, and NCO Net. Staff members have inter alia S-1 Net, MI Net, S3-XO Net, LOGNet, SAMS, LandWarNet, Information Ops, Fires Net, Maneuver Support Net, Medical Knowledge Net, SimOps Net, KMO Net, Civil Affairs Net, and Spiritual Leaders Net. Currently expanding functional nets include Counterinsurgency, Foreign Security Force, Domestic Operations, Financial Management, Lessons Learned Integration (L2I), and Recruiting ProNet. All are in varying stages of maturation.

The secret of all of these forums is that they foster sharing of data and information in turn developing shared knowledge and actionable understanding. Leaders connect and collaborate with friends, coworkers, and peers around the Army . . . those known and those who should be known. Sharing can be rank- and duty-specific discussions, review of common areas of interest and concerns, or shared experiences discussing various successful solutions. Now that sharing can be extended to joint and interagency ToL waging the Long War both overseas and supporting homeland defense.

Special topics networks can connect and collaborate with Subject Matter Experts wherever they may be in the world. The online social networks at BCKS essentially provide a means for Army personnel to solve their problems in an environment free of past constraints (geographical, organizational, or functional area). Peer groups or hierarchical groups or leader teams are formed as Soldiers share. Most important, KM/BCKS functions essentially bottom up, drawing on the great Long War experience of junior leaders in America's Army. Comparable disaster relief experience abides with National Guard leaders in each state. They too are experienced KM/BCKS users, certainly capable of advantaging KM/BCKS in the event of domestic WMD attack.

As KM/BCKS proliferates, new applications multiply. For example, the ARFORGEN Road to Deployment prepares units to deploy into combat by conducting virtual Right Seat Rides introducing incoming leaders to their peers currently deployed.[11] Units at Home Station conduct individual, team, or collective training or staff exercises based on "in Area of Responsibility (AOR)" intelligence, thus improving situational understanding. The unit in AOR conducts combat missions or civil-military operations and transfers tacit and explicit knowledge to the incoming unit—Army, joint, or interagency.

Now KM is being institutionalized in Brigade Combat Teams (BCTs) as a two-officer, two NCO Battle Management KM cell assigned the following functions and responsibilities:

- Provides Battle Command KM capabilities to the Commander and staff through the integration/management of information and Army Battle Command Systems (ABCS), optimized for situational understanding.
- Develops and manages a Knowledge Systems Architecture in support of the operational mission and strategies.
- Applies in-depth knowledge and understanding of current and future operations by leveraging the Operational and Knowledge Systems Architectures processes/products to enable timely knowledge transfer.
- Incorporates and manages a set of integrated applications, processes, and services that provide the capability for Command Post Operations.
- Supports 24-Hour Operations for unitary command post (minimum mission essential for most likely configuration: Main + Tactical Command Post [TAC] Combined).
- Develops KM plan in accordance with CDR guidance to include Commander's Information Requirements.
- Tailors KM plan to support Command Post SOP.
- Assists in organizing a Common Operational Picture for the command.
- Continuously monitors the external Information Environment and recommends changes in the info management plan.
- Develops file and data management procedures.[12]

Thus, KM "enhances battle command." Other KM missions develop as they address current issues—providing a "better way."

As BCKS builds, it seems useful to view this emerging KM capability from a broader end-game perspective. The overarching challenge KM addresses is rapid conversion of data and information to knowledge and understanding "actionable" in the Long War, be it international or domestic in homeland defense. To generate effective, efficient, grouped, and virtual conversion, the Army needs both widespread collaboration practices and supporting tools. Both appropriate KM practices and usable KM tools are comparable in importance to successful daily operations, equivalent in the conduct of day-to-day operations to the necessity of possessing fully available pure water and consistent usable electricity. Neither is inexpensive. but both are necessarily ubiquitous for both international and domestic operations.

Collaboration practices are just ways to share using the Internet. Most leaders today are accustomed to threads of discussion of e-mail. Increasingly, that will become "video phone"-type discussion. In time there will be increased sharing by the use of avatars; that is, the digital representation of you and digital representations of others meeting perhaps around a digital table in a digital world. But all merely apply Information Technology to permit you to "get together" globally, synchronously. Then there are various asynchronous ways to collaborate: requests for information (RFI) or searching a database such as the Warrior Knowledge Base (WKB) of BCKS or the various data and information resources of the Center of Army Lessons Learned (CALL) or common multiple addressee e-mail. All can be applied cross-culture joint, interagency intergovernmental, or multinational (JIIM). The constraints are not science, solved by IT technology; the constraints are cultural, addressed by the art of encouraged collaboration enabled by KM capabilities stimulated by encouraging the development of teams.

KM/BCKS tools are the various Professional Forums or Structured Professional Forums when the Proponent is disseminating professional doctrine or tactics, techniques, and procedures (TTP). All in BCKS are facilitated by a trained person who, among other support of discussions, maintains an operational security overwatch. Other tools are the various Knowledge Nets and Unit Nets described earlier.

So the essence of successful and growing KM/BCKS is near-continuous collaboration exemplified by multiechelon, multifunction peer and hierarchical sharing, bottom up, by "passionate professionals." They are digital natives enthusiastically teaming and sharing in selfless service to America's Army; that is, leaders at all levels wanting to improve themselves and to support their teammates also engaged in the Long War.

Security is an ever-present concern. Three Company Commanders in Iraq may have an excellent conversation about Company administration that is unclassified yet protected from eavesdropping by Al Qaeda because the thread of discussion is inside AKO with a security-credible changing password. But the moment they compare notes on tactics, techniques, and procedures of their operations in Iraq, the content becomes classified and needs to be moved to the secure AKO (AKO-S). The facilitator is there to coach such transfers.

It would be naive to think that America's Army is the sole possessor of digital natives. Al Qaeda has many, as well as increasingly sophisticated IT support. The title of a recent article in *Armor* magazine says it all: "The Poor Man's FBCB2: R U READY 4 the 3G Celfone?"[13] Enemy imagination and competence in the use of cell telephones in the improvised explosive device (IED) fight must be assumed to exist in Al Qaeda KM.

COMMANDER LEADER TEAMS

The third leg of the three-legged ToL stool consists of various ToL, often commanders in the military services.[14] Because of IT, leader teams can function grouped or distributed globally, connected by the Internet, unclassified or secure. Teams may consist of peers—leaders grouped in a unit staff; leaders who are action officers in various departments or agencies of the U.S. government working a common problem such as HIV/AIDS in Africa; or platoon leaders in a rifle company. Other leader teams are hierarchical—the chain of command, for example, brigade commander to battalion commander to company commander; or combatant commander to combined joint task force commander to brigade combat team commander; or various chains of functional support or joint chains of coordination.[15] Leader teams crisscross homeland defense—federal, state, and local jurisdictions; military services; and various JIIM organizational combinations. They consist of leaders in organizations and of contractors hired to support operational requirements. Now, in the Long War, most teams also cross multiple cultures. So, CLTs are everywhere, linked by IM and collaborating through KM practices and tools to generate shared knowledge and actionable understanding.

As they collaborate they may, and hopefully will, create the shared skills, knowledge, and attitudes characteristic of team leadership across the most diverse teams. Aided by team-building tools provided by KM, the CLTs develop shared trust, shared vision (or common CLT mission), and shared competence (in mission tasks), and they share confidence (in ability to accomplish the mission). When these four SKAs are shared by all members of the CLT, that CLT becomes high performing, at least in assigned mission execution and hopefully in broadening areas of responsibilities.[16] When they do not, as discussed earlier with respect to contractors in Operation Iraqi Freedom, there can be disastrous results.

The most effective HP CLTs, particularly virtual teams, are those generated from the bottom up through KM, since they are generally spontaneous and self-reinforcing. As a result, shared trust becomes the single most important SKA. This relative importance is accentuated for JIIM due to the common, widely varying cultural lenses of each interagency, intergovernmental, or multinational leader in those leader teams. The capabilities of IM can be combined with the tools and practices of KM to generate and sustain JIIM HP CLTs. That combination of IM, KM, and CLT programs is ToL.

The importance of CLTs becoming high-performing rapidly, effectively, and efficiently justifies exceptional support programs. Fortunately, leaders in America's Army are accustomed to the structuring of training with various highly effective training exercises. The development and fielding of structured SKA learning exercises should not be difficult, particularly when new IM capabilities such as participatory media (Second Life, Facebook) are available. Current Combat Training Center scenario and cue content (described in Chapter 5) could be made readily available to support learning exercises distributed through participatory media. We advocate such advanced learning efforts, particularly for JIIM CLT applications.

ToL may seem new, but it isn't. At the Stryker Center at I Corps, Ft. Lewis, Washington, ToL has been implemented "reaching forward" and "reaching back" between deployed and deploying Stryker Brigade Combat Teams (SBCTs) for years. ToL practices have been embedded in all SBCTs to varying degrees. Now the challenge being executed by Forces Command is to extend ToL to Infantry BCTs (IBCTs) and Heavy BCTs (HBCTs) and translate these "best practices" to address Long War cross-cultural JIIM challenges. The next step is to extend these ToL across domestic jurisdictions and functions to support homeland security and homeland defense.

TEAMS OF LEADERS

The potential of ToL seems very high both within America's Army, in Homeland Defense, and in the broader Long War environment. Likely, ToL future capabilities and developments should be nurtured, for they appear highly promising. For example:

- Support of intensive hierarchical and peer collaboration generating self-correcting "workarounds" can be exceedingly useful at friction points of competing, occasionally conflicting, time-sensitive Army, Department of Homeland Security, Department of Defense, or ongoing Department of State transformation programs. BCKS collaboration can be encouraged to provide action-enabling lubrication of personal relationships. In effect, ToL/KM collaboration is molded to lubricate improved management practices whether for domestic defense or overseas interagency operations. Application of ToL to support increased federal–state collaboration in homeland defense seems both useful and necessary.
- Intensive collaboration such as extensive coaching and mentoring of subordinates inculcated within a functional culture can provide intense training and learning in an operating as well as a generating force environment. Perhaps leader preparation, after Initial Entry Training (IET) socialization, could be entirely conducted by coaching and mentoring in the unit or organizational environment up to the platoon sergeant level and for all company-grade officers. Shaped branch cultures combined with warrior values can become a powerful ToL/KM engine particularly as units transition between kinetic combat and non kinetic stability operations.

An example of a new opportunity provided by ToL/IM could be availability of "on demand" mentoring and coaching, whenever and wherever, for individual leaders and leader teams. Institutionalized, this could portend revolutionary changes in Army training and learning. Exported to JIIM CLTs, comparable coaching and mentoring could coalesce and generate high-performing leader teams more rapidly in various interagency organizational combinations. Exported to state and local emergency action teams preparing for weapons of mass destruction (WMD) contingencies, the virtual mentoring could provide team preparation resources that might not be otherwise available to isolated localities.

Collaboration, collaboration, collaboration! Lest we appear overly biased as to its importance, recently the Director of National Intelligence released his "100-Day Plan for INTEGRATION and COLLABORATION"—his emphasis. The number one program goal is to "create a culture of collaboration." ToL is at heart intensive collaboration stimulated to override frequent individual and team reluctance to share information and improve decision-making. Power is sharing—not hoarding—information!

ToL reshapes the normal dimensions of time and space to support interagency collaboration:

- The Internet Protocol (www) compresses distance such that when enabled with social networking software, peer or hierarchical ToL can confer "across the table" globally and routinely. The physical locations of decision makers and staff at any level, particularly the operational (regional) level, become irrelevant.
- Time can be manipulated. The past can influence as experienced former leaders provide longitudinal expertise. They can explain why the situation is as it is, as they support their successors. This spring, five former Assistant Secretaries of State (1977 to 1997) met at the Council on Foreign Relations to discuss Africa policy. Such concentration of expertise and experience, or perhaps timely counsel of the past five ambassadors to Country X, could be available to contemporary decision makers routinely. The future can be shaped also as those likely to assume future responsibilities are "brought forward" to participate in current interagency leader teams. Taking advantage of the "best practice" precedents of Stryker BCTs that routinely "reach forward" and "reach back" from deployed leader teams to those scheduled to replace them will facilitate seamless transfers of authority and responsibility. With intensive collaboration, normally sequential processes can become near simultaneous.
- IT/KM provided in profusion to experienced digital natives of the Millennium Generation who seek characteristically to collaborate and to team can provide decisive national advantage as ToL are created essentially reinforcing America's Army Soldiers who are "digital natives." The multitasking capability of the Millennium Generation already oriented to teambuilding and collaboration is a decisive national military strategic advantage. World-class expertise can be made available to support policy collaboration. Experts can become available across traditional program stovepipes enabled by IM and KM tools. Tools—for example, proven collaboration software, leader-encouraged Professional Forums, functional Knowledge Nets, and Action Teams of leaders, multilevel and multifunctional as assembled across JIIM jurisdictions—can be available. These ToL/IM and ToL/KM tools permit extraordinary pooling of expertise within ToL/HP CLTs.

- Due to the intensity and frequency of commitment to combat, most leaders of America's Army know each other—in person or by reputation. Why search databases when relatively small pools of subject matter experts know one another through past or present service (6,000 Foreign Service officers, comparable numbers of military service functional experts)? There are, at most, two degrees of separation. No one is more than two to three leader contacts away—an associate who knows another who knows another who is THE actual Subject Matter Expert for America's Army. IM and KM that permit me to consult responsively with the three leaders whose advice I most respect—such as my predecessor in command, my Ranger buddy, and my brother-in-law—also permit me to consult with THE expert perhaps to create a ToL. I may be able to short circuit the cognitive hierarchy by going directly from data to understanding, coached by THE expert whom I can contact through a mutual contact. Accelerated conversion of data and information to shared knowledge and shared understanding by expert intervention is a likely Long War breakthrough.
- Through intensive collaboration—appropriately molded to stimulate shared trust, shared vision, shared competence, and shared confidence—powerful and effective cross-cultural communication is developed. Sharing establishes or enables cross-cultural, high-performing team building across the JIIM environment.

These several ToL characteristics, stimulating intensive collaboration, promise startling change in joint and interagency program formulation and implementation. They should apply equally to intergovernmental and multinational collaboration.

We suggest that ToL can be shaped to support the collaboration culture of individual commands and agencies as a central supporting capability that could be provided to all leaders and leader teams in a U.S. Combatant Command, a joint and interagency community. ToL could manifest itself generally as described in the following example of "a way" ToL could support fighting HIV/AIDS within a geographic combatant command. "The way" would be determined by the particular command, department or agency.[17]

An Africa Command (AFRICOM) ToL could support the President's Emergency Plan for HIV/AIDS Relief (PEPFAR, administered by the U.S. Agency for International Development, or USAID) as a contribution to the success of an important, complex, public, and private multinational effort. Multiple knowledge nets and forums (communities of practice) could be encouraged among leaders and teams of leaders across the various concerned U.S. government departments and agencies and then across the Global Fund, the World Bank, the Joint United Nations Program on HIV/AIDS (UNAIDS), private organizations, various medical communities, multinational contributors, and both governance and health systems in African countries. These IM communication tools and complementary KM social bonding and shared understanding development processes could generate continuous discussion of multiple topics among and between the various leaders routinely grouped into multilevel Action Teams addressing specific issues, teaming and then regrouping as circumstances require. Some of these Action Teams are small, private, and secure—conducting ongoing actual policymaking. Other teams are huge—leaders brought together globally, virtually and across jurisdictions, responding to shared concerns and generating shared actionable knowledge and understanding.

Lest the above appear unlikely, exactly these sorts of collaborations have developed in the Army logistics community. From a handful of concerned visionaries several years ago, LOGNet, a typical Knowledge Net, has grown to include more than 17,000 active participants collaborating to generate shared knowledge and actionable understanding across logistics functions and organizations of the Department of Defense. Deliberate Knowledge Net growth planning became growth by spontaneous combustion as leaders recognized significant value added to routine job performance. Now logistics decision processes modify to benefit extensive collaboration. Decision centers of gravity for department-wide logistics policies and programs seem likely to shift.

ToL enables continuous collaboration among peers and within decision hierarchies. For specific policy planning and execution, broad collaboration congeals into collaboration within command, agency, or interagency Action Teams of selected leaders supporting established decision processes. But all have collaborated informally beforehand as peer or hierarchical leader teams at and between country team, regional, and national strategic levels. As virtual teams—high performing as they develop shared trust, shared vision, shared competence, and shared confidence—their locale on the ground becomes irrelevant at any level of governance. And sequential decision processes may become truncated as continuing collaboration permits near-continuous decision-making.

These potentials seem equally applicable and attractive at strategic, operational, and tactical levels as various combinations of Civil-Military Operations Centers (CMOCs) and Joint Interagency Coordination Groups (JIACGs) become HP CLTs by taking advantage of ToL.[18] Strategic benefits can be enormous. Consider the quantity and quality of the U.S. response to the earthquake in Pakistan and the tsunami in Indonesia—both "front line" states in the Long War. That timely, effective humanitarian assistance generated effective, nationally important, strategic communications. The absence of strategic collaboration among and between teams of leaders is equally stark as seen in inadequate early Green Zone governance of Iraq or uncoordinated Homeland Security/Federal Emergency Management Agency (FEMA) support during Hurricane Katrina in the Gulf of Mexico.[19]

We suggested above various applications of ToL to the President's Emergency Plan for HIV/AIDS Relief. Other applications of ToL may be profoundly intergovernmental and multinational in nature supporting international military force interventions on postconflict stability operations. These operations, whether under the governance of the European Union, NATO, or the African Union, are foreseen to often require a decade of presence to be effective in suppressing conflict in complex environments such as those in desperately poor countries in Africa.[20] Now another portfolio of ToL capabilities becomes relevant; that is, those capabilities proven in sustaining near-seamless transition from one unit to another in Operation Iraqi Freedom. "Right seat rides" to prepare replacement multinational force leaders; development of longitudinal leader teams to ensure institutional memory of relations with national leaders within the multinational force; adaptation of learning best practices to form high-performing multinational teams of leaders prior to arrival in-country of replacements during the decade-long commitment—all are proven ToL capabilities that seem applicable to multinational postconflict stability operations.

At the geographic combatant command level of operational responsibility, ToL is currently engaged in support of Commander, U.S. European Command as U.S. Africa Command is formed during Fiscal Years 2007 and 2008. Developing an organizational framework to improve interagency collaboration is explicit in conceptual guidance from General John Craddock, Commander, U.S. European Command:

> Africa Command must be interagency from the start, because of the challenges on the continent.... *The problem is there are so many different (agency) stovepipes. We've got to get these stovepipes connected horizontally.... I think AFRICOM may be the spearhead—the pioneer here ... but I think there will be spin-offs and best practices we can use in re-crafting the combatant commands....* [emphasis added] We'd like to populate the interagency group with decisional authority rather than having them reach back to Washington for a decision.... It would enable greater opportunities for fast decisions and be able to do things on a higher-tempo basis.[21]

ToL has been charged to support program design and activation in this important national interagency effort within the U.S. European Command to improve national security policy formulation and execution. Clearly, ToL must evolve to be responsive to important joint and interagency decision processes at every level. Intergovernmental and multinational processes next?

This example just scratches the surface of probable ToL applicability. Tactical-level applicability for America's Army has been demonstrated with the various SBCTs. I Corps at Ft. Lewis, the home base of Stryker development and SBCT fielding, maintains a Stryker Knowledge Net that includes extensive Lessons Learned content that supports preparation of SBCTs to deploy. SBCTs preparing to deploy maintain continuous Professional Forums across functions with SBCTs in combat. Leader team formation and sustainment is well addressed in Army leader development doctrine for tactical application.[22] HP CLT generation is a central objective of the ARFORGEN Road to Deployment formulated in 2006 by then Lt. Gen. David Petraeus at U.S. Army Training and Doctrine Command's Combined Arms Center. ToL is launched effectively for present commitments both within America's Army and in the larger JIIM arena. But ToL can and should be significantly more for the future.

Think ToL again for futures. It enables one to move beyond past constrictions of time and space and cultural reticence to collaborate in seriously addressing a new and necessary framework for cross-cultural decision making for the Long War.

Blending the developing capabilities of ToL and those of the Future Combat System (FCS) seems a natural. The experimental development capabilities of Ft. Bliss (Future BCT) should lead to exploitation of ToL support of battle command as incremental FCS improvements occur. The FCS fielding plan envisages years of "spin outs" of advanced capabilities. Just as Combat Training Center "combat" experience supports introduction and Army assimilation of new capabilities, the ToL combination of IM, KM, and CLT development ensures leader team collaboration across "spin outs" so there are no surprises to leaders out in units. Peer leader teams can and will collaborate to introduce new capabilities.

ToL collaboration becomes routine. Quality Soldiers—currently highly experienced in the Middle East—remain experienced fighting the Long War either personally or through gaining experiential knowledge as they associate with peers in ToL. The abiding experiential challenge is to draw upon ToL to generate continuing vibrant, bottom-up, shared "voices of experience" generating knowledge and understanding through KM supported by global IM while continuously updating Army learning as they form CLTs. This is precisely what is being done, initially so that all of the SBCTs forming CLTs can share experiences, globally. The SBCT Warfighters' Forum will be followed by similar forums for light and heavy BCTs supporting home station unit preparation for Long War deployments. There could be similar experiential development enabled by ToL in other federal departments directly supporting the Long War overseas or engaged in homeland security in the United States.

Another futures application of ToL is to accelerate adaptation to the unexpected. An abiding overarching strategic issue is composing the Army philosophically and practically "to turn on a dime" with respect to continuing readiness for various conventional conflicts requiring offensive, defensive, and stability operations. These operations range from global "World War" to counterinsurgency (COIN) while fighting asymmetric counterterrorists—akin to maintaining robust health while containing a dangerous very long-term infection effecting both domestic security and international security interests. In all of the contingencies or "hedges" we will discuss, ToL should be a central element in the planning and preparation, both for domestic emergencies and internationally.[23]

While advancing on multiple fronts for a prolonged period is challenging, the difficulty can be eased by advantaging two important military institutional precedents, TRADOC and SOCOM, and by drawing on the boundless potential of a third, the citizen-Soldier, particularly the Army National Guard—exploiting the abiding strengths of America's Army. A skilful combination of policies and programs drawing on these three should respond fully to the challenge. ToL "lubricates" these interactions.[24]

TRADOC is the institutionalization of balanced Service support to generate and rebuild existing forces and develop future forces—exploiting a proven incubator of innovation over three decades despite severe resource shortfalls. To those roles now add overwatch of various mobilization hedges—"spiral support" of the seven imperatives from objective to interim to legacy to hedge force.[25] Transformation becomes continuous, unending exploitation of the unique advantages of America's Army. However, surplus resources need to be available for the "architect of the Army" to be able to respond proactively to targets of both necessity and of opportunity. For example, the recent requirement to turn the Army from midintensity to counterinsurgency operations or to shift from direct combat to indirect advisory force development. Both have proven to require substantial resynchronization of doctrine tactics, techniques, and procedures (TTP), training, and leader development (DTL). The tools of KM—Knowledge Nets such as COIN Net, Professional Forums such as Companycommand@army.mil, and Action Teams formed across generating and operating forces—supported effective resynchronization. Such support should become routine for America's Army addressing kinetic and nonkinetic operations—joint and interagency.

SOCOM is highly credible, mission-focused joint unit excellence demonstrating extraordinary innovation and competence addressing new forms of conflict such as counterterrorism. Elite forces directing precision munitions in Afghanistan as reported in the media are likely a "tip of the iceberg" in highly adaptive tactical innovation. This was important highly preferential interagency collaboration between the Central Intelligence Agency (CIA) and SOCOM.[26]

KM can reinforce cascading excellence of SOCOM as peer and hierarchical ToL collaborate and share best practices. As they develop the shared trust, shared vision, shared competence, and shared confidence characteristic of high performance, they should accelerate the pace of transformation, particularly the translation of high performance to JIIM. They are effectively accelerating the rate of "cascading excellence." All is applied not just to direct action but also across the range of stability operations.

Both SOCOM and TRADOC are important organizational initiatives. Now combine the two drawing on the expanding capabilities of ToL. How could they combine ToL to create an interagency whole much greater than a mere sum of the parts? How would these organizational innovations combine to generate relevant new capabilities? How much introduction of what would be required at each echelon, when?

We suggest the development of ad hoc organizations of highly variable composition composed from individuals, small teams, or small units from BCTs or Support Brigades designated to be prepared, on demand, to support SOCOM. Without regard to service category—AC/RC/Department of the Army Civilian or Contract individuals would become highly competent/cohesive teams (by function) added to core functional mission teams patterned on SOCOM Special Forces Alpha teams or Delta teams. Perhaps habitual associations could be established to permit formation, contingency training, and sustainment of high-performing SOCOM Plus teams created by capability "plug ins" appropriate to mission requirements. These should be interagency teams. Clearly, R&D would be required to reduce significantly the time required to apply ToL to form highly competent, cohesive teams of leaders at all echelons, across battle functions and various cultures. And TRADOC would have to prepare "war reserve" Training Support Packages on call to support leader team building. That support would seem to be the next breakthrough in leader development.

ToL advances in creating very high-performing leader teams will be particularly useful in asymmetric operations. For example, a critical offensive counterterrorist capability will be the ability to create rapidly (in hours not days or weeks) high-performing, multifunctional, multicultural leader teams, both vertical and horizontal, adapted to the culture of the particular Common Operating Environment (COE). Operational interagency teams, drawing on hierarchical and peer ToL advantaging IM capabilities and KM tools, should be capable of rapid adjustment in composition and in mission execution to "stay ahead" of morphing local terrorist cells, which will be continually changing their method of operations to remain effective. The issue is the provision of highly proficient teams composed of individuals possessing the greatest conceivable capability to influence the local counterterrorist situation in collaboration with local authorities. Perhaps these teams could come from the USAR and draw upon the cultural learning associated with various state associations developed through the many Army National Guard State Partnership Programs supporting international security cooperation. What a fine opportunity to draw on ToL practices to develop culturally "tuned" leader support for SOCOM Plus deployments to those overseas states.

The major challenge is not to modify the performance of all-purpose groups to dominate a local situation. Rather, it is to draw on ToL to bring together the precise interagency expertise required to dominate the local situation (the stability operations "niche") and to rapidly create a high-performance team built around those dominating capabilities whether applied to counterterrorist operations, COIN operations, adviser training, or any other operation required to win across the spectrum of conflict. Capability to effect such rapid cross-cultural leader bonding in ad hoc, hybrid military/civilian organizations would be a national asset comparable to stealth or network operations. The capability is coming in emerging ToL initiatives, but development needs to be shaped to tactical purpose as suggested by and then embedded in TRADOC and probably in Joint Forces Command supporting other agencies.

Sustainment of highly capable counterterrorist and stability operations forces plus highly credible hedges becomes a new aspect of military deterrence. The actual competence and deterrent credibility of these forces would be sustained by a substantially larger TRADOC charged to maintain proofed and in-being "cutting edge" global dominancy in each of the seven DTLOMPF imperatives.

EMPLOYMENT OF THE OBJECTIVE FORCE (SOCOM PLUS) IN INTERNATIONAL COUNTERTERRORISM OPERATIONS

Long War counterterrorism capability follows the SOCOM quality precedent.[27] Continuing terrorism today is the most likely near-term threat to national security. SOCOM Plus is maintained as the joint and interagency objective force—the leading edge of all seven DTLOMS imperatives. Supported by each of the Services and relevant U.S. federal agencies—land, sea, and air and ToL—SOCOM Plus establishes the "mark on the wall" for future international counterterrorism operations as it operates, drawing on highly flexible interagency combinations that are highly entrepreneurial in nature.

A hypothetical response to a WMD attack either in the United States or abroad could be:

- Counterterrorist forces (Delta Force) and direct action forces (Ranger Regiment) supported by appropriate Service units all formed into highly proficient land (Brigade Combat Team "ready forces"), sea, and air teams, hopefully augmented by local national counterterrorist organizations to kill terrorists and to destroy their enabling infrastructure.
- Simultaneously, joint SOCOM and interagency teams augmented by high-performing functional teams prepared by TRADOC or Joint Forces Command (JFCOM) to support operations in the specific COE and other U.S. security and intelligence organizations bring local leaders cross-culture (civilian, military, nongovernmental organizations [NGO], economic, religious) together into high-performing counterterrorist teams of leaders competent to modify policies and programs as required to conduct counterterrorist and stability operations.
- SOCOM Plus leaders are trained to develop and sustain local leader teams. Weapons would consist of nonlethal weapons, then lethal—all "brilliant" munitions—as required. ToL would be able to draw on a precise combination of land, sea, and air capabilities and other interagency tools—"arrows in the quiver"—as needed to dominate particular terrorist situations. These teams would be provided access to reinforcing national assets through the

U.S. Ambassador and the appropriate Military Command authority. It is to be hoped that a substantial part of the combat force would come from allies established in the particular COE. The objective is to achieve local diversity matching the local population so that local security organizations representative of local cultures—ethnic, religion, and so on—are at the cutting edge. They could be augmented—stiffened—by Special Forces teams or Ranger-Delta type U.S. forces either from SOCOM or the Army BCT "ready" forces/Support Brigade support capabilities described above developed and sustained as effective peer and hierarchical teams through ToL.

- Reinforced by extensive application of ToL, SOCOM Plus is elite in every aspect. It consists of extraordinarily competent, very high-performing inter-agency teams (units) with capabilities maintained across all battle functions. This capability could be provided as required from existent standing forces. Sustainment of extraordinary cross warfighting mission area excellence is the Title 10 responsibility of each of the Services. For the Army, this is a major responsibility of TRADOC providing intensive leader development, unit training, proven doctrine TTP, and proven organizational configurations appropriate for multinational, multiservice, multicivil organizations. Conceptually, this would be quite similar to early Army Strike Force conceptualizations in the 1990s, but now integrated into the modular Brigade-based force.
- This vision, enabled in time for legacy forces, will also serve well to sustain the proactive professional ethos that has characterized the U.S. Army in the past, for it is a vision of extraordinary professional excellence across the breadth of America's Army. This approach also may be applicable for justification to generate robust reinforcing U.S. agencies otherwise unable to provide competent support to JIIM operations. America's Army could provide trained retirees seconded to support ailing U.S. agencies unable to maintain their personnel commitments to JIIM organizations until these agencies are able to "bulk up" for the Long War.

This model for grouping excellence has been confirmed over time by the third of the near revolutionary very high impact Long War multipliers in the process of routinely addressing natural disasters; that is, the Army National Guard serving as an operational force while strengthening homeland defense in conjunction with federal, state, and local authority.

THE ARMY NATIONAL GUARD: VITAL MULTIPLIER OF AMERICAN POWER

A vital force multiplier and partner with TRADOC, SOCOM, and our active forces is the Army National Guard. It is the land power muscle reinforcing state and local authority to secure homeland defense and mitigate natural disasters while serving as operational, standing national land power forces as they continually transform. The Army National Guard is now within the select very best of armies in the world, having some 30 percent of Soldiers combat-experienced with increased field grade leader experience due to Long War commitment that began with divisional-echelon commitments and command in the Balkans.

ToL would support homeland defense within the United States. The military expertise would be provided by the National Guard of each state under the command of the governor with such support as required being provided to the National Guard by the Active Army and the Army Reserve. New authorities, responsibilities, and associated resources will be required to better support the Army National Guard in its enlarged role in America's Army.

Aggressively led, particularly since 9/11, the National Guard fully matches SOCOM and TRADOC in potential as a vital Long War multiplier. The Guard is within 2 percent of the mandated strength for 2006 having increased end strength by over 13,000 during a year of Guard combat in Iraq and Afghanistan. It is combat trained and experienced to standard—a highly credible member of the operating forces expecting to deploy routinely but at roughly half the pace of the active force thus doubling the at home time in acknowledgment of the competing business–military service time constraints of the citizen-Soldier.

Simultaneously, the National Guard of the states and territories is an agent of each of the most important commanders in homeland defense—the state governors. The Guard combines superb military task competence with ToL prepared in elaborate continuing professional development committed to defense of the homeland. This is well-institutionalized continuing education far beyond the reach of any other branch of federal or state government in one of the premier learning organizations in the world.

No other organization within the Department of Defense has the Guard combination of size, skills, training and experience, dispersion across the nation, command and communications infrastructure, and the legal flexibility to support civil authorities at a moment's notice. It is notable that in six and one-half days, the Guard deployed over 50,000 Soldiers from every state to support disaster recovery operations after Hurricane Katrina.[28]

These are challenging times. Fortunately, America's Army is ready as it is reinforced by the capabilities of ToL. Institutionalization of processes of adjustment represented by TRADOC and SOCOM ensures timely, appropriate responses to evolving challenges to our great nation. The Army National Guard knows the path; it accelerates accepting responsibilities for defense of our homeland, at home and abroad since 9/11.

These can be the vital enablers of continuing Transformation. SOCOM effectively shapes new joint and interagency warfighting capabilities. TRADOC ensures DTLOMPF-balanced land power prepared for conventional and asymmetric kinetic and nonkinetic conflict from objective forces to hedges. The ARNG serves as an operational force while strengthening homeland defense in conjunction with national, state and local authority.[29] All three draw on the "reinforcing rods" that are the IM, KM, and Leader Team building resources of ToL.

In sum, ToL is collaboration—intensive sharing—peer and hierarchical, generating teams as shared data and shared information become shared knowledge and shared understanding within the team. Stimulated and supported by IT, aided by new learning tools and practices to intensify collaboration, this KM sharing can encourage development of HP CLTs as the SKA of team leadership are generated. ToL proliferates. Now it must become interagency, intergovernmental, and multinational to prevail in the Long War.

8

Homeland Defense: First Responding

KATRINA PROVIDES, AND its aftermath provided, a startling example of the need for creating an effective, no-notice command and control capability available to take charge in major domestic emergencies until federal, state, and local authorities can assume responsibility. This applies to both natural disasters and to major acts of terrorism (weapons of mass destruction [WMD]) on American soil. We believe this capability is latent in America's Army.[1] It needs to be realized. Furthermore, we believe that the Army possesses well-established "best practices" that can serve federal, state, and local governments in homeland defense just as they supported Army rebuilding after Vietnam and again today rebuilding from operations in Iraq.

As acknowledged explicitly in "A Failure of Initiative," "The need for assistance is extreme during the initial period of a catastrophic hurricane, yet the ability of state and local responders to meet that need is limited. That is why it is so important for the federal government, particularly Department of Defense resources, to respond proactively and fill that gap as quickly as possible. Because it takes several days to mobilize federal resources, critical decisions must be made as early as possible so that massive assistance can surge into the area during the first two days, not several days or weeks later."[2]

There is no desire here whatsoever to impugn the good work done by emergency planners and first responders in the past. Nor do we overlook the thoughtful efforts of the Department of Homeland Security, U.S. Northern Command, or the many states and organizations like the Homeland Security Policy Institute at George Washington University—one of many organizations seriously working homeland defense and security. There has been much serious response work accomplished of which they can be justifiably be proud. Through the efforts of concerned federal, state, local, academic, and business organizations, new equipment has been provided and better communications systems integrated; seriously better training is now provided in many locales. An encouraging indicator of successful collaboration was the effective unified response to the I-35 bridge collapse in Minneapolis, Minnesota, in August 2007. Likewise, the federal and state response to the massive fires in southern California in October 2007 seems to have been much more effective.[3] All ponder the best paths to improved pre-WMD event planning. But in the face of the potential challenges, from a no-notice attack like 9/11 (but with nuclear effects) or an evolving, short-notice, or no-notice natural disaster (Hurricanes Katrina and Rita) to an enemy WMD attack, these good works are solid and competent but not yet major-league efforts.[4] Now the challenge has reached World Series proportions, in terms of demanding exceptional highly competent no-notice performance across multiple federal, state, and local public and private organizations in the face of a major disaster.

This is not a "more of the same is better" situation. It is time to call upon the only organization in the United States possessing the size and competence to address this situation at practically every level of federal, state, and local governance—America's Army. What seems required is a major redefinition of America's Army responsibilities, authorities, and capabilities in response to major disaster whether terrorist or natural. Either can be extremely disruptive of every aspect of U.S. strength and, therefore, deserves the best the nation can muster in response.

The challenge is to advantage the strengths of America's Army. One aspect of strength is the nature of America's Army itself—a combination of federal and state, national regional and local (AC/ARNG/USAR). A second and equally important aspect is America's Army's Soldier-leaders, active and retired, who since about the mid-1980s have been trained and educated to standard in a large, exceptionally good learning organization in the federal government and, in the case of the National Guard, the most consistently competent organization in state public service. These leaders are smart, motivated to superior performance, highly skilled, very experienced in adverse environments, and wholly dedicated to service to nation. Most important, leaders all, they are exceptionally adaptive, taught practically, globally, in harm's way. They are a vital national command, management, and organizational resource that, active and retired, spans about every physical jurisdiction and interest in the United States. The Appendix portrays the ubiquitous presence of America's Army in Georgia. This type of presence is typical in every state, and it represents an enormous national resource that is generally unrecognized and not taken advantage of by state or local governments or by the general public.

A third strength is America's Army as a highly adaptive learning organization with firmly embedded best practices to respond to change advantaging the twin revolutions of information management (IM) and knowledge management (KM)—the melding of diverse teams of leaders through intensive grouped and virtual collaboration. In contrast to every other agency of federal and state governance, interagency collaboration within and among active, National Guard and Reserve is simply not an issue in America's Army. The three components are bonded by extremely strong shared values of duty and service beyond self to nation reinforced daily in combat and in the most effective continuing education programs in any United States institution.

The objective of America's Army as first responder could be to provide highly adaptive, functionally competent leaders and teams of leaders to support planning processes if asked and then to be immediately available to provide direct support to state and local political, economic, and social leaders during the most sensitive period of any crises, the first 72 hours. These Army leaders would then withdraw as federal, state, and locally generated disaster support assumes necessary disaster "command and control."

A second and reinforcing aspect of America's Army support to homeland defense could be mentoring and coaching application of institutionalized lessons learned from Army rebuilding after Vietnam to restructuring of homeland defense under the Department of Homeland Security, to the emergency governance of the various state and local jurisdictions, and to the robust multifunctional support of the Department of Defense represented by U.S. Northern Command. Several strikingly successful Army initiatives have been competency-basing personnel to uniformly applied tasks, conditions, and standards; assimilating both learning practices and essential infrastructure for intensive individual, team, and organizational learning (Combat Training Center [CTC] paradigm); establishment of a logical, persuasive rational for allocation of resources (the "imperatives"), and recognition of a continuum of service to Nation cross-component, active and retired. Each of these initiatives is now being reinforced by an evolving Teams of Leaders (ToL) program combining IM, KM, and hierarchical and peer leader team building. Designed to support joint, interagency, intergovernmental, and multinational operations overseas, ToL can apply with equal effectiveness to homeland defense.

America's Army is an absolutely relevant contributor to a national solution to a substantial challenge such as revealed by Hurricane Katrina and foreseen with a pandemic such as avian flu because of the basic characteristics of this army. That is, there exists an exceptionally capable active Army with a clear, abiding role to support the reserve components—both state and local Army National Guard (ARNG) and the regional, federal, functionally oriented U.S. Army Reserve (USAR). That federal, state, and local combination of leader preparation, of uniform competence standards (common task-based training), and of all-terrain, all-weather equipment is designed to be responsive to both hostile attack and to natural disaster relief as comparable important national challenges.

The domestic role of federal authority is to support the state, then the state to support local authorities. That is top-down support to sudden, largely unpredicted bottom-up requirements. Top down–bottom up interfaces of IM and KM appropriate to typical warfighting are equally relevant to federal–state support to bottom-up local disaster requirements in terms of thinking through the challenge of providing highly responsive, competent, and immediate support to local command and control to counteract the effects of domestic WMD.

Because of its inherently federal, state, regional, and local character and functional expertise that extends across every area of disaster support, America's Army routinely conveys most current leader "best practice" across the nation. After all, landpower competencies fundamentally address people performing under stress. An excellent example is current America's Army predominance in KM within the Department of Defense particularly in creating IM vehicles to generate and proliferate shared knowledge and shared actionable understanding. The growing Battle Command Knowledge System (BCKS) stimulates important learning among "passionate professionals" such as those on Companycommand.mil and NCO.net. Both are available as Professional Forums on the Internet through Army Knowledge OnLine (AKO). Now AKO evolves into Defense Knowledge Online (DKO) with two million participants and growing and built to provide redundant, continuity of operations in emergencies. BCKS, also growing rapidly, now supports over 100,000 leaders across the Active Army, the ARNG, and the USAR. Broad leader forums grow at every level—squad leader through very senior unit leaders. Today, they meet online to discuss professional issues. BCKS also has Knowledge Nets where leaders with specific functional interests meet. Logistics Net thrives today with subgroups for Medical, Supply, and Transportation. Similar nets are growing for engineers, communication, and about every other area of landpower capability including units across corps, divisions, and brigades in Army Forces Command Warfighter Forums.

An important IM and KM capability sits ready to support homeland security. Small groups living in the same geographic area could meet across component and across support function to discuss likely disaster support issues—to plan then to execute when emergency occurs.

America's Army support competence is legion—a source of national respect and support. Corps of Engineers River and Harbor competencies are understood and generally respected. Similar competencies exist across combat support and combat service support functional areas that would need to become operational amid devastation. And in each of these functional areas, there are abiding links with the appropriate civilian industry. That individual leader cross-walk between America's Army and civilian expertise is a central, very important, continuing Army Reserve regional capability that could be expanded today drawing on the power of functional knowledge nets stimulated by BCKS.

Imagine the power of leader Professional Forums grouping by urban area—state or multistate region—perhaps inviting federal, state, and local emergency officials to join. All areas of commercial competence apply. For example, ask the medical Soldier/leaders on Logistics Net to invite local and regional medical physicians and managers, as well as local Red Cross leaders and commercial medical suppliers to join the local Army Professional Forum. That Forum could be a "rally point" on a regional Medical Forum supported by the various included state Medical Societies. Together, these would work through coordination of responses to likely disasters. More important, this would create teams of functional experts used to working together available to respond for the always unexpected "big one." Expertise could be expanded as appropriate, with construction engineers, transportation companies, communications companies, and so on. The functional expertise of Army Reserve Soldiers grouped nationally by area, military, or civilian business competence is all encompassing.[5]

IM and KM combined can convert federal–state–local "top down" to ready "bottom up" disaster area functional expert teams available locally to support advance planning and perhaps provide near-immediate support when the WMD attack or massive natural disaster such as an earthquake occurs drawing on the deliberate robustness of an Internet designed to withstand nuclear attack to communicate. When expert teams form based on IM and KM, effective ToL programs are present.[6] Top-down authority would be expected to participate, to listen to, and to understand "bottom-up" issues and provide counsel when there are relevant top-down national doctrine, tactics, techniques, or procedures that must be followed to receive top-down support. Perhaps of equal merit, as a result of participation in the various functional Knowledge Nets, functional leaders would have a superb "www Rolodex" of who to go to get action and to correct glitches when the disaster occurs. Think of this as a highly decentralized national fall back for workarounds far more effective than a disaster Google because it is based on leader teaming by function developing shared trust and shared competence among and between leaders at every level well before the disaster occurs.

Current, quality, top-down support is provided routinely from state to local cities and towns by trained ARNG personnel. The National Guard routinely translates federal competencies and physical capabilities to local political and emergency support institutions—a very important function frequently:

- Training local officials (elected and appointed) in crisis management, supporting crisis decision—showing "how to" to local teams of leaders. Or setting the emergency support example with state regional commands working with state and local emergency management leaders.
- Using tactical communications to support first responders.
- Providing "best practices" counsel on application of IM/KM.

America's Army pattern of interlocking federal–state and national, regional operations could be drawn upon practically to reduce, if not overcome, many federal–state tensions in coordinating disaster relief. No other federal or state organization has such wide-ranging capability and competence wholly focused to act in concert despite extraordinary stress.

They act in concert because they share important values. These shared Army values are inculcated in a work (tactical) context through routine institutional training/education and cross-assignments. Common task-based training with a clear mission orientation is reinforced by intensive simulation-based preparation of individuals, teams, and units to accomplish assigned missions that are routinely updated because training is a centerpiece of force deployment readiness—the ARFORGEN Road to Deployment.[7]

Promotion and assignment are military competency-based with a politically-based patronage application incorporated routinely for state National Guard Adjutant Generals who are routinely politically aligned with the state executive (governor) they serve. This is a unique and supremely valuable blending of state political governance and actionable understanding of America's Army capabilities, operating routinely in extremely close collaboration developing the shared trust that is essential to high performance in crisis.

Quality control across America's Army has been institutionalized, as the reserves were building during the Cold War:

- Readiness Groups, now a Reserve Training Command with Active Components (AC) providing training support to Army Guard and Army Reserves.
- Some AC personnel seconded to RC command, and vice versa.
- Federal inspection of proficiency, and governance, with Federal resources covering 75 percent of costs.

Now with abiding unit presence in Army posts (homesteading), the active force should be able to provide continuous direct support to state and local institutions. These same support interactions are sought in reverse for Army Family Readiness Groups of active and reserve units deployed in combat. Should the nation now extend these federal support counseling/advisory emergency planning practices through ARNG (and USAR for individual functional expertise) to states and to selected high risk local areas?

These programs represent enormous advances in leveraging the multiple strengths of America's Army across the entire institution. The nation as a whole benefits. But for all practical purposes, none of the competence-generating processes previously described are present or are affordable for federal agencies such as FEMA or state organizations. This is a weakness in our national security posture that can and should be corrected, using these programs as models and the expertise available in America's Army for assistance. An important point is that they currently exist and can in many ways be exploited by other agencies rather than undertaking expensive efforts to duplicate them. We will discuss several solutions to this issue.

The wheel does not have to be reinvented. Just ask several of the millions of retirees who have experienced and understand America's Army policies and programs to suggest how to apply these best practices to improve national security performance, be it federal, state, or local.

The basic capability is that the National Guard in America's Army is highly competent and will respond appropriately. As expressed by the Director of the National Guard Bureau, "No other organization has our combination of size, skills, training and experience, dispersion across the nation, command and communications infrastructure, and the legal flexibility to support civil authorities at a moment's notice." To support Hurricane Katrina, the National Guard deployed over 50,000 Guardsmen from every state and territory in six plus days "the largest, fastest military response to a natural disaster in the history of the world."[8]

The Guard is the Department of Defense, U.S. Northern Command, Army North (ARNORTH) "first responder" that can rapidly be reinforced by active forces' functional support and likely USAR functional leaders leading teams previously developed as ToL. That is Professional Forums and Knowledge Nets teaming nationally, routinely, but then regrouped regionally by volunteers—"concerned passionate professionals" to provide action teams of local expertise when and where disaster occurs.

Both ARNG and USAR would likely need primarily command and control (C2) reinforcement from within America's Army to address major disasters within a state if that support is sought by higher headquarters to extend beyond the first 72 hours plus "issue handover" time.

Where there is multiple-state disaster, higher federal military authorities, National Guard Bureau and ARNORTH as a subordinate command of U.S. Northern Command, would direct America's Army in support of every function during the initial 72-hour period before federal, state, and local governance assumes command and control in consonance with a top-down national response plan (with the exception of law and order where existent national, state, and local law prevails). The ready teams of USAR-sponsored functional expertise assembled drawing on Knowledge Net associations could be regional not local.

Were it just that simple. Federal, state, and local collaboration remains a highly sensitive issue. "'In my 19 years in emergency management, I have never experienced a more polarized environment between state and federal government,' said Albert Ashwood, Oklahoma's emergency management chief and president of a national association of state emergency managers."[9] Federal command and control of the National Guard during disasters both natural and hostile has been and remains a controversial area of federal versus state jurisdiction. Dismayed by the inadequate federal response during Hurricane Katrina, Congress approved Public Law 109–3864, broadening presidential authority to federalize the National Guard and authorizing military forces to suppress domestic violence, obstruction, and resistance to federal law and federal court orders. There is continuing opposition to these provisions. "Members of the National Governors Association, the National Sheriffs' Association and the Adjutants General Association of the United States told the Senate Judiciary Committee that their organizations oppose a provision of the 2007 Defense Authorization Act that grants more power to the president to federalize Guard forces for domestic purposes."[10] This a fine example of the creative tension characteristic of the multiple jurisdictions included in America's Army.

In sum, a major national challenge is rapid establishment of expert governance, leader teams, to direct and coordinate responses—local, state, and federal. America's Army can provide highly useful and necessary support in rapid effective coordination of responses to domestic WMD—using appropriate "best practices" of the U.S. military multiplied by U.S. industry.[11] This is a challenge very similar to that routinely faced and met in America's Army—similar to the leader team challenge associated with Army quick response to deployments in ad hoc modular organizations configured frequently "on the fly." But now include private industry that possesses the state of the art best practices as well as continental scale resources. For example, America's Army has transportation and supply capabilities (know how) but doesn't approach the practical knowledge or "reach" of UPS or FedEx or WalMart or IBM or Microsoft.

How to better draw on remarkable individual leader and leader team competence existent today within America's Army be they active, citizen-Soldiers, veterans, or retired? The Army today is investing heavily in linking individuals with similar functional skills into high-performing ToL. Drawing on the Internet and current developing Army practice in BCKS, virtual teams of volunteers mentored by volunteer USAR leaders could be created by function at the local state and national levels and prepared as virtual functional leader teams using emerging emergency decision exercises. The actual team to execute that function in a particular disaster could be drawn from the larger virtual team, credentialed by appropriate local, state, or federal authority and then committed to support recovery from that disaster. Lest this appear impractical, exactly these sorts of capabilities to build competent ToL in organizations composed only after the specific contingency is known are used very successfully in military operations globally today. An excellent example of ad hoc emergency support was the joint military and civilian response to the tsunami in Indonesia in 2005.

Posse comitatus or America's Army subordination to state or local police authority remains an issue as illustrated previously in legislation accompanying the 2007 National Defense Act. We believe this is a false issue and represents outdated attitudes and misunderstandings, which ill serve the security interests of the American people. The concerns focus on usurpation of local and state political authority, especially in the area of law and order. This misses the point. The larger challenge is rapid provision of world-class advice and counsel to elected and appointed state and local officials to support good timely decisions in either 9/11 or Hurricane Katrina situations (WMDs). There remain effective checks on Army intervention at state and local levels. Aggressive national media accompanies every disaster promoting the "blame game" to increase media revenue 24/7. There is an elaborate local, state, and national political infrastructure watching closely, intensively on behalf of the disaster's victims. Local and state bureaucracies aggressively monitor external intervention. America's Army chain of command is highly competent. These safeguards were known by the Founders but not with the effectiveness today's constraints of the visual impact or timeliness of television.

Perhaps the most useful Army capability supporting Hurricane Katrina operations could have been effective, mobile command and control organizations prepared to command in extremity or, more likely and preferable, to advise and provide appropriate staff and communications support to those actually in command. America's Army has many combinations of highly mobile command and control (C2) globally capable in the Active Army and trained and ready in each state within the National Guard. These constitute rapidly available, highly competent C2 cells that could provide "plug-in" functional technical management competence that could be placed in direct support of state and local authority. This was neither a capability nor a requirement foreseen by the writers of the Constitution. America's Army routinely supplements C2 to support military operations with Allies. Why not similar C2 support for desiring but unpracticed governors and mayors at times of national disaster? This does not represent military assumption of control within the United States but rather military assistance as has been provided for years in foreign military assistance programs.

We envisage America's Army responsibility to be to set up, very rapidly, within 2 to 4 hours or less, command and control modules across emergency functions—federal, state, and local. They are not there taking over "command"—rather to advise federal, state, and local "commanders" and provide control and communications for command use.

These Army capabilities would have been very helpful during Hurricane Katrina. They also could support improved Army readiness for extended combat operations across the spectrum of combat operations. Each component of America's Army can play a role that complements and reinforces the other components' capabilities:

USAR. Develop and maintain national functional expertise with individual ready reservists (IRRs) maintaining new functional virtual teams within the Battle Command Knowledge System on Army Knowledge on Line (AKO) becoming Defense Knowledge Online (DKO). Sustain virtual ToL in each major function with knowledge nets and various professional forums. These teams would coordinate "best practice" for supporting that function during disaster. Those committed to support a particular disaster would transition from virtual planning team to actual execution team. The USAR-mentored virtual functional teams could prepare virtual planning exercises, develop common techniques and procedures, and create common Rules of Emergency Operation in coordination with federal, state, and local authorities. And there may be more.

New, expanded USAR learning competencies have developed in the stress of Army overcommitment to operations in the Middle East. Army reserve training infrastructure has been consolidated in one command with increasing generating force responsibilities for both individual and collective training. Increasingly the USAR provides supporting infrastructure for implementation of the CTC learning model. Now the CTC model is applied locally as part of the ARFORGEN Road to Deployment. That highly effective experiential learning model could be expanded to include initial and sustaining learning for the emergency response teams suggested above perhaps distributed regionally, nationally.

ARNG. Support planning and provide coordination resources to state emergency management planners. Prepare for integration of "plug-in" capability from other states or functional capabilities brought in by USAR leader teams proposed above from across U.S. industry. Orchestrate pre-disaster America's Army support to other federal, state, and local authorities.

Active Army. Support ARNG (by state) and USAR (by function) disaster planning:[12]

- Establish stand-by command and control for near-immediate on site disaster governance including providing Joint Task Force command under U.S. Northern Command to direct immediate Department of Defense support for major no-notice domestic WMD or disasters, then transition governance and functional resources to Department of Homeland Security.
- Provide quality control of the command and control capabilities of the various America's Army combinations supporting domestic WMD responses.
- Develop ground rules for Army support of domestic WMD.

Prepare common definitions, common techniques and procedures, and common Rules of Conduct for each function—extending what could have been developed by the USAR functional teams across AC and ARNG and using doctrine, techniques, and procedures developed by the Department of Homeland Security. These common interagency "ground rules" could be equally useful supporting Long War interagency operations overseas.

Several examples of doctrine, techniques, and procedures could draw on successful precedents developed in training America's Army for stability operations, such as:

- Prescribe level of planning detail required by echelon of responder:
  - Participation how far down by the layers of "doers"?
  - How complex the situations presented?
  - How bad the situation?
- Prescribe level of execution rehearsal detail:
  - Talk through.
  - Walk through: "rock drill" type rehearsal.
  - Walk through: actual time and space on the ground, real time.
- Prescribe team detail (hierarchical and peer leader teams):
  - Department heads.
  - Department subordinates.
  - Teams: actual cross function by jurisdiction.

In sum, in association with the Department of Homeland Security, and in support of the U.S. Northern Command, America's Army supports planning, preparation, and execution stages of immediate, major WMD disaster response. Together, the Department of Defense, Northern Command, America's Army, and the Department of Homeland Security prepare common procedures and rules of support. They provide individual leader and leader team training both virtual and grouped in proven National Training Center-type learning environments developed together by the Department of Defense and Department of Homeland Security.

When disaster occurs, America's Army provides command and control support including communications and near-immediate (2 to 4 hours) start up disaster-relief functional expertise preparing prioritized concept plans responsive to what has actually occurred not what was planned in advance, however elegantly.

An example of disaster support operations for a large city (larger than 500,000) could be:

PLANNING

Active Army. X Corps, Division, or Brigade Combat Team has a habitual support responsibility to the city (one of many). Under this agreement, X Corps, Division, or BCT support crisis action planning. They establish, assign, and train active Army command and control assets to be provided immediately to city political leaders. Corps or Division coordinate with the state ARNG commander to provide initial immediate support resources not within the state nor likely to be immediately available from functional teams.

Where home stations of active forces precludes effective habitual support relationships—simply too distant—the appropriate State National Guard Joint Combined State Strategic Plan (JCSSP) designates the responsible National Guard or Army Reserve headquarters.

ARNG. Primary America's Army support to the governor and Mayor. Provide worst-case resource requirements beyond the capabilities of the state to National Guard Bureau and the ARNORTH Commander through the sponsoring active Army Corps, Division, or BCT or other Reserve Component headquarters.

USAR. Individual Ready Reservists designated and expert in functional areas (transportation, construction, supply, medical, communications, and so on) form Professional Forums and Knowledge Nets of national virtual functional teams of leaders. These teams include the national expertise in that particular functional area be it in business, academia, federal, or state service. In support of the Department of Homeland Security, they plan "bottom up" as a group for national, state, and local disaster recovery operations in their functional area, and provide emergency headquarters as requested within the National Guard Joint Combined State Strategic Plan.

PREPARATION

Each element above conducts virtual and grouped exercises supported as required by America's Army, the Department of Defense–Northern Command, and the Department of Homeland Security.

EXECUTION

Active Army. Fly in command and control to the mayor (on the ground two to four hours after the WMD). Resources provided as direct support to state ARNG.

ARNG. Command and control of state and reinforcing ARNG resources as determined by the National Guard Bureau and the U.S. Northern Command

USAR. Virtual functional leader teams in disaster area become actual on the ground functional teams immediately supporting appropriate local functional authority.

HOW IT MIGHT "COME TOGETHER"

To go beyond generalities, consider how the nation might respond to a pandemic.[13] For example, assume that the greater Atlanta area might be struck with a major outbreak of avian flu. This would impact a multicounty area, with a population of several million people. In a worst case, masses of infected persons would overwhelm local emergency rooms and clinics. It might be necessary to quarantine the region to prevent the spread of the disease by people fleeing the scene or entering it by both land and air. This would be far beyond the capability of any local authority.

Under our concept, coordinated planning support to requesting federal, state, or local leaders planning for such a disaster would be the general responsibility of U.S. Army North (Fifth Army) under the supervision of U.S. Northern Command. ARNORTH would assign specific general planning responsibility to the Georgia National Guard or perhaps the U.S. Army Infantry Center at Ft. Benning, Georgia, or the 3d Infantry Division at Fort Stewart, Georgia. Whichever is designated as lead would be responsible to maintain a standing command and control capability to provide assets to Atlanta within 2 to 4 hours should the WMD have occurred with no notice. In this case, to support planning to address the medical aspect, ARNORTH would coordinate with the U.S. Army Reserve Command to designate a Reserve medical support command (perhaps the 3rd Medical Brigade in Decatur, Georgia) to coordinate with the Centers for Disease Control and Prevention, if asked, in anticipating treatment requirements and for stockpiling and distributing vaccines and medical supplies. The Reserve medical brigade, if asked, would support planning with state health authorities to identify and prepare treatment facilities. It would also, if asked, plan with the Veterans Administration to involve veterans' hospitals in dealing with large numbers of victims. The Reserve medical brigade would be the "last resort" default medical planner for developing this comprehensive response if called upon by federal, state or local authorities.

To implement a quarantine, the Georgia National Guard (or the Infantry Center at Ft. Benning or the 3rd Infantry Division at Ft. Stewart if designated the lead support role) would work with requesting state and local authorities. A major role would be required of the Georgia Department of Defense and its Adjutant General, who directs the 48th National Guard Brigade. Also involved in the planning would be the Georgia Department of Transportation and local and state police organizations, as determined by state and local governance. One of the reserve military police commands (such as the 220th Military Police Brigade from Gaithersburg, Maryland), as well as a transportation element (perhaps the 143rd Transportation Command from Orlando, Florida) could play leading roles in assembling functional police or transportation support if asked by Department of Homeland Security or Georgia or Atlanta authorities. Airspace control would require support by the Federal Aviation Authority and the Air Force and Navy organizations at Dobbins Air Force Base and elsewhere. The Georgia Federal Emergency Management Agency would participate in the planning process on behalf of Homeland Security for support requirements they can provide. These would be incorporated into the overall plan.

All of these requirements and a host of others would be broken down into specific tasks for all participants as parts of first local, then state, and then federal response on a prearranged basis. Note the profound bottom up bias built in to the response. The local leader knows best what has to be done in what order of priority. "Higher" exists to support lower "on the ground"!

This type of preparation cannot be done in an extemporaneous fashion in the midst of a crisis. Clearly, this is a huge challenge. It is feasible but not desirable for the Army to take the lead in initiating such detailed planning. But the abiding competence, experience, and values of selfless service to nation of its Soldiers—present and past—mandate a reinforcing role when called upon by federal, state, or local authorities. Failure is simply not an option. Without meeting these planning and execution challenges, the results of a pandemic, or other major crises, would likely be panic, chaos, perhaps civil disorder, and needless loss of life, as occurred in the Hurricane Katrina disaster. It should be obvious that far more than simply developing and stockpiling effective vaccines would be necessary. Similar plans could be put in place for other areas throughout the country and for various types of emergencies.

There are many other measures to be taken to improve U.S. response capability. Resource allocation and priorities should be evaluated for active and reserve elements charged with greater responsibility. This should be reflected in the Department of Defense force development and budgeting. Greater use should be made of the talent currently available in the superbly prepared retired military community existent in each state and most localities. Emerging KM and IM technology could be used to assist in forming functional teams responsive to unexpected contingencies. This is current practice in the growing Army Battle Command Knowledge System actively supported by the Army Reserve. ToL programs currently in pilot development for European Command then potentially Africa Command may provide additional policies and programs for Northern Command and the various states.

CONCLUSION

In sum, there are now threats of near coequal seriousness: high, mid- and low-intensity conflict across a spectrum of conflict of offensive, defensive, and stability operations and domestic WMD (9/11, natural disasters such as Hurricane Katrina/Rita, pandemics). It is incumbent on the United States to draw on contemporary mid- and low-intensity military experience across function in addition to engaging the experience of very competent leaders (active, citizen-Soldier, veteran, and retired) who are available to counsel, supported by emerging IM and KM generating shared actionable understanding. No federal, state, or local agency can match the predictable individual and team competence possessed in the aggregate by America's Army leaders—serving, veteran and retired. It is there. Thousands of leaders with proven competence in service to Nation, built over decades at a cost of billions of dollars—a vital national resource addressing the complexities of the Long War.

The good news is that now the "awful" such as WMD–nuclear, chemical, biological, or San Andreas catastrophic earthquake has become believable. "Awful" has become a serious issue that must be addressed. The United States is lucky again just as we were when the Czech Coup alerted us about the intentions of the Soviet Union in 1948 confirming the establishment of NATO. 9/11 and now Hurricane Katrina enable serious national programs addressing domestic WMD.

We caveat however that what we propose is only for the most serious events—major overwhelming national disasters such as Andrew and Katrina as hurricanes, major earthquake or major urban or multi-state WMD. Of course, America's Army has to be prepared to act as the last resort—not only provide assured competent functioning command and control available within 2 to 4 hours for 72 hours but also a satisfactory default to restore governance where federal, state or local fail. Resources may have to be provided America's Army—likely to the National Guard or Army Reserves—to provide an absolute, certain, available, default capability. That should be determinable from the various Lessons Learned reviews of 9/11, Katrina, and

Rita and then the application of analytical processes proven during the past several decades.

For example, it seems likely to be necessary to think through force development from a new perspective. Rather than the traditional force sizing of readiness for one or two Major Regional Contingencies (MRCs), we should use current Department of Defense force capability planning guidance plus ability to support one or two Katrina's simultaneously with command and control and initial coordination of functional support as the major Department of Defense force sizing requirement. Different deployment rules/mission execution force requirements would be established for America's Army such as immediate command and control (2- to 4-hour availability) then Reception, Stationing, Onward movement, Integration (RSOI)—turn over to other agencies as more capabilities arrive combining Department of Homeland Security, relief agencies such as the Red Cross, and major industry supporting by function—all agencies or corporations needing information and mechanisms for effective coordination as they stream into the WMD/disaster area. Then America's Army reverts to subordinate support relationships under Northern Command as agreed by various federal, state, and local authorities.

Time-phased force deployment requirements will probably be required. Take lessons learned from 9/11, Katrina, and Rita—sum lessons learned requirements by function then translate to priorities for functional capabilities if no-notice attack occurs. What percentage of what capabilities within what function where—regionally and locally—by when? Beyond vital first responders, and immediate command and control provided by America's Army existent headquarters, who provides what within 4, 12, 24 hours, and so on. Size America's Army to provide until relieved by responsible authority after 72 hours—a standard doctrinally based "battle handover" issue, practiced and executed routinely throughout America's Army.

This is a huge additional mission. Some will fret that America's Army will sacrifice too much warfighting capability or responsiveness. Perhaps—but consider:

- Army recruiting sufficient to sustain a volunteer force in an extended Long War is at risk. The news still appears good for 2007 despite several monthly quota shortfalls; but, as one reviews in Chapter 4 what has had to be done to generate success, there is serious unease. America's Army (Active, Guard, and Reserve) needs as many friends and supporters as it can muster in local communities to sustain the volunteer force for the Long War. National value-added in support to domestic WMD will be evident.
- American youth today want to team to address national problems. They want to defend the country.
- Thirty years after institutionalizing an extremely effective, competency-based, national, service-oriented learning system, there are hundreds of thousands of competent, experienced former officer or NCO leaders, not

serving today but retired or wounded or who went on to other jobs who could be called upon to reinforce any component of America's Army to provide the First Responder capabilities required.[14] Accrual of more years of service to support defined benefit retirement and quality health care (TRICARE) becomes more attractive year by year to veterans as industry reneges on vested retirement. Costs could be supported by whatever federal agency benefits, most likely the Department of Homeland Security since the objectives are wholly in support of that mission.

This is important new wine but there are old bottles available. Which old bottles for what purpose? The next issue becomes one of hedges. What is actual, what is hedged?

9

Hedges: Planning for the Contingent

America's Army must sustain full-spectrum readiness either in-being or as credibly available potential capability; that is, readiness to support national responses to weapons of mass destruction (WMD) at home, as well as provide land power to conduct offensive and defensive campaigns in major conflicts against major global peers while fighting a continuing Long War with primarily stability operations. To be ready for such breadth of security challenges, the nation has to decide what to be prepared for and what to hedge. What support can be expected from allies? Perhaps of greatest importance in addressing an inordinately complex threat environment, what collaboration and mission support can America's Army expect from other agencies of the federal government, such as the other military services and the various Departments of State/USAID, Treasury, Justice, and Homeland Security?

America's Army is Army Strong, to draw on a current recruiting theme. With personnel diversity well institutionalized, consistent competency-based development of superb leaders reinforced by a great learning organization, and robust depth provided by balanced imperatives (DTLOMPF), America's Army—both serving and retired—can be both remarkably responsive to address full-spectrum land power responsibilities and fully capable of supporting the totality of federal, state, and local governance becoming more robust to handle their "fair share" of national security responsibilities. Realization of these capabilities is central to understanding hedging national security, both requirements and capabilities.

America's Army is no "one trick pony." It demonstrated its abiding competence recently in the Balkans. With NATO allies, there have been recent clear successes. America's Army went into Bosnia-Herzegovina in 1995 as the Implementation Force prepared to fight midintensity combat to secure a fragile cease fire despite a brutal, widespread civil war that was partially religion-based. The Army, sized to dominate the local situation and fully prepared to fight to secure a peace, conducted highly effective nation building and peacekeeping operations. There is little reason to believe that an army led by veterans of the Balkans who knew the size, organization, and doctrine required to prevail in Operation Iraqi Freedom could have not achieved results comparable to the Balkans had they not been so ineptly directed by the civilian political leadership.[1] This is not to infer that errors were not made by Army leaders insensitive to a deteriorating and changing situation, slow to modify the force doctrine and training; and inattentive to basic command responsibilities. But America's Army was and remains a fully adaptive organization prepared to adjust doctrine, tactics, techniques, and procedures, as has been demonstrated subsequently in Iraq. But adapt to which of a wide family of full-spectrum missions? Which missions? What about the other missions? What to hedge and how to do it?

An abiding perennial defense issue is "how much is enough"? What percentage of precious national resources should be devoted to defense in what areas? This is a particularly vexing question when there appears to be a narrowing array of "good" defense policy choices available and there are compelling national social policy competitors for resources. The quandary increases as the Long War proceeds amid considerable uneasiness about both national military strategies and possession of actual capabilities necessary to enable those strategies.

Operation Iraqi Freedom proceeds amidst considerable uncertainty about the merit of current national defense policies, allies' unease about U.S. national security policies and programs, and growing prospects of widening religious conflict in the Middle East spreading outward from civil war in Iraq; all provoked by inept U.S. intervention and exacerbated by skilful terrorist operations to destroy the public comity and trigger a violent civil war not unlike what occurred in the Balkans with the fragmentation of Yugoslavia in the 1990s. Where elections occur, terrorist groups, often better serving local voters than local governance, won recently. Despite U.S. and NATO efforts, the Taliban reemerged in Afghanistan, and that country is now rapidly expanding its lead as the global opium producer. Nuclear proliferation spreads with North Korea nuclear-capable but ostensibly shutting down production facilities and Iran a nuclear aspirant.[2]

Against this temporary but certainly unfortunate national security situation, America's Army is seriously depleted with combat losses requiring massive national reinvestment to reset the force and to complete other substantial Department of Defense-directed changes to about every facet of Army readiness. The Army moves midstride in midstream of major challenges, vitally dependent on a steady annual flow of billions of dollars to rebuild basic capabilities. Unit performance remains stellar. Officer and noncommissioned officer (NCO) leaders are seriously stretched but unbroken in spirit or in capability. Reenlistment remains high. But significant seed corn has been consumed. America's Army has been underresourced for years by two consecutive Administrations mesmerized by the lure of high technology permitting quick cheap victory—Kosovo, Afghanistan, and Iraq—through top-down net-centric use of brilliant firepower—commonly air power.

The Chief of Staff commented recently on this corrosive resource deficit while addressing the Army at the 2006 Association of the United States Army

(AUSA) meeting. He recalled "bitter lessons" of unpreparedness that have plagued our history:

> We now find ourselves fighting a protracted war, and with defense expenditures less than 4% of Gross Domestic Product (GDP) and a declining national budget deficit. Compare this to World War II when we committed 38% of GDP to defense, or Korea at greater than 14%, and Vietnam at approximately 10%. In fact, since 1968, our GDP has grown by over 300%, our defense budget a little over 68%; in 1968 our deficit was 2.8% and rising and in 2005 it was 2.6% and declining. Since 1984, procurement and RDTE accounts as a percent of Army budget declined from 31% to 17.5%."[3] And then the attrition of extended commitment to the Long War—now longer than World War II—began, exacerbated by the converging pressures of Transformation execution described by the Director of the Army Staff as "like designing an aircraft in flight.[4]

Such is the record of inadequate bipartisan national security governance over an extended period.

The Army Chief of Staff makes a persuasive case, but a national mood of great frustration concerning the apparent ineptness of federal governance both in war (Iraq and Afghanistan) and in natural disasters (Hurricanes Katrina and Rita) and Homeland Defense (Trade Towers, anthrax, bird flu) erodes the probabilities that financial support of the amounts the Army needs and expects will be provided. So, it is appropriate to think through the overarching force design of America's Army and the various "Plan Bs"—the hedges—that prudence demands be enabled. How much of which, when, to ensure the desirable future? Which are the "must" policies and programs and which can be deferred until a more certain need develops or perhaps more favorable resource support emerges? Then, what are the hedges that prudent national security demands if the "must" programs are invalidated by unanticipated events?

Fortunately, the United States addresses this current perplexing situation in the Long War, largely limited to the Middle East, as the dominant global military power.

There are no fully capable peer competitors for the proximate future in land, sea, or air that could provide a "clear and present" danger directly influencing defense resource allocations. Aside from the frustrations of Iraq and Afghanistan, we know only that serious conventional full-spectrum military threats involving offensive, defensive, and stability operations are certain to emerge and that we must be prepared to sustain our dominant traditional national defense superiority when they do appear. And we know that tough resource decisions are coming as the Nation ponders costly, necessary adjustment of Social Security and health care while the Long War continues.

So, what to "buy"? And equally important, to defer capabilities in which defense areas? Where and how to "not buy"? That is, can we accept material shortfalls with confidence that we can develop the requisite national defense material capability—the necessary hedge—required to win (to get well) faster, better than can any emergent competitor?[5] Given the current dominance of human interactions across civilizations—global terrorism—state or religion-based—should the primary foci be on developing superb leaders and teams of leaders supported by timely, effective doctrine and training rather than material? Focus intensely on developing adaptive leaders prepared to advantage generated or unanticipated change?

Known defense shortfalls can be dangerous, providing a rationale for disabling neglect of defense preparation which, in turn, can become quickly a slippery slope to military impotence. Shortfalls simply cannot be permitted to put the present at unwarranted risk. Young Soldiers are in harm's way today. They deserve the "best" as they, the deployed forces of all Services, daily face certain threats. Moreover, immediately available military capabilities deter those tempted to damage grievously important U.S. interests.

So decisions where to take cuts and not impair important existing capability, then, how to correct those cuts, if wrong, are terribly important issues of national defense policy. For example, serious cuts in human intelligence gathering capabilities lured by the chimera of high technology "spies in the sky" led to serious shortfalls in intelligence afflicting all national intelligence. No human intelligence Plan B seems to have been sustained. Human Intelligence (HUMINT) capability rebuilding proceeds, but regrowth of capability requires multiples of years. During the gap, the United States is partially blind. No hedge, or if there was a hedge, it was not exercised when the magnitude of the deficiency appeared for tactical forces in Desert Storm now over a decade ago.

We describe the Army repetitively as the unique product of democracy, nation, state, federal republic, and continent. What do these overarching imperatives mandate for America's land power weighing "how much is enough"? Should these decades until a peer competitor arises be a period of land power quality or of land power quantity? By quantity, we seek land power in being sufficient to "win" against any combination of opponents rapidly with forces-in-being whenever the National Command Authority (NCA) directs. A peer competitor threat is a traditional threat; a nation-state possessing capabilities to conduct mid- or high intensity conflict directly threatening vital national security interests. Quality is considerably fewer forces in being but with essential land power capabilities for offensive, defensive, and stability operations sustained on the absolute front edge of contemporary technologies. If the answer is a smaller, qualitatively superior force, then how to correct known deficiencies in order to restore military supremacy if that answer proves wrong? What are the necessary hedges? How might Long War capabilities have been impaired and then repaired, rapidly?

Perhaps we need to rethink what is a peer competitor? Implicit in discussing peer competitors is an assumption that the peer is a nation state. Perhaps the more immediate risk could be "peer" global religion or "peer" nonstate terror. Now, is the more appropriate hedge likely to relate to social behavior rather than material capability?

Quality and quantity are highly subjective terms often subject to misinterpretation and distortion. One person's quality becomes another's "gold plating." Focus on quantity can become reliance on ill-prepared, ineffective "cannon-fodder" to a critic.

The Army in World War II best represents national focus on quantity. Protected by sea power, an enormous military capability was built to defeat the Axis Powers. Drafted soldiers were representative of all strata of American society in a national total effort to match a global threat. As manifested in equipment such as tanks and aircraft, quantity generated its own quality in tactical excellence. Today, quantity could be active standing forces across all battlefield functions immediately available to fight and win simultaneously in multiple theaters with that capability sustained irrespective of threat build ups either overseas or domestic such as WMD risk to Homeland Defense.

Quality, on the other hand, can be considered as:

- "The best, not just the satisfactory" in important components of military capability.
- "World class" when comparing capabilities internationally.
- Superior capability to "switch gears" in response to sudden and perhaps unexpected changes in military requirements such as from midintensity to COIN to the greater complexity of civil war in Iraq.
- Routine exceptional task/mission performance. This exceptional performance might be described as consistent performance in the top 30 percent of a distribution of task and mission performance of individual, team, and collective tasks in typical Army missions executed across a broad spectrum of conflict. ALL individual, team, and collective tasks are performed in top 30 percent of the distribution, half of the tasks performed in top 10 percent.[6]

U.S. land power today is fully accustomed to quality, the hallmark of most Army activities for the past several decades despite the erosion of resource support. Quality has developed as both the reality of current military capability and an important expectation of future capabilities through a variety of recurrent actions taken after Vietnam:

- Quality through steady improvement in the capabilities of reserve forces, although reserves may no longer be the hedge as greatly as in the past since many are now considered and are designated operational forces.
- Quality provided by all-volunteer accessioning of highly capable Soldiers who stimulated quality practices essential to retention while generating significant resource advantages, such as significant reductions in support force requirements. There were substantial reductions in the generating force

training base and substantial increases in reliance on civilian contract combat service support permitted by accessing highly competent volunteer Soldiers.

- Quality by rebuilding an expanded force post-Vietnam that generated competitive advantage with respect to the Warsaw Pact in Europe during the Cold War. An agile force, "David vs Goliath," all part of a robust NATO alliance which clearly succeeded in the Cold War, supported by effective strategic deterrence.[7]
- Quality in demonstrated force agility such as when America's Army adjusted rapidly, effectively, from near total midintensity focus in countering the Warsaw Pact, a capability evident in Desert Storm, to a peacekeeping operation in Bosnia. Drawing on learning organization development, Combat Training Center (CTC) rotations were created to prepare Division to Squad levels for Low Intensity Conflict (LIC) with dominant midintensity conflict capability. Then the organization was precipitously reoriented to peace enforcement to near peace keeping—learning through practicing civil governance and negotiations then community building with three distinct highly antagonistic religious ethnic groups in Bosnia. It worked beyond expectation.

  Appropriate adaptive behavior prevailed. For example, the Arizona Market—invented by a bright Brigade Commander—restarted free enterprise in a highly sensitive area. The Intervention Force was sized to fight with sufficient force to be wholly credible and was amply supported by the U.S. Air Force and fully coordinated with French and British Implementation Forces. The CTC scenarios started with tough midintensity combat then with a peace treaty and enforcement of a Zone of Separation between fighting forces in training vignettes of increasing complexity particularly for young leaders. Ten years later, two Armies—Bosnian Federation and Bosnian Serbian, formerly in full unrestricted combat—have transitioned to a combination of the two into one Army. That is a notable peacekeeping achievement combining successfully military, political, economic tools themselves strengthened by the active support of NATO and the carrot of European Community membership.[8] That was effective force agility enabled by a clearly quality America's Army.

One apparent lesson from the Balkans intervention applicable to hedges is the import of training a quality unit to fight low-intensity conflict with clear ability to escalate to midintensity. That evident capability was an important source of credibility in the Balkans. And as the situation waxes and wanes in Iraq, low-intensity conflict mixes with COIN operations. It is easier to transition from midintensity to COIN than the reverse once a pattern of COIN operations is established.[9] This was also observed personally in multiple IFOR/SFOR unit training periods at a CTC. The challenge of shifting from midintensity conflict to COIN and vice versa in military units is a challenge of sustaining quality small unit leaders—prior training of leaders and teams of leaders to be full-spectrum capable JIIM teams in particular. This is an abiding challenge for America's Army as a learning organization.[10]

What a contrast with the Balkan deployments when Iraq and Afghanistan came! Underresourced from the start and misunderstanding the emerging nature of Iraq conflict exacerbated by inept national decisions such as disbanding the Iraqi Army, the Army got behind the power curve. The recovery and reorientation led by Gen. Petraeus has been remarkable, but it may have come too late if Iraq descends into the ethnic cleansing and overt religious war so successfully arrested in Bosnia.

- Quality enabled generational experimentation: the Air Assault Division and TRICAP linked helicopter mobility to combined arms warfighting later reflected in Operation Just Cause in Panama, Operation Desert Storm in Iraq and most recently in extended peacekeeping and peace enforcement in the Balkans (Operations Joint Endeavor then Joint Guard then Joint Forge) and combat in Afghanistan and Iraq. Experimentation continued to assimilate the digital revolution—Louisiana Maneuvers, Force XXI, Strike Force, Objective Force Transformation and various Army Warfighting Experiments (AWE). Most currently, assessment of an Interim Brigade Combat Team (IBCT) lead through the innovation of Stryker BCTs to today's Brigade-Based Modular Force. Consistent futures experimentation continues as Future Army Systems (FCS) establishes a Future BCT at Ft. Bliss—serious quality futures work.
- Quality institutionalized by creating Training and Doctrine Command (TRADOC), an organizational approach to reinforce quality effecting change by embedding organizationally balanced focus on now seven imperatives of doctrine, training, leaders, organizations, materiel, personnel, and facilities (DTLOMPF). AirLand Battle doctrine development was backed by focused material acquisitions (the Big Five—Abrams, Bradley, BlackHawk, Cheyenne/Apache, and Patriot), Division 86 organizational development, Soldier and leader development, and professionalization of the NCO Corps combined clearly rebuilt the Army post-Vietnam. The current Army Plan does the same to a substantially greater potential if it is funded to completion.

These well-institutionalized, highly successful integrated force development best practices could apply far more broadly across federal agencies building to robust competence to fight the interagency Long War. Thousands of TRADOC leaders, serving and retired, are available to explain what worked in embedding quality in America's Army. And they are available to counsel translation of clearly successful policies and programs to current federal, state, and local organizations.

In addition, an important new fighting organization was created largely drawing on land power experience. That was Special Operations Command (SOCOM/USASOC), combining ready joint capabilities across the spectrum of conflict and new, highly responsive, joint counterterrorism capability drawing on competent light infantry made even better. Clearly, SOCOM is a model of successful quality force generation drawing very effectively upon capabilities across national institutions. It is an important precedent in joint force development that seems particularly appropriate for fighting international terrorism.

Now in the Long War, fault line conflicts proliferate where nationality, race, or religion contest. Our national experience, somewhat bitter because it seems to have been unexpected, has been conflict with or within Islam in the Balkans and Iraq. In both cases, we underestimated initially the explosive effect of suddenly releasing tremendous pressure to suppress fault line conflict from a totalitarian dictator—Tito in Yugoslavia and Saddam in Iraq. Along a fault line, quality has a different dimension—diverse race, religion, and language working together competently in hierarchical relationships is exceptional, actionable quality. Our diversity is a great strength of America's Army that should permit us to easily adjust across fault lines. And where opponents contest, to stand back protected by our racial, national, and religious diversity and allow them to destroy each other rather than us?

Quality has in fact been the well-lauded keynote of Army capability since the rebuilding post-RVN—arguably paced by quality accessions. TRADOC and SOCOM are particularly important quality precedents for Transformation—one in executing Service responsibilities, the other in joint warfighting.[11] Both could serve as a policy and resource example of what will be required across federal agencies both for the Long War and to establish interagency capability hedges.

QUANTITY VERSUS QUALITY

The rational national leader wants both—affordably. But with constrained resources, conscious choices are necessary. Alternatives are "fewer but clearly better" or "more but less capable"—assuming roughly comparable resource cost for each alternative.

Resource requirements are seldom equal. The policy and program challenge is: avoid fewer, less capable (a recipe for failure), or more, better which "breaks the economy" in responding to alternative, equally important requirements such as economic growth, social welfare and public works in a democracy. Overtly losing in conflict is not an acceptable alternative. Who wants to volunteer to serve with "losers"? Quality can trade off quantity only above a floor of nationally acceptable risk in which the preservation of national values and resources are assured. And there must be quality capability "floors" such as sustainment of nuclear deterrence safeguarding vital national military capabilities.

It is not an either/or proposition, however. Theory addresses the extremes (poles). Reality is more complex—searching for "more and better" and avoiding "less and worse" than any likely opponent or coalition of opponents. It is the search for a "sweet spot" of quality sufficient to accomplish assigned missions while maintaining agility and flexibility to respond to surprise. An example of such strategic surprise occurred in the 1970s. The Israeli 1973 Yom Kippur War was an effective post-Vietnam wake-up call to the need for Army modernization to deter the Warsaw Pact in Western Europe.[12] Devastation of the New York Trade Towers by Al Qaeda was also a wake-up call, but now it is to asymmetric threats. The danger of misjudging asymmetric threats was reinforced in Lebanon in 2006 by the tactical and operational military surprise created by Hezbollah fighting Israel. Hamas and Hezbollah delivered effective wake-up calls.

"Fewer but excellent" continues to be preferable to "more but average" for America's Army. Neither quality nor quantity is attained with any specific size or capability. Nor does the distinction necessarily relate to any specific threat. Rather it is an issue of capabilities—a present orientation for quantity fighting the Long War, a future orientation for quality addressing hedges? Past accomplishments focusing on quality augur future success pursuing quality in the current international environment particularly given the substantial broadening of the potential spectrum of conflict. That spectrum includes WMD, home defense to asymmetrical threats such as cyber war, as well as the more conventional threats ranging from midintensity (North Korea) to counterinsurgency (Iraq and Afghanistan) to the range of Security, Stabilization, Transition and Reconstruction operations (SSTR) present and growing in Africa. Quality bests quantity in better responding to change—expected and unexpected—such as religious or ethnically based civil war along fault lines as has occurred in the Balkans and Iraq.

HEDGES

Perhaps more important than either quality or quantity, however, is practical policy and program recognition of the requirement to develop hedges. Hedges are highly credible military capability alternatives consisting of compensating corrections to either quality-based or quantity-based programs should futures projections prove wrong. A hedge is the quick fix (Plan B) to a known agreed shortfall in defense capability.

The focus of national defense policies and programs needs to be on quality. But, simultaneously, there needs to be much more attention to creating and maintaining hedges for traditional warfighting capability particularly as necessary focus is directed currently at countering terrorism. In sum, shortfalls are implicit in any quality defense strategy. Policies and programs to fix those shortfalls (hedges) are as important to the nation's defense as are the clear, evident, strengths of quality focus. Because of that importance, America's Army should base hedges on reinforcing national strengths. Those strengths are the characteristics of America's Army as they are required to hedge proficiency across the full spectrum of conflict. For example, the challenge of hedging training for midintensity conflict in Korea for Corps and Divisions recycling for deployments to Iraq. Preparation for SFOR/IFOR in the Balkans was hedged from the start. Combat training center preparation was modified to be split between demonstrated midintensity capability while preparing for stability operations maintaining a Zone of Separation between combatants. A similar training hedge is necessary today to retain mounted Abrams and Bradley fighting capability with the near total current emphasis on dismounted stability operations. Hedges live—they are a day-to-day Army readiness issue.

Effective hedges need to be:

- Potentially decisive if implemented—they would clearly make a difference at the strategic, operational, or tactical levels.
- Assimilated by the military. The Air Assault Division was clearly a quality success, although it required generational adaptation similar to development of USMC amphibious capability and USN carrier aviation in the Interwar Period. To be a genuine hedge, that particular military capability has to be perceived as having been assimilated so that it will be employed properly when fielded. It has to be credible as the product of balanced DTLOMPF development.[13]

The toughest hedge issue may be assimilation of cultural shifts to accommodate new operating environments. For example, the Army baseline preference for midintensity kinetic operations—the clarity of direct action—is trained routinely exceedingly well in the Combat Training Center learning model and the Army Training System. That natural warrior preference makes it difficult to prepare the leaders and the teams of leaders for full-spectrum operations. In the Iraq case, a difficult transition to nonkinetic COIN—particularly when the engine of change, TRADOC, remains severely underresourced to adjust integrated doctrine, training, and leader development (DTL). But as a superb learning organization, the Army knows how to provide full-spectrum learning experiences to both individuals and teams of leaders drawing on the Combat Training Center learning model perhaps distributed interagency to train to COIN or some other SSTR operating environment. This was done successfully in the Balkans, but at that time it had to be grouped learning. Information management (IM) and knowledge management (KM) combined with leader team building now permit virtual, distributed joint, interagency and intergovernmental cross-cultural preparation building high performing teams of leaders.[14]

Exactly such a grouped and distributed intensive learning environment was created successfully to adapt the Army to COIN operations for Iraq and Afghanistan in the ARFORGEN "Road to Deployment" in 2006 and 2007. A new doctrinal COIN manual was developed and then implemented with effective training across a large organization very rapidly. That demonstrates a highly credible hedge capability to adapt. Potential enemies must be made to believe that the hedge is in fact "doable" in America's Army within a federal republic and democracy. Doable means not only physically attainable but also certain of an assured timely national decision to execute to permit the necessary build up and probable national public support of sufficient duration to ensure success. There lies the importance of the current all-volunteer force that keeps public attention/concern tolerable—because "they" have volunteered, not been drafted. Sustainment of recruiting and reenlistment of the volunteer force in 2006 despite buildup of America's Army by 30,000 Soldiers is a notable achievement that reinforces credibility.

Willingness to suffer first another Pearl Harbor or Trade Towers catastrophe is unacceptable as a triggering call to execute a hedge to stimulate building quantity military capability. Conversely, the United States gains triggering credibility from past performance—the credibility of sole use of nuclear weapons against an enemy in war. George Kennan once described the United States as a sleeping dragon that suddenly awakens and destroys all in its path. Less extreme alarms must be credible, but there is highly believable uncertainty associated with past U.S. national military responses—evidenced post–World War II by unanticipated actions in Korea, Iraq, and perhaps in combating terrorism. There is a strain of national unpredictability that should support the credibility of hedge policies.[15] This may have been reinforced by recent U.S. operations in the Middle East. If there is uncertainty with respect to U.S. military operations globally, the uncertainty should relate to duration not initiation. A nation contemplating indirect nuclear terrorism against America could consider that "the wounded party might not be over-concerned with proof of ownership. The most likely target, the United States, has invaded two countries and toppled their governments, inflicting thousands of casualties in the process, largely because of these states' associations, proven in one case but merely assumed in the other, with an attack that killed 3,000 Americans. How might it respond to an attack that killed perhaps half a million citizens, devastated Manhattan or Washington and crippled the national and global economies?"[16]

Nevertheless, the general lesson seems clear. Hedge strategies rely on national acceptance of triggers mandating execution of the hedge. Some might see hedges as an artful return to the disastrous "ten-year" policies of the British during the Interwar Period as described well by the Kagans in *While America Sleeps*.[17] The comparison is unpersuasive. Defense issues (how much is enough?) are consistent presidential campaign issues. Defense gaps are a staple of presidential politics.

Prolonged debate endures about a vital national security issue: national missile defense. While there is always international unease about a potential "Fortress America," the clarity of consistent national support for some highly credible national missile shield is remarkable—across both Democratic and Republican Administrations. Development issues center on "how to," given genuine technological uncertainties, not "if" the defense is to be built. Post-9/11, debate on allocation of strategic defense resources seems certain to broaden with believable WMD (anthrax, nuclear, and chemical) threats. But the central national concern, credible defense, is a persistent subject of lively national debate as has become the reaction to recent North Korean nuclear tests and U.S. efforts to generate a multinational response.

The importance of collective security is refreshed in the Balkans and Afghanistan. U.S., and of equal importance, NATO, policies prevail in the Balkans—after an admittedly disturbingly slow start.[18] It seems likely that NATO, now European Union forces, will eventually be present somewhere in the former Yugoslavia for the foreseeable future and that the pursuit of terrorism in "revolving coalitions" will continue but that, too, is a public reminder that freedom isn't free.

U.S. forces are continually in the public view in harm's way across the globe. A past dysfunctional "zero casualties" mandate due to uncertain national support for minor contingencies in a democracy was a genuine problem influencing commitment during the Clinton Administration; but, the U.S. military is certainly not out of sight, out of mind. Counterterrorism operations will maintain this visibility as has been the case since 2002.[19] The current Administration restates the Al Qaeda threat regularly to generate security policy support. A recent National Intelligence Estimate is explicit: "We judge the US Homeland will face a persistent and evolving terrorist threat over the next three years. The main threat comes from Islamic terrorist groups and cells, especially Al Qaeda, driven by their undiminished intent to attack the Homeland and a continued effort by these terrorist groups to adapt and improve their capabilities."[20]

The public issue seems likely to be duration not initiation of U.S. interventions particularly in response to domestic terrorism. This is born out by the continuing debate about level of presence in the Middle East as it slides into complex regional religious conflict. That conflict added to global Al Qaeda combined with U.S. reliance on oil imported from the region ensures continuing U.S. military presence in the region and resulting concern about U.S. military capabilities.

Furthermore, there is broad public recognition of a growing Chinese threat, perhaps partially racially based, but nonetheless effective as a generator of continuing public concern about defense readiness. Nuclear espionage and IEW collector interceptions stimulate public perceptions of danger.

Most significantly, the U.S. defense budget remains enormous yet level or declining proportionate to U.S. economic growth. U.S. defense expenditures in 1999 during the "peace dividend" were greater than NATO Europe, Russia, China, Iraq, and North Korea combined.[21] That preponderance with respect to other states continues. That does not mean that the resources are sufficient as concern has been expressed by a recent Army Chief of Staff nor distributed as effectively or as efficiently as they might be, but continuing national defense focus is exceptional. Increased resource support to America's Army to correct extraordinary current shortfalls within the overall defense budget may be problematical.

America may not be best at rational allocation of defense resources but she is certainly not sleeping post-9/11.[22] The British precedent of the 1930s does not apply. Hedges with appropriate triggers are not only desirable and feasible for the United States as the Long War and Transformation evolve, but they are essential to cover the inevitable shortfalls in a quality force's capabilities for major conflict with peer competitors. Hedges for conventional conflict, certainly—but whatever remains appropriate for conventional conflict, hedges are different for ethnic/religious war that is normally generational in nature. Balkan religious strife still smolders despite important European Union participation incentives that are likely more than will be available to encourage collaboration among factions in the Middle East.

Has the hedge lead time changed? Perhaps there is no longer an X year rule? Or should the decision rule be something other than a time period that in the past was essentially equipment production rate-based? Or alternatively with new emphasis on highly responsive adaptability across balanced DTLOMPF could there be new, shorter lead times?

The design of hedges will be influenced by the nature of the baseline quality force itself. That force is highly likely to draw upon the considerable strengths of land power in the United States as it is rebuilt in the Army Plan. Recall that America's Army is unique, formed as it is from a combination of democracy, nation, state, federal republic, and continent.[23] Each of these elements puts special requirements on the nature of the quality force and the derivative hedges. The importance of these unique characteristics of America's Army is so great that explicit recall of this description seems warranted as we consider hedges.

Democracy. A "citizen's army"—competent, confident Soldiers (leaders) prepared (motivated, disciplined) to fully advantage their natural capabilities while excelling as members of teams and teams of teams. They are generally self-starting, prepared to thrive when offered "bottom-up" opportunity to influence decisions. Decentralization is oxygen.

Nation. National distribution of Soldiers by race, religion, gender, and ethnic background at every level of responsibility.

State. Possession of credible capability to build capabilities to defeat any land power threat to the United States when and as the threat arises. Inter alia this means that there is a very substantial reservoir of highly competent combat leaders—active and recently retired—prepared to command at higher echelons if a hedge is executed and a rapid buildup occurs.[24]

Federal republic. A steady state division of effort has been created assigning specific responsibilities to each of the three components. That division of effort is:

- *AC*. Dominate OCONUS threats with support by operational reserve forces. Maintenance of the reservoir of long lead-time expansion capability (actual and latent) that constitute nationally agreed credible land power hedges.
- *ARNG*. The guts of quantity-based land power—partially in the operating force, partially reserve forces. The National Guard is the center of gravity of homeland defense as politically savvy supporters of state executive authority (Adjutant Generals) share authority and responsibility with peers—experienced National Guard warfighters (Officers of the Line), all supported by active Army and Army Reserve units. National Guard Adjutant General—National Guard unit commander associations are the closest and most important federal-state program execution relationships in the United States.
- *USAR*. Maintenance of highly specialized "exotic" national capabilities such as cyber defense, bio defense, and community management/Civil Affairs, (individuals and units) difficult to sustain in either active or National Guard organizations due to the nature of skills required.

Continent. Global land power capability in all conditions of terrain and weather.

These general characteristics of a quality-based America's Army generate specific, abiding requirements for each of the seven DTLOMPF imperatives. These requirements both reinforce maintenance of the standing quality force and, equally important, they become the practical policy and program foundation for the development and sustainment of requisite credible hedges.

To support likely hedges, the quality force needs:

- *Leaders*. quality leaders at all grades—the single most important assets in the quality force. Prepare all Soldiers Corporal and above as leaders.[25] That leader quality is the best insurance that America's Army can rapidly transition back and forth between kinetic (midintensity) and nonkinetic (SSTR) operations. Prepare adaptive, self-aware leaders for assumption of responsibilities at three to five echelons higher postmobilization or upon a national decision to implement an appropriate hedge.[26] In all areas, cultivate and institutionalize leader and teams of leaders' abilities to assimilate change more rapidly than national peer rivals (singly or in coalition).[27] KM applied decentralized by Generation Y "digital natives" offers national strategic advantage here. Teams of Leaders programs exploit this advantage (see Chapter 7).

- *Personnel.* Sustain enhanced professional development to develop and retain military leaders, uniformed and civilian. Consider programs such as service with industry, tours supporting state and local government, and extended sabbaticals. Lateral midservice entry should be encouraged to attract highly competent individuals possessing world-class expertise into the USAR.[28]
- *Doc TTP.* Appropriate to the preponderance of highly qualified, motivated leaders, design flexible, eclectic, tactical doctrine to dominate opponents across the broadening spectrum of conflict. Implement broad prescriptive doctrine with highly decentralized "bottom up" adaptation of tactics, techniques, and procedures as is being done now fighting the Long War. Accommodate joint and combined forces at all levels of conflict.
- *Material.* Plan Modular Force capabilities with variable survivability, lethality, and mobility all backed by modernized legacy forces. Ensure "reach down" to legacy or coalition capabilities. Ensure that an expansion baseline of low and mid intensity material capability embedded in the Army Plan is maintained.
- *Organization.* Sustain ad hoc, hybrid organizations, which can be readily modified to support both kinetic and nonkinetic operations and add situationally dependent battlefield functions (maneuver, fire support, logistic support, and so on), as well as joint or combined forces as required to dominate local military requirements.
- *Training* evolving into *Learning* (training and education). Maintain individual, team, and collective learning occurring to standard in institution, self-development, and unit domains. Increase CTC participation as a practical leader development instrument. Develop leader training ("Lehr") units to provide quasi-combat experiences to leaders not assigned to TOE units so that a reservoir of highly competent combat leaders is maintained with active, National Guard, and Army Reserve Soldiers.
- *Facilities.* Support the current Army Plan—Modular Force, Army Force Generation, Base Realignment and Closure (BRAC).

However capable the quality force, there will be shortages. If the seven imperatives have been supported in the quality force as suggested earlier, rapid expansion to build the agreed hedges should be feasible. If they have not been supported, tough hedge priority decisions are required. If post-Iraq reset of material and force relocation in the United States are not fully supported and perhaps further end strength increases are denied, new hedge priorities will be required. We suggest the revised priorities should be:

- Adaptive leader, leader team generation for joint, interagency, intergovernmental, and multinational operations.
- Expand from baseline midintensity conflict readiness with equal priority to offensive, defensive, and stability operations. That is both kinetic

operations—current midintensity conflict operations and nonkinetic cross cultural "soft" operations, such as counterinsurgency receive substantial emphasis.
- After Leader, support equal DTOMPF (for balance) or in order Leader, Doctrine, Training, Personnel then Organization, Materiel, Facilities (L,D,T,P then OMF) acknowledging the momentum of transformation. DTL synchronized to be mutually reinforcing should be the top priority imperatives.

Specific hedge design depends upon the nature of shortfalls between the quality force and the desired dominating quantity force. Hedges could be present across all battle functions or targeted to specific high-risk areas. It may be prudent to design hedges to support specifically the most challenging circumstance, which is World War scale mobilization (nation at arms) that would be large-scale conventional conflict among nation states and domestic attack with WMD.

Another World War stimulating transition of land power from exceptional quality to significant quantity would cause great change to America's Army. The all-volunteer force disappears. More nationally representative soldiers would arrive with the draft Army with profound policy implications such as:

- Much higher percentage of lower mental category soldiers in poor physical condition.
- Transition to a mobilization production base.
- Activation of a standby mobilization training base.

Under circumstances such as these when a full mobilization hedge is implemented, policies and programs appropriate for each of the seven imperatives during hedge execution might be:

- *Leader*. Prepare for actual postmobilization position drawing on leaders developed previously by active force (combat, combat support, and combat service support) leaders prepared to serve three to five echelons higher).
- *Personnel*. Accessions increased as structure increases to overmatch the peer competitor (five- year rule?).[29] Assume World War II draftee mental and physical characteristics (more characteristic of general population—more lower mental capability personnel).
- *DocTTP*. Narrow focus to actual conflict.
- *Material*. Execute a previously agreed multiyear rule—overmatch the then peer competitor. Support new economy "mass production"—whatever forms it takes.
- *Organization*. Balanced combat, combat support, and combat service support Brigade Combat Teams.
- *Training*. Individual, team, and collective training, all in unit. Maintain task, condition, standard, and the quality force learning structure. Increase

hands-on training to accelerate leader development. Distributed quality control of training provided by the institutional base that is focused on leader preparation.
- *Facilities*. Rapid expansion to expand force generation capabilities.

Development and maintenance of the DTLOMPF hedge described above would be truly challenging. It portrays the most difficult case. That is expansion to a level of national mobilization comparable to World War II. The discussion relates to America's Army. Important contributions would be made by the other military services and other federal agencies. Presumably, there would have been accompanying national military policy decisions to follow "five- or ten-year rules" for buildups that seem certain to vary as immediate threats such as counterterrorism arise. There would be a much shorter response time for some. Shortfalls in the quality force would have been determined, and a prudent national security community would have done essential planning for hedge execution. Alternatively, with the new emphasis on highly responsive adaptability across balanced DTLOMPF advantaging growing KM might there be new, shorter lead times—another role for Teams of Leaders?

If this World War example seems extreme, select another such as the early Cold War two and one-half war strategy of the Kennedy Administration that well exceeds current war planning. From that, estimate likely shortfalls then think hedges.

The above are of course ultimate, overarching hedge requirements. The need for hedges in a narrower sense can be illustrated by two examples that might also be considered exemplary contingency planning. Elsewhere we have discussed the possibility of a collapse of the North Korean regime. We have also described at length our view of an appropriate role for America's Army in domestic emergencies. In the case of a North Korean regime collapse, there could be an enormous humanitarian crisis involving refugees within North Korea and spilling over its borders, armed conflict involving elements of North and Korean forces and those of the United States, Chinese intervention, and other unanticipated results, perhaps occurring simultaneously, perhaps involving tactical nuclear weapons. How should we be prepared to hedge against such a development? What resources would be required? With careful analysis through war gaming and intelligence, our forces in the region could develop a number of scenarios for execution if necessary, identifying anticipated resource and mission requirements. It would also involve other U.S. agencies, such as the State Department, to prepare for dealing with other nations in the region, especially China and Japan. A regime collapse may never occur. But if it does, we should not be caught flat-footed, playing catch up in the midst of a major crisis.

As we have discussed, we should also hedge against major domestic emergencies, such as we endured during Hurricane Katrina. In our discussion, we posited a major avian flu pandemic in one of our major cities. We suggested that currently existing resources in the Army Reserves and the National Guard could play an invaluable role in assisting state and local authorities in planning for such a crisis and identifying resources in advance to assist in implementing effective responses. In this case, an appropriate hedge requires little in the way of additional materiel or financial resources. It does require new thinking, however, and a willingness to "think about the unthinkable" and coordinate with various teams of leaders before a crisis hits. That too is effective hedging.

That is the central issue of these observations. Little if any planning in likely hedge areas is underway. Design of the Army Modular Force focuses on creating a quality force. Quality not quantity prevails, correctly. Hopefully that force will reflect the strengths of America's Army. That seems to be generally the case. However, competing national resource demands will generate inevitable shortages—areas of defense risk. Incomplete transition to the Brigade-based Modular force seems certain given competing national requirements such as medical care and social security. Should hedges be established in the event of incomplete transformation reset and realignment of bases? Think *hedges*!

Nor should hedge development be limited to responsibilities of America's Army. Any response will involve inevitably the other agencies of federal and state governance. These agencies need to be provided comparable robustness to that provided to the Department of Defense by Executive and Legislative governance. To win the Long War, State/AID, Justice, Treasury, Homeland Security, and the other departments and agencies all require experience-based learning opportunities; continuing education programs and competency-based personnel development in programs of balanced DTLOMPF applied to their federal or state mission. Leader development extends beyond civil servants in the federal and state governments. It is equally important to prepare political appointees—an essential element of patronage within a democracy. These leaders require experience-based learning opportunities too, perhaps as a precondition to appointment.[30] Both requirement and performance results have been validated again and again by America's Army. The results of failure to resource other agencies have been painfully evident in Iraq and Afghanistan.

There is no body of thought or institutionalized effort focused on design of hedges to cover the Long War shortages comparable to that devoted to building the future quality force. That is a serious omission that requires correction. Support of hedges may mandate significant national military policy and program changes as described earlier, which should be developed and supported up front, not hidden in unfunded requirements. Neglect here is a recipe for near disaster—the British experience between the world wars. An interagency response is essential.

It is to be hoped that the strengths of America's Army can strengthen the national solution.

10

Conclusions

OUR PURPOSES

AT THE OUTSET and throughout this work, we have stressed the urgent need for more competent interagency implementation of national security policy. We have also expressed our conviction that the creation of a more effective model for such implementation can and should draw upon the human and institutional resources of America's Army. We believe that many of its practices can serve as useful examples for other agencies of government. We fully recognize the indispensable roles of the other armed services. Air and sea power are essential to America's position as a great power. Our focus is on the Army because it is most affected by the radical transformations underway in the security environment, and it must also change to meet new circumstances. But we also believe that its distinctive qualities and programs are uniquely suited for improving competence in the security establishment as a whole. Such national competence is also essential for America's Army itself. As an instrument of policy, it operates within the broader framework of national security strategy. It can live up to its responsibilities only if the United States as a whole has the capacity and the appropriate framework for competent joint and interagency operational effectiveness at home and abroad.

THE UNIQUENESS OF AMERICA'S ARMY

We believe America's Army can make essential contributions to our national security because of several distinct attributes:

- Multidimensional synergy.
- Concepts-based institutional imperatives.
- Comprehensive long-range planning and programming.
- Internalized cultural values of service, discipline, high standards, and institutional loyalty.

Multidimensional Synergy

In Chapter 3, we described the character of America's Army as being ultimately derived from its nature as a ground force, distinct among the armed services. While this is fundamental, the Army cannot be fully comprehended by this basic feature alone. America's Army as a land power reflects the characteristics of the United States of America as a democracy, as a nation, as a federal republic, as a state, and as a continent. Singly and in combination, these are the practical sources of how its characteristics interact to become strengths and how they frame its responses to challenges.

This is of particular importance today. Taken together as a synergistic entity, America's Army is a federal, state, and local resource woven into the fabric of the nation at every level. With shared values, shared socialization, common experiences, and a unifying mission, the active forces, the Army Reserve, and the Army National Guard routinely perform on a "horizontal" interagency basis absolutely integrated in support and in combat—practicing collaboration found to be so difficult for other agencies of government. And due to its multilevel presence in American life, it is "vertically" integrated with a seamless propensity to translate policies into action with effective implementation processes well institutionalized from top to bottom. Again, this is a difficult task for other agencies organized to support a function at just one level—federal, state, or local. These characteristics of America's Army are of huge importance for shaping the necessary collaborative national responses for the Long War.

This has been enhanced by the professionalization of the noncommissioned officer corps. Its status has been immeasurably improved since Vietnam. In every village and town in America, there is an Army presence, normally in the person of young leaders—highly competent officers and noncommissioned officers—if not in active service, then retired or separated, proud of his or service to nation. This is serious grass roots involvement in American life. This integration of competence within a shared culture of service beyond self to Nation into the fabric of our populace at every level in every locale has no parallel elsewhere (see Appendix).

Concepts-based Imperatives

This synergy did not occur by accident. In Chapter 6, we indicated that the synchronization of concepts-based imperatives were critical in the rebuilding of the Army in the aftermath of Vietnam. Concept-based requirements in Doctrine, Training, Leader Development, Organization, Materiel, Personnel, and Facilities have provided integrating focus throughout the active and reserve components. All march to the same drummer. This framework as an interior management approach enables America's Army to institutionalize uniform adaptation to remarkable change effectively and rapidly. This has become ingrained in the culture of America's Army—in its genes if you will. There is nothing comparable, either in the other armed services or in other federal agencies such as Homeland Security. It is a national resource that should be treasured and used for the benefit of the nation as a whole girding for the Long War.

Comprehensive Long-Range Planning and Programming

If viewed in perspective, the initiatives being undertaken in The Army Game Plan are extraordinary, even historic, for an army fully committed at war. In the face of a complex, uncertain world, the Army must focus on fundamental, basic, even generic requirements. It is doing so. The Army Game Plan is based on four main pillars:

- Provide relevant and ready landpower.
- Train and equip Soldiers and grow adaptive leaders.
- Sustain an all-volunteer force.
- Provide infrastructure and support.

Each of these is critical and interconnected. All Soldiers who serve are contributors to the overall success of the effort, and all are valuable. Many of the tasks to be performed are not glamorous. The Soldier responsible for ensuring family housing maintenance on an obscure Army post may receive no accolades, but his or her work is helping to create an environment in which heroism can flourish in dignity. Every soldier's work is ennobling.

The Game Plan is much more than a set of principles. We describe the full range of programs that are designed to make them a reality:

- *The Army Force Generation Model* is a readiness model for both active and reserve components. Its purpose is to provide rapidly deployable forces to combatant commanders on a sustained basis to fill specific mission requirements.
- *Future Combat Systems* are designed to replace equipment designed for an earlier era, and exploits advanced and emerging technologies.
- *Brigade Centric Modular Force* is the conversion of the force into self-contained full spectrum units that can be "plugged in" larger forces quickly and effectively.
- *Repositioning the Force* is designed to more closely align our forces with the demands of the post–Cold War era.
- *Growing Adaptive Leaders* focuses on evolving its training and education systems to build "pentathletes, with multiple skills, adaptive, and capable of operating at higher levels of authority.

Taken together, these programs are not only ambitious, but also revolutionary for an Army at war. We strongly endorse the Army Game Plan. It is a remarkable achievement for an Army that is too small and in the midst of a war that has already lasted longer than World War II. It is vital that the superb visionary Army Plan be provided the significant resources that will be required to make it a success in the years ahead.

Institutional Values

The inner strength of America's Army is not quantifiable but is its most important attribute. In an age of self-gratification and materialism, we witness hundreds of thousands of young Americans laying their lives on the line for what they believe America stands for. There is an ingrained culture of service beyond self, subordination of the personal to the greater good for the institution and for the nation that they serve. This is a product of the Army's history and its representation of the American people. This is the reason that our public stands behind our troops in spite of widespread discontent with the conduct of the war in Iraq.

The Army instinctively recognizes this. It is reflected in the continuing adherence to "Duty, Honor, Country" at West Point, down through the inculcation of "Ranger values" at Ft. Benning. It is not contrived. It is genuine. It is an essential cultural refection of the American society from which our soldiers are produced. It is of transcendent importance that national leaders do not simply view America's Army as another claimant for national resources, or attempt to exploit it for political ends. No other institution in America offers this magnitude of devotion and discipline. Our national leadership must advantage these unique characteristics responsibly and wisely.

AREAS OF CRITICAL IMPORTANCE

We discuss a number of areas of vital importance for America's Army in the years ahead, all of which are addressed in the Army Plan. These include sustaining excellence in the Volunteer Force. This is essential for achieving the complex tasks demanded of a professional force of an essentially fixed, even modest size. Related to this is a discussion of the Army as a learning organization, we believe the most effective in the federal government. This is far more than simply emphasizing education, but includes the institutionalization of a concepts-based requirements system, supporting balanced synchronized development of the "imperatives" of Doctrine, Training, Leader Development, Organization, Materiel, Personnel (Soldiers), and Facilities (DTLOMPF). The Training and Doctrine Command (TRADOC)—the crown jewel of America's Army—is the institutional mechanism for sustaining and leading a continuing revolution in highly effective individual, leader team and organizational adaptation to change.

In our discussion of knowledge management, we describe the means by which the expanding revolution in information technology must be exploited to carry out the difficult missions of the future. We are convinced that this requires a new operational concept combining information management, knowledge management, and very high performing leader teams, which we term Teams of Leaders (ToL). This goes beyond a requirement for America's Army, but will also be a key to effective joint, interagency, international, and multinational operational effectiveness for the entire national security establishment. Object lessons for the urgency of such an approach are many, ranging from the inadequate national response to the Katrina disaster to our travails in Iraq.

We devoted a chapter to response to domestic emergencies, and the key contribution that America's Army can make in this area. This chapter explains not only direct application of Army capabilities but also how the highly effective engines of change institutionalized in the Army can be applied much more broadly to national security challenges.

In Chapter 9, we discussed preparation for threats and conditions that cannot be predicted with certainty, but which potentially pose serious security problems. These include large-scale conventional conflict, nuclear proliferation, security impacts of climate change and major domestic emergencies, either natural or man made such as major WMD attacks. It must be understood that our ability to respond adequately to requirements beyond the capacity of standing forces or their current posture depends heavily on leveraging the quality of the force throughout the Army's components. This is a serious issue for military leadership.

CONCERNS FOR THE FUTURE

While we believe that America's Army is on the right track, we are concerned that our nation and its leaders must better understand how it should be employed, and what will be required for effectiveness in waging the Long War.

Quality and the All Volunteer Force

The nation and its leaders must comprehend the full significance of the evolution of America's Army since the Vietnam era. By opting for a volunteer force over conscription for a comparatively small force of essentially fixed size, we made the determination that we would rely on quality rather than quantity for our security. Volunteers with relatively longer enlistments fostered greater professionalism, training, and skills than any draftee force could achieve. This has been a great positive. But it has also meant that we must leverage the quality of the force to meet greater demands with a smaller standing force with the unlikely prospect of rapid expansion.

This is reflected in our work. We have stressed "force multipliers" and "cascading excellence," for example as priority elements of Army capability.

This has also required that we place greater reliance on the reserve components, especially the National Guard, to leverage the capability of the total force to meet contingencies beyond the capabilities of active units. In our discussion of "hedges" it is clear that we rely upon a culture of excellence throughout the Army institution. Indeed, this is the basis for our insistence that we view the family of Army components as a unitary total force: "America's Army." This goal of pervasive quality has been largely achieved. Viewed in perspective, the Army Plan is a comprehensive effort to enhance and sustain quality and excellence in the years ahead.

What concerns us is that the Army's ability to maintain the qualities it requires will be undermined by lack of understanding, insufficient support, and inappropriate employment. We have seen disturbing evidence of these in recent years. The cumulative effects of these shortfalls have created major stresses for the institution and its people. It is a backhanded compliment to the power of institutionalized change over the past several decades that the Army is as strong, resilient and positive as it is today. Severely stretched the "rubber band" hasn't snapped.[1] Should this under support continue it will be difficult to take on successfully the complex demands of the Long War. It is not our purpose to critique the conduct of operation Iraqi Freedom. But it is necessary to reflect on the impact of that commitment on America's Army and learn from it for the future.

Strategic Misemployment

In Iraq, our all-volunteer force was required to take on by default an enormous nation-building mission and an extended occupation in a hostile environment. As pointed out earlier, the force created since the Vietnam era was neither designed nor intended for this. It was not supposed to be this way. Restricted by too few forces in country, caused by Secretary Rumsfeld's summarily eliminating units recommended by subsequently fired Army leadership, Army leaders had assumed and planned that a large role in the aftermath of major combat operations would be performed by the Iraqi Army. It was anticipated that large scale U.S. troop withdrawals could begin in a matter of months after the fall of the Saddam regime. This was made impossible by the abrupt and unexpected decision to dissolve the Iraqi Army by Ambassador Paul Bremer on May 23, 2003.[2]

Whether this plan would have succeeded or not can never be known. But it would have been consistent with the qualitative character of America's Army, which has the need and the capability to multiply its own strengths by working with and through third and local parties, a primary requirement of stability operations. The active Army is a highly professional force, limited in size, designed for dominance on a high intensity battlefield, for highly specialized missions, and leveraging its qualities to multiply its effects in a variety of missions.

Mismanagement

Misemployment combined with inept Department of Defense management of such force has revealed the inadequate size of the Army for large, extended operations. The manpower requirements of the occupation required the large-scale deployment of the National Guard. This is at odds with its intended purposes also. The citizen-Soldiers of the Guard are designed for support of state and local governments as required by state authorities. In addition, it provides additional resources as a hedge for potential large-scale conventional operations which require forces beyond the capability of the standing Army.

The nature of the occupation adds additional burdens on Army manpower and resources. America's Army must provide the bulk of logistical support in the theater, not only for itself, but also for the Iraqi and coalition partners, and for the large Marine Corps contingent. And there has been an extraordinary expansion in use of contractor personnel often apparently beyond effective control of either U.S. or Iraqi governance. As a result, the number of actual "boots on the ground" in Iraq is a small proportion of the total Army force in country. The manpower crunch was demonstrated by the difficulty in fielding a comparatively small "surge" force.

We were struck by the obvious lack of understanding of the character of today's Army during the debate over the "surge." Respected defense intellectuals proposed without hesitation that we immediately deploy tens of thousands of new combat troops to the theater.[3] It was as if we were still in the era of the draft, not acknowledging that our limited forces were already over committed. Obviously, the Army must respond to crucial circumstances. However, if it is to be expected to conduct large, long campaigns, it must not be subject to arbitrary manpower limits.

This is not to argue the merits of our commitment in Iraq. It is to underscore the importance of several points we have made previously in our analysis. First, national leaders must fully comprehend the actual capabilities and limitations of our all-volunteer force structure and employ it appropriately in the future. This also means that Army manpower limits must not be held arbitrarily low as we enter a new era. The requirements of the Long War will likely place greater demands on America's Army as it involves conflicts among peoples. It is not warfare between weapons systems, but interaction among groups and individuals on the ground.

Nation Building by Default

The ongoing experience in the Middle East gives urgency to our proposals for ToL to provide more effective implementation of security policy by the nation as a whole. As pointed out, it fell to the Army to manage the major occupation following the fall of the Saddam regime. Effective interagency operations were notably absent in Iraq. This must be remedied in the future even if an increased burden is placed on America's Army transferring its post-Vietnam lessons learned to the broader federal department and agency community.

Inadequate Resources

We believe that America's Army is under funded. This along with personnel shortages has widespread, pernicious effects. The Walter Reed scandal is an example of cutting corners by an organization that was suffering overload, although strong leadership should have prevented such a disgrace. We believe that our national leadership should review the allocation of defense resources among the armed services. There has been an apparently immutable division of funds between the services for many years. The Army share is about 24 percent. This is not parochial special pleading. We do not disagree that all armed services play essential roles, and vital programs must be funded. But it strikes us as questionable that our largest service, which suffers 90 percent of the nation's combat casualties receives only a quarter of its defense resources and is a distant third in line for appropriations.[4] To his credit, the Army Chief of Staff successfully challenged this arrangement recently. The standard formula remains unchanged, however.

We do not offer a precise funding target for America's Army, because it is unclear to us what the true costs of a new strategy will be. The Army Plan identifies large financial requirements to fulfill its objectives. These are important needs that must be met. But it is our view that the Long War will demand much more of the Army in the future, especially if has an expanded new roles in national security strategy. We have suggested that it take a far greater role in improving federal departments and agencies that have proven inadequate for effective implementation of policy, and that America's Army can serve as a model for support of stability operations.

These roles will require substantial investments in intellectual and human capital required for engaging in new forms of warfare. It was pointed out earlier that the Army support structure is markedly smaller than those of the other services. Yet we foresee escalating requirements placed on TRADOC, SOCOM, and on the COCOMs as they gear up for the Long War. And the United States must retain its capacity for conventional wars and other contingencies, as new powers, such as China, translate growing economic power into military capabilities.

A new study by the Association of the United States Army, "Establishing Strategic Vectors," lays out in clear terms the magnitude of the tasks ahead. To mention only a few: "What are the strategic requirements of the twenty-first century? Are joint forces (Army, Marines, and special operations forces) properly sized and structured to provide the capabilities needed to perform the missions the nation will require? How does the Army best leverage its human and financial resources to ensure that it remains the world's preeminent landpower?"[5]

We believe that a comprehensive review of Army resource requirements should be conducted in tandem with the development of a new national security strategy. It should not be constrained by previously established guidelines for budget submissions by the armed services. American security will depend largely on the ability of America's Army to maintain a clear qualitative edge to deal with all challenges.

Our point in describing the current challenges facing the Army is that lack of understanding, manpower, and funding can make the pursuit of quality, upon which the future of our security depends, extremely difficult, as immediate longer term needs are sacrificed to meet short-term emergencies.

Understanding the Long War

A fundamental concern is that our national policies do not reflect comprehension of the true nature of the threats posed to us in the Long War. We pointed out that this war is ongoing in multiple "theaters" by nontraditional means, and the opponents we face are undergoing constant evolution, seeking new ways to destabilize the regimes and institutions of order and stability. This will demand imagination, resilience, and new approaches, involving all elements of our national power. Debate over security continues to reflect a traditional mindset, focusing on budgets, force levels, and weapons systems. This must change.

A NEW STRATEGIC FRAMEWORK FOR A WORLD TRANSFORMED

Long wars pose an extraordinary challenge to impatient, materialistic democracies such as ours. But we have been there before and have been successful. The West, led by the United States, prevailed, due to the tenacity and steadfastness of the American people, throughout the half century of the Cold War. Public support was vital, as it is today. But public support requires an informed populace and national leadership to guide it. At the dawn of the Cold War in April 1950, the United States published a 58-page document, designated NSC 68: United States Objectives and Programs for National Security. This established and communicated a framework that defined the challenges facing the nation. It served to organize the nation's resources in pursuit of a common goal. Much of today's security posture and programs is the product of NSC 68.

In our view, the United States needs a new statement of strategic direction. Early in our work, we suggested a strategic framework in very general terms. We proposed re-examination of a strategy of containment as offering potential. This does not imply a passive security policy, nor did the containment strategy of an earlier era. All instruments of national power, including engaging in extended conflict in Korea, Vietnam, and elsewhere were employed as necessary.

We do not presume that this concept briefly described in Chapter 1 constitutes a fully developed national strategy. But the nation needs to start somewhere in seriously examining its overall approach for the years ahead. Any national security strategy for the future must take into account not only the Long War, but also the complete range of interests the United States has as a global power. This was easier in the bipolar world of the Cold War. But the world we face today must be confronted as it is. Intelligent planning for the future cannot be achieved in an unrealistic strategic vacuum.

It is our concern that we are uncertain, nationally, as to where our vital interests lie, and confused as to how to proceed. This is entirely natural. We face new enemies, threats, and conditions we only dimly understand. But we must learn fast if we are to be secure. A major element of NSC 68 was devoted to "the underlying conflict in the realm of ideas and values," description of the nature of the conflict, and extensive analysis of Soviet intentions and capabilities. We must undertake the same learning process.

At some length we have suggested how the United States might be more effective in the implementation of national security policies. America's Army can play a vital role in that. We are confident in its enduring commitment to service and capacity to learn. It is making every effort to confront the unprecedented challenges facing us today. Through applications of "best policies and practices" that matured as the Army rebuilt from Vietnam, America's Army could be a vital part of a larger national effort in support of a clear national strategy.

THE LONG WAR AND POLICY IMPLEMENTATION

We devoted Chapter 2 to a new and highly complex threat to American and international security, global terrorism. We analyzed this new threat, how it is evolving, and what it will require of our defense establishment and of America's Army in particular. The Long War must be fought on multiple fronts simultaneously, from the Middle East, to hometown America, to areas threatened by instability and insurgency such as the Horn of Africa. We conclude that to be effective, we must exploit the capabilities of all federal, state, and local agencies involved in national security both overseas and at home.

Confronting this threat requires more than simply updating previous counterinsurgency doctrine of the past. Jihadism has become a global movement with many dimensions. It has become much more decentralized both globally and in contested theaters. Unlike twentieth-century insurgencies, it aims primarily at destabilizing institutions of government and the forces of order. It is "open source" relying heavily upon the Internet and autonomous operations of disparate groups and individuals. It is an elusive, invidious enemy, challenging and bringing into question the relevance and effectiveness of traditional instruments and responses to violence by ourselves and our allies. We have yet to fully comprehend the nature of this evolving threat and how to combat it effectively.

We conclude that in the face of this new threat more effective interagency implementation will require greater decentralization of operational authority and resources to ToL who, bottom up, are best suited for understanding then meeting the unique challenges at national, state, and local levels.

THE NEED FOR GREATER DECENTRALIZATION

Large, centrally directed programs and organizations have difficulty functioning with selectivity and precision. Examples are Homeland Security and other large bureaucracies with programs such as efforts to control immigration. An inevitable consequence of globalization is decentralization in virtually every sphere. We have described how al Qaeda has become more influential globally by decentralizing and that on the insurgency battlefields in Iraq and elsewhere insurgents are decentralized also. We must respond in kind. We have no choice but to fight on this battlefield, unfamiliar as it is. This does not mean that there is no role for policy guidance. There must be a central vision but decentralized execution, especially in tribal societies.

Decentralization also shields against overall systems destabilization and ineffectiveness. All does not depend on effectiveness at all levels. Organizations and their leaders must possess flexibility and resilience to avoid systems failure at their level. Organizations must not be "brittle," subject to destabilization under stress, and capable of rapid adaptation as situations change. This depends on the right kind of people in a structure that empowers them to operate to their full potential. The key is "alignment" of decentralized operations with overall strategic goals. America's Army with its multilevel synergy has mastered this and extends the advantage with information management and knowledge management blended into ToL.

CONCLUSIONS

Our conclusions fall into two categories: those focusing primarily on America's Army itself in preparing for the future, and more general conclusions regarding the national security framework in which the Army operates.

America's Army

The Army Game Plan. We have devoted considerable discussion to the Army's initiatives to meet the demands of the future. We believe it is on track and correctly identifies the capabilities it must have for success in the years ahead. This vital effort must be supported and sustained.

TRADOC. Our analysis of the Game Plan confirmed the centrality and importance of the Training and Doctrine Command. In the Long War it must serve as America's Army's learning center and much more. Force Generation and multiplication will depend on the Army's ability to understand the challenges it faces, then to develop rapidly the responses and leaders to prevail. This means assimilating new ideas, procedures, methods of learning and the application of knowledge and actionable understanding. Major new organizational structures must be absorbed as well as next generation equipment as part of the Future Combat Systems. "Pentathletes" must be produced throughout the ranks. We believe that it's potential to meet these challenges is insufficiently recognized or exploited. We urge that TRADOC be funded at levels sufficient to be the force generator that it can be and should be.[6] TRADOC simply can no longer be regarded as a somewhat dysfunctional generating force "cash cow." It is in fact the "crown jewel" secret of America's Army successes. Support accordingly. Other federal and state agencies should consider comparable organizational change.

Capability multipliers. Special Operations Command (SOCOM) plus TRADOC supported by the National Guard. The Special Operations Command will be a key to success in the Long War. In understanding our unconventional enemies, their cultures, and how to combat them, SOCOM's role in defeating global insurgency will be vital. While conventional operations will remain important, an increased role for our unconventional Soldiers is inevitable. SOCOM is a natural and necessary partner as TRADOC generates synchronized balanced doctrine, training and leader development in meeting the new challenges. SOCOM's expertise can inform the remainder of the force through TRADOC while the latter can provide vital intellectual and organizational depth to America's Army efforts. Both of these organizations should receive priority funding as should the citizen-Soldiers who provide the essential foundation for America's Army. As highly competent citizen-Soldiers simultaneously supporting State Governors in Home Land Security and America's Army as deployable operating forces, the Guard is a national treasure.

Cascading excellence. In our view, the Army Plan understates a very high potential "cascading excellence" breakthrough. The synergistic and combined impacts of the updated synchronized imperatives referred to earlier (Doctrine, Training, Leader Development, Organization, Materiel, Soldiers, and Facilities), rigorous training throughout the force to Tasks, Conditions, and Standards, real-time lessons learned and experience from combat, and the Combat Training Center learning model, combined with revolutionary advances in knowledge management, can create a cascade of excellence across the force that can be of enormous significance. Army leaders should view these elements as part of an integrated whole, and exploit their combined effects to the fullest. All of the essentials are there. Institutionalization of the vitally important shared warrior ethos is but a launch pad to extraordinary excellence. These proven organizational best practices should be studied for application across the diverse federal and state agencies responsible for national security—domestic and overseas.

Knowledge management and ToL. We consider the lead America's Army is taking in the new areas of information and knowledge management to be a vital, indispensable element of future national security. This is not limited to simply the mastery of technology. It is embedded in the ToL concept to enhance national security policy implementation in Joint, Interagency, International, and Multinational operations. The pioneering work taking place in our Combatant Commands, led by the Army, is an innovative response to the transformation of the international security environment. It must continue. Furthermore, it should be expanded and applied much more broadly throughout the national security establishment.

Army veterans. There are millions of dedicated retired Army veterans. Among them they have a wealth of experience and expertise across the full range of both active and reserve force competencies. They know how the Army rebuilt and how that experience can improve significantly the performance and coordination of federal and state agencies. Many would welcome a chance to be of service although they are no longer in uniform. This is an asset that is underused. We encourage new programs to provide trained leaders from this pool to bring great capability to federal, state, and local levels. An example would be assisting in disaster relief planning and execution.

NATIONAL POLICY AND IMPLEMENTATION

Applying the Capabilities of America's Army: Much of the foregoing work has been devoted to examining and improving the capabilities of America's Army. This is important in its own right for the nation's premier instrument of integrated multifunction, multilevel (federal, state, and local) national security. But we see enormous potential in applying these far more broadly in the service of nation. One of our goals is to propose means by which the implementation of security policy can be made more effective in the future. It is our strong conviction that these unique capabilities can and should be fully exploited, in perhaps unprecedented ways, to achieving this goal. Below are our views on how this should be accomplished.

Stability Operations: A National Responsibility

As the premier land power element of our national security, America's Army will inevitably be expected to carry a large part of the responsibility for stability operations, as we are conducting in the Middle East. Furthermore, it has vastly more direct experience in such missions than any other agency of government. It also has the vital logistical infrastructure to sustain stability operations. We sense a disturbing lack of capacity in the nonmilitary federal departments and agencies of our nation to be effective in such operations, although many patriotic and talented Americans are fully committed to them.

National Security Presidential Directive (NSDM) 44 establishes policy guidelines for interagency efforts concerning stability and reconstruction efforts. This is a beginning. In our view much more needs to be done. We believe that the nation should look to America's Army proven practices as a model for Joint, Interagency, Intergovernmental, and Multinational (JIIM) support of stability operations for national regional commanders (COCOMs). This would clarify responsibilities, draw upon clearly successful development models proven within America's Army and promote coordinated and timely planning among diverse organizations of government. Furthermore, it should not be construed only as a response resorted to once a crisis situation has developed. It has great application in the prevention of crises and insurgencies. It should be viewed in some circumstances as preemptive nation building and insurgency prevention.

This concept applies equally to responding to major domestic emergencies. As we discussed in Chapter 8, large domestic emergencies such as the impact of Hurricane Katrina require concerted, coordinated, teamwork by multiple state, local, and national agencies. A domestic WMD attack would presumably take place without warning making an adequate response even more difficult. Serious planning can dramatically reduce the costs and impacts of such disasters. Much of the chaos and loss of life, not to mention American credibility, could have been avoided with appropriate advanced preparation. We believe that America's Army is ideally suited to take the lead in collaborative planning for such events, following the ToL concept in our domestic environment.

Proposals

In closing, we make the following general proposals to national authorities and to the leadership of America's Army to emphasize what we consider to be crucial.

National Authorities:

- Provide a new strategic formulation that reflects the new security environment and provides guidance to our national security establishment. This new framework should include decentralization of the operational implementation of policy. It should adopt the Team of Leaders collaboration concepts for national, state, and local operations.
- Improve the capabilities of all national security agencies to operate effectively in policy implementation. In doing so it should look to America's Army as a model for competency-based leader and leader team development and institutional reform, and adopt its proven developmental capabilities and practices for other agencies.

- Fully fund the Army Game Plan and increase funding for America's Army support of extra-Army responsibilities supporting federal, state, and local adaptation to policies and programs to win the Long War.

Army Leadership:

- Maintain the primacy of the Army Game Plan as the road map for the future.
- Refine the ToL concept and promote it as a federal, state, and local model, assisting other agencies.
- Continue to analyze the evolving nature of global terrorism and develop refined policies and programs to prevail.
- Encourage and support federal and state study of clearly successful policies and programs for broader application. Candidates are balanced development of DTLOMPF imperatives, performance-based individual development, continuing professional education, experiential learning (the Combat Training Center model), and ToL advantaging bottom-up team building across JIIM jurisdictions.
- Develop adequate hedges for important contingencies that cannot be met with existing forces, maintaining the quality of the All-volunteer force.

While the security challenges facing the United States are formidable, we believe we have the capacity for meeting them successfully. The unmatched and enduring strengths of America's Army are essential national assets that must be fully employed in the interests of the American people in the new era we face.

Appendix: America's Army—Distinctive Characteristics

THE MAP ON the next page illustrates the pervasive presence of America's Army throughout the United States. Portrayals of other states would reflect a comparable pattern. (Active forces are not included due to space limitations.) No other national government institution has such a deeply rooted, community-based presence in American life.

While the magnitude of this presence is impressive, of particular significance are the distinctive characteristics of this family of organizations:

- It is a community of shared values of service to nation, and with common experiences.
- This community reflects and serves the public interest at the federal, state, and local levels.
- These institutions are organically linked and integrated, both "vertically" from local to national and "horizontally" between components and units. Ultimately they answer to a common authority. This enables the marshaling of multiple, mutually reinforcing capabilities across jurisdictional lines.
- The elements of America's Army share common standards of training, performance, and quality established by the U.S. Army.
- This institution is reinforced by the large veteran population, which also shares the values and experiences of the uniformed members of America's Army.
- Active-duty personnel and veterans of the past twenty-five years are talented Americans, educated, trained, and proud of their demonstrated service to the nation. Today's Soldiers are recruited from the 7.1 percent of the age-eligible population that meet Army mental and physical requirements and are high school graduates.

These are the qualitative characteristics of this vast institution that multiply its effectiveness and should be fully utilized by the nation. It is ideal for inter-agency operations, and can serve as a model.

Locations of Army National Guard and Reserve Activities in the State of Georgia

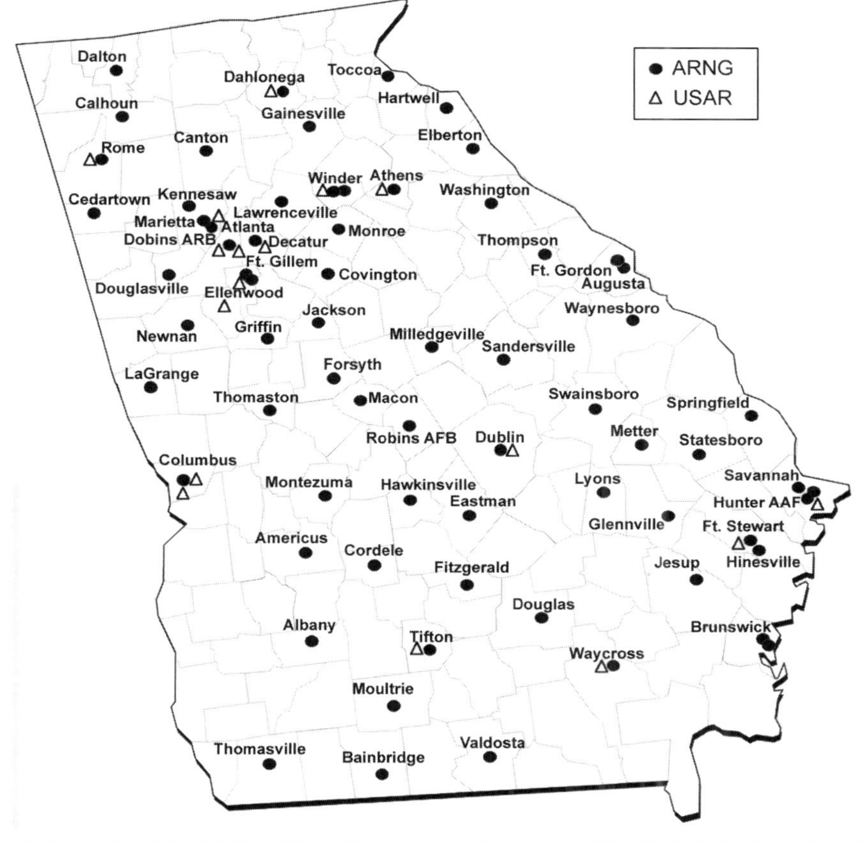

	Veteran Population	Retiree Population
Georgia	768,675	83,438
U.S. total	26,549,704	1,944,111

Demographics (Total Army)	% Male	% Female	% White	% Minority	Size (%)
Active	86.0	14.0	61.6	38.4	502,790 (48.4)
Guard	86.5	13.5	74.5	25.5	346,288 (33.3)
Reserve	76.7	23.3	59.5	40.5	189,995 (18.3)
Total					1,039,053

Sources: Veterans Administration; Georgia National Guard; *Army Times*, October 15, 2007.

Abbreviations

AAR	After Action Review
ABCS	Army Battle Command System
AC	Active Component—"Regular Army"
AFQT	Armed Forces Qualification Test
AFRICOM	Africa Command
AKM	Army Knowledge Management
AKO	Army Knowledge Online
AKO-S	Secure AKO (for classified communications)
ARFORGEN	Army Force Generation (model)
ARNG	Army National Guard
ARNORTH	Army Component U.S. Northern Command
ARTEP	Army Training and Education Program
ASVAB	Armed Services Vocational Aptitude Battery
AUSA	Association of the United States Army
BCKS	Battle Command Knowledge System
BCT	Brigade Combat Team
BCTP	Battle Command Training Program
BRAC	Base Realignment and Closure
CALL	Center of Army Lessons Learned
CCTT	Close Combat Tactical Trainer
CENTCOM	Central Command
CIA	Central Intelligence Agency
CITV	Commander's Independent Thermal Viewer
CJTF	Combined Joint Task Force

CLT	Commander Leader Team
CMOC	Civil-Military Operations Center
CMTC	Combat Maneuver Training Center
COCOM	Combatant Command
COE	Contemporary Operational Environment
COIN	Counterinsurgency
CPX	Command Post Exercise
CRAF	Civil Reserve Air Fleet
CS	Combat Support
CSS	Combat Service Support
CT	Counterterrorist
CTC	Combat Training Center
DAC	Department of the Army Civilian
DARPA	Defense Advanced Research Projects Agency
DBST	Digital Battle Staff Trainer
DHS	Department of Homeland Security
DocTTP	Doctrine, Tactics, Techniques, and Procedures
DTL	Doctrine, Training, Leader Development
DTLOMPF	Doctrine, Training, Leader Development, Organization, Materiel, Personnel, Facilities
EFP	Explosively Formed Projectiles
FBCB2	Force XXI Battle Command Brigade and Below
FCS	Future Combat Systems
FIST	Fire Support Team
F2C2	Future Force Company Commander
HP CLT	High-Performing Commander Leader Team
HUMINT	Human Intelligence
IDF	Israeli Defense Force
IED	Improvised Explosive Device
IET	Initial Entry Training
IFOR	Implementation Force (Bosnia)
IM	Information Management
IRR	Individual Ready Reserve
IS	Information Systems
JCSSP	Joint Combined State Strategic Plan
JFCOM	Joint Forces Command
JIACG	Joint Interagency Coordination Group
JIATF	Joint Interagency Task Force
JIIM	Joint, Interagency, Intergovernmental, Multinational
JMTC	Joint Multinational Training Command
JRTC	Joint Readiness Training Center
KM	Knowledge Management
LDX	Leader Development Exercise

METL	Mission Essential Task List
METT-TC	Mission, Enemy, Troops, Terrain—Time, and Civil Considerations
MILES	Multiple Integrated Laser Engagement System
MiTT	Military Transition Team
MOS	Military Occupational Specialty
MRE	Mission Rehearsal Exercise
NCA	National Command Authority
NCO	Noncommissioned Officer
NCOES	Noncommissioned Officer Education System
NTC	National Training Center
OC	Observer-Controller
OJCS	Office Joint Chiefs of Staff
OPFOR	Opposition Force
PRT	Provincial Reconstruction Team
QDR	Quadrennial Defense Review
RC	Reserve Component—Army National Guard and Army Reserve
SBCT	Stryker Brigade Combat Team
SES	Senior Executive Service (U.S. Civil Service)
SFOR	Stabilization Force (Bosnia)
SKA	Skills, Knowledge, Attributes
SOCOM	Special Operations Command
SOF	Special Operating Forces
SSTR	Stability, Security, Transition, and Reconstruction Operations
STANAG	Standardization Agreement
STX	Situational Training Exercise
TCS	Task, Condition, Standard
TES	Tactical Engagement Simulation
TLD	Training and Leader Development
TLDP	Training and Leader Development Panel
TOL	Teams of Leaders
TPFDL	Time-Phased Force Deployment List
TRADOC	Training and Doctrine Command
TRICAP	Triple Capability Division (1970s test)
TTAS	Two-Tier Attrition Screen
TTP	Tactics, Techniques, Procedures
USAR	United States Army Reserve
WKB	Warrior Knowledge Base
WMD	Weapons of Mass Destruction
WWW	World Wide Web (Internet)

Notes

Preface

1. Zeb B. Bradford, Jr., and Frederic J. Brown, *The United States Army in Transition* (Beverly Hills, CA: Sage Publications, 1973).

2. For a brilliant discussion of this, see Fareed Zakaria, "The Deepest Political Divisions," *Washington Post*, January 7, 2008.

3. Gordon R. Sullivan, "America's Army into the Twenty-First Century," National Security Paper 14 (Washington, DC: Institute for Foreign Policy Analysis, 1993); and Gordon R. Sullivan and Frederic J. Brown, "America's Army," *Military Review* 82 (March–April 2002): 3–8.

4. See Hans Binnendijk, "At War But Not War-Ready," *Washington Post*, November 3, 2007; and Max Boot, "Send the State Department to War," *New York Times*, November 14, 2007.

5. Editorial, *New York Times*, March 18, 2007.

6. The seriousness of this scandal was immediately apparent. See Zeb B. Bradford, Jr., "Army's Reputation Takes a Hit," *Atlanta Journal-Constitution*, May 13, 2004.

Chapter 1

1. Editorial, *The Economist*, June 30, 2007.

2. Editorial, *Financial Times*, May 25, 2007.

3. Vali Nadr, *The Shia Revival* (New York: W. W. Norton, 2006), 246.

4. For a full discussion of this subject, see Robert D. Kaplan, "When Korea Falls," *Atlantic Monthly*, October 2006.

5. An Israeli air strike in Syria has raised questions about a potential nuclear program in that country, possibly supported by North Korea. This reinforces concerns

about nuclear proliferation by the North Korean regime in spite of ongoing international negotiations to dismantle its own nuclear program. See Eban Kaplan, "Nuclear Questions Aimed at Syria," Daily Analysis, Council on Foreign Relations, September 26, 2007.

6. Elizabeth Economy, "The Great Leap Backward? The Costs of China's Environmental Crisis," *Foreign Affairs* 86 (September–October 2007): 38–39.

7. Ibid., 40–41, 43.

8. Ibid., 44–45.

9. "A Troubling Middle Eastern Era Dawns," *Financial Times,* October 17, 2006.

10. Gen. Peter Schoonmaker, Annual Army Chief of Staff Address to the Eisenhower Luncheon, Annual Meeting and Exposition of the Association of the United States Army, Arlington, VA, October 10, 2006.

Chapter 2

1. For a chronology of three decades of terrorist activities, see *Financial Times*, July 7, 2007.

2. Rupert Smith, *The Utility of Force: The Art of War in the Modern World* (New York: Knopf, 2007), 280.

3. Ibid., 5.

4. Paul Haven, "Al-Qaida on Air," Associated Press, July 13, 2007.

5. Ibid.

6. Ibid.

7. Eric Hoffer, *The True Believer: Thoughts on the Nature of Mass Movements* (New York, Perennial Classics, 2002), 85.

8. Mitchell D. Silber and Arvin Bhatt, *Radicalization in the West: The Homegrown Threat* (New York: New York City Police Department, 2007).

9. Steven Erlanger, "A Life of Unrest," *New York Times Magazine*, July 15, 2007, 47.

10. John Robb, *Brave New War* (Hoboken, NJ: John Wiley & Sons, 2007), 94.

11. Ibid., x.

12. Ibid., 113.

13. Erlanger, "Life of Unrest," 44.

14. U.S. Department of Defense, *Military Support for Stability, Security, Transition, and Reconstruction (SSTR) Operations*, DoD Dir 3000.05 (Washington, DC: U.S. Department of Defense, 2005).

15. U.S. Department of the Army, *Counterinsurgency*, FM 3.24 (Washington, DC: U.S. Department of Defense, 2006).

16. For an insightful yet deeply disturbing analysis of ineffectual national efforts to coordinate agencies, see Nora Bensahel, "Organizing for Nation Building," *Survival: The IISS Quarterly* 49 (Summer 2007): 43–76. Comparably inept federal–state collaboration for homeland security is described well in Spencer Hsu, "States Feel Left Out of Federal Emergency Planning," *Washington Post*, August 8, 2007.

17. For a detailed analysis of FM 3.24, see *The Army Magazine Guide to Counterinsurgency* (Arlington, VA: Association of the United States Army, 2007).

18. For a discussion of the criticisms of FM 3.24, see Frank Hoffman, "Neo-Classical Counterinsurgency?" *Parameters* 37 (Summer 2007): 71–87.

19. Quoted in Frederick W. Kagan, "Why We're Winning Now in Iraq," *Wall Street Journal*, September 28, 2007.

Chapter 3

1. Unique Army strengths are from Sullivan and Brown, "America's Army," 3–5.

2. Samuel P. Huntington, *Who Are We? The Challenge to America's National Identity* (New York: Simon & Schuster, 2005), 212.

3. We acknowledge the superb service of the U.S. Marine Corps, an outstanding fighting force of which the United States should be very proud. The Corps is an essential Sea Service.

4. For reasons unique to their functions, the Coast Guard does not fall under posse comitatus.

5. The length of the "dwell time" at home has been suggested to be five rather than six years. Time will tell; all schedules are in disarray because of the level of commitment to operations in Iraq and Afghanistan.

6. U.S. Department of the Army, Office of Army Demographics, September 30, 2005.

7. Donna St. George, "Yearning to Be Whole Again," *Washington Post*, November 24, 2006.

8. Jeff Tietz, "The Killing Factory," *Rolling Stone*, April 20, 2006, 58.

9. The description and discussion of Army goals is from U.S. Department of the Army, Office of the Chief of Staff, *2006 Game Plan—United States Army* (Washington, DC: U.S. Department of Defense, 2006).

10. Ibid.; and *Profile of the U.S. Army: A Reference Handbook.* Arlington, VA: Association of the United States Army, 2005.

11. Another enormous beneficial difference is the presence of a strong noncommissioned officer corps protecting the Army from becoming "broken" during the current period of great stress on the organization.

12. Jim Tice, "Casey Pushing Four Major Initiatives," *Army Times*, October 2007.

Chapter 4

1. The importance of a shared culture of service beyond self to nation and to organization cannot be overstated. Apparent lack of a shared culture of service appears to impair efforts to recruit Department of State foreign service officers in Iraq. See Karen DeYoung, "Envoys Resist Forced Iraq Duty," *Washington Post*, November 1, 2007.

2. Samuel P. Huntington, *The Soldier and the State* (Cambridge, MA: Belknap Press, 1959), 10. Huntington attributes this phrase to Harold Lasswell.

3. Michael Sharra, *The Killer Angels* (New York: Ballantine Books, 1975).

4. The power of such diversity is reflected in the national pride and international notice evident when both the space shuttle *Discovery* and the International Space Station were commanded by women in October 2007.

5. Huntington, *Soldier and the State*, 11.

6. It is this complex uncertainty that distinguishes the ground military from any comparable business decision-making environment and questions the relevance of much academic leader development research.

7. "Mosaic" is the term used by CENTCOM and the media to describe varying, highly adaptable patterns of operations conducted in Operation Iraqi Freedom.

8. This chapter reflects these changes and expands significantly on Frederic J. Brown, "Leaders for America's Army," *Military Review* 83 (May–June 2003): 69–78.

9. President George W. Bush, Graduation address at West Point, June 1, 2002. Available at: http://www.whitehouse.gov/news/releases/2002/06/20020601-3.html.

10. U.S. Department of Defense, *Quadrennial Defense Review Report* (Washington, DC: U.S. Department of Defense, 2006), 3, 19.

11. U.S. Department of Defense, *Military Support for SSTR Operations*, 2.

12. See Chapter 6.

13. U.S. Department of the Army, Office of the Chief of Staff, *2006 Game Plan*, 2.

14. Ibid.

15. America's Army as described in Sullivan and Brown, "America's Army."

16. But this advantage may not remain unique, as millions worldwide become highly proficient at using cell phones. See Capt. Daniel Helmer, "The Poor Man's FBCB2: R U READY 4 the 3G Celfone?" *Armor* 115 (November–December 2006): 7–10.

17. Donna St. George, "Yearning to Be Whole Again," *Washington Post*, November 24, 2006.

18. "Army Meets 2006 Goal," *Military Officer,* December 2006, 34.

19. U.S. Department of the Army, DAPE-MPW-PD, "Information Paper," *Army Retention*, September 7, 2006. As attrition has grown in recent months, bonuses of up to $35,000 have been added for captains in an extensive incentive program described in Ann Scott Tyson, "Army Offers Big Cash to Keep Key Officers," *Washington Post*, October 11, 2007.

20. A notable contribution to reenlistment has been an abiding, very serious effort to upgrade Army posts to support readiness and quality of life. This effort is well summarized by *Installations as Flagships for Soldier and Family Readiness and Quality of Life*, Torchbearer National Security Report 23 (Arlington, VA: Association of the United States Army, 2007).

21. For an extensive discussion of leader team development and performance, see Chapter 7.

22. Lt. Gen. John Riggs, "The Objective Force in 2015," in U.S. Department of the Army, Office of the Chief of Staff, *2006 Game Plan*, i.

23. U.S. Department of the Army, Office of the Chief of Staff, *2006 Game Plan*, 8.

24. ARFORGEN is discussed in detail in Chapter 5.

25. Gen. (Ret.) Barry McCaffrey, Remarks at the 2006 MOAA Military Professionals Symposium, November 16, 2006.

26. This position was first stated vehemently early in the rebuilding after Vietnam by Frederic J. Brown, "The Army and Society," *Military Review* 72 (March 1972): 3–7.

27. One set of criteria could be arrival in the United States before the age of sixteen, and residence here for five years. See Brigid Schulte, "Why Won't We Let Them Fill the Ranks?" *Washington Post*, June 3, 2007.

28. "Married in America: The Frayed Knot," *The Economist*, May 24, 2007.

29. Gen. William Wallace, "TRADOC Commander's Perspective," presented at the 2007 Armor Warfighting Conference, Fort Knox, KY, May 2, 2007.

30. U.S. Department of the Army, Training and Doctrine Command Headquarters, DCG IMT, "The Human Dimension in Full Spectrum Operations," presentation, 2006.

31. "Married in America: The Frayed Knot," *The Economist*, May 24, 2007.

32. Jane McHugh, "War Worries," *Army Times*, March 21, 2005.

33. Michelle Tan, "Sign-Up Boon for 45 MOSs," *Army Times*, June 11 2007.

34. Vince Crawley, "DoD Offers More Money to Keep Spec-Ops Troops," *Army Times*, February 7, 2005.

35. This is due to the foresight and impact of Sen. John Warner of Virginia.

36. The Congressional Budget Office asserts that military pay is fully comparable to civilian pay for comparable jobs. See Rick Maze, "A Fresh Look at Pay," *Army Times,* July 16, 2007.

37. Rick Maze, "A Bigger Military in the Long Term," *Army Times*, December 11, 2006. A current estimate is that each increase in Army end-strength of 10,000 Soldiers costs $1.2 billion, up from $700 million in 2001—in part due to various enlistment bonuses and other incentives. See Ann Scott Tyson, "General Says Army Will Need to Grow," *Washington Post,* December 15, 2006.

38. Tom Philpott, "Army Signs More Dropouts," www.military.com, November 22, 2006. Available at: http://www.military.com/features/0,15240,119382,00.html.

39. This assessment is based on personal observation and comments from Observers/Controllers at various Combat Training Centers.

40. Lt. Gen. Steven Blum, "Army and Air National Guard Core Capabilities: Talking Points," presented at the Army War College/George Washington University Homeland Defense/Eisenhower Series Homeland Security Symposium, Washington, DC, November 13, 2006.

41. Rick Maze, "Panel OKs Guard 'Empowerment,'" *Army Times*, May 21, 2007.

42. ARNG Divisions were highly successful Total Force AC-RC composite organizations serving in Bosnia.

43. Maj. Gen. (Brevet) Emory Upton was the preeminent Army futurist of the 1870s and 1880s. He was a strong and controversial advocate of reliance on the regular army over militia forces.

44. Blum, "Army and Air National Guard Core Capabilities."

45. All are captive to personal experiences. As 4th Army commander, one author was surprised to discover that he had USAR units that were indisputably world class. In one case, a technical intelligence unit was in fact the leading edge of the R&D side of one of the major medical manufacturers in the United States. In another case, a port engineering unit was the premier unit of its type in the United States—the technical support for the Army Engineer School in this area, with staff officers who flew in from all over the United States to be present at drills. In the Civil War, Western Union ran the Army telegraph. In World War II, RCA and AT&T came to the Army en masse.

46. National Guard Bureau Fact Sheet, "State Partnership Program," November 13, 2006.

47. SOCOM Plus is discussed in Chapter 7.

48. See Chapter 7.

49. For a more complete discussion of high-performance team requirements, see Frederic J. Brown, *Preparation of Leaders* (Alexandria, VA: Institute of Defense Analyses, 2000); and Frederic J. Brown, *Vertical Command Teams* (Alexandria, VA: Institute of Defense Analyses, 2002).

50. Riggs, "Objective Force in 2015," 13.

51. Bradford and Brown, *United States Army in Transition*, 110.

52. Ibid., 111.

53. Warfighting Mission Areas: Focused Logistics, Battlespace Awareness, Force Application, Force Protection, Net-Centric, Force Management, Training, and Command and Control. Business Mission Areas: Acquisition, Financial Management, Human Resource Management, Installations and Environment, and Logistics.

54. For an excellent discussion of hard and soft power, see Joseph S. Nye, Jr., *The Paradox of American Power* (New York: Oxford University Press, 2002), 4–12.

55. For discussion of the potential of professional forums supporting chains of command in "double knit" data, information, and knowledge sharing, see Chapter 5.

56. For a theoretical discussion of a learning and teaching organization that uses Special Forces as a "best practice" model for business, see Noel M. Tichy, *The Cycle of Leadership* (New York: HarperCollins, 2002), 2–19.

57. Warrant officers are important but not discussed here. By and large, they are gold-collar.

58. SMA (Ret.) William Gates, Interview in *All We Could Be*, videocassette (First Person Productions for the Association of the United States Army, 1996).

59. Riggs, "Objective Force in 2015," 7.

60. E-mail correspondence from LTC Doane to Dr. Quinkert, Army Research Institute, March 20, 2003. This was advocated most recently by the Department of Defense in 2007. See Donna Miles, "Flexibility Encouraged to Promote Reserve-Component Service," American Forces Press Service, June 22, 2007.

61. Stephen Barr, "A Push to Create a Fresh Class of Public Servants," *Washington Post*, March 23, 2007.

62. Mary Beth Sheridan, "For Unusual Task Force, an Unprecedented Mission," *Washington Post*, March 12, 2003.

63. Army leaders are aggressively recruited by U.S. industry, especially by Jack Welch, formerly of GE, and Home Depot.

Chapter 5

1. Doctrine, Training, Leader Development, Organization, Material, and Soldier, subsequently expanded to include Soldier in Personnel and Facilities and described generally as the imperatives of Army development. DTLOMPF is discussed extensively in Chapter 6.

2. This chapter revises and expands considerably on Frederic J. Brown, "Three Revolutions: From Training to Learning/Teaching and Team Building," *Military Review* 83 (July–August 2003): 54–62, to address the Long War and the impact of both information technologies and knowledge management.

3. U.S. Department of Defense, *Quadrennial Defense Review Report*, vi, vii.

4. The context for JIIM is described in Riggs, "Objective Force in 2015."

5. The description that follows is detailed to encourage actionable understanding of how Army training evolved and how that progress might now be applied between agencies.

6. This was a major effort directed by Gen. Bill DePuy and then–Maj. Gen. Paul Gorman from 1973 to 1977.

7. The foundational requirement is U.S. Department of Defense, *Military Support for SSTR Operations*. SSTR is described as a core mission "given priority comparable to combat operations" (p. 2).

8. This assessment is based on personal observation of five to ten such exercises conducted at Hohenfels and Ft. Polk by both Active Army and National Guard Divisions prior to deployment to Bosnia in IFOR or SFOR.

9. Popular management literature extols the Army CTC AAR process as a superb example of a teaching organization practicing a "virtuous teaching cycle." See Tichy, *Cycle of Leadership*, 3.

10. This is especially true when this assessment is communicated rapidly among commander peers on emerging Professional Forums and Knowledge Nets such as companycommand.mil.

11. For an appreciation of this domestic interagency learning requirement, see Zeb B. Bradford, Jr., and Frederic J. Brown, "America's Army as First Responder," Landpower Essay 06-1 (Arlington, VA: Association of the United States Army, 2006).

12. Less the obvious stress created by actual KIA or WIA.

13. This aspect is discussed at length in Chapter 6.

14. This was a notable contribution of Gen. Carl Vuono, later Chief of Staff of the U.S. Army.

15. Lt. Gen. William Steele and Lt. Col. Robert Walters, "Training and Developing Leaders in a Transforming Army," *Military Review* 82 (September–October 2001): 10.

16. Call to Duty Boots on the Ground, CPA, October 2006.

17. For an excellent summary of the TLDP, see Joe LeBoeuf, "Case Study No. 3: The 2000 Army Training and Leader Development Panel," in Don M. Snider and Gayle L. Watkins, eds., *The Future of the Army Profession* (New York: McGraw-Hill, 2002), 487–504. A revised Army Training and Leader Development Strategy, intended to provide measurable training and leader development goals, is in final draft and is expected to become part of the Army Campaign Plan in August 2007.

18. See U.S. Department of the Army, *Training the Force*, FM 7.0 (Washington, DC: U.S. Department of Defense, 2002), I-4. "L" had always been part of DTLOMS and later DTLOMPF. A major effort by CSA Gen. Dennis Reimer concentrated on TLS to complement the continuing emphasis on DOM.

19. This challenge first emerged for company-sized maneuver units when the TOW was fielded. With a range of 3,000 meters and a night sight, it was exceedingly difficult to replicate combat cues for routine training. Only battalions—and in some cases only higher-level units—had the resources to support company TOW training. Thus began the recent centralization of Army training.

20. Frederic J. Brown, "Executive Summary," in *Training Third-Wave Landpower: Structured Training* (Alexandria, VA: Institute of Defense Analyses, 1993).

21. "Hedges" are discussed in Chapter 9.

22. This is one of several "secrets" of exceptional leader competency in Special Forces Delta Force units.

23. For example, a recent CG of the NTC trained there as a battalion and then a brigade commander, as the head of both battalion and brigade OC teams, and as Chief of Staff for NTC. What relevant experience: he now commands a division in Baghdad!

24. A separate but important issue discussed elsewhere is whether or not sufficient resources were provided to TRADOC to assess and then revise the doctrine TTP being trained at the CTCs. See Chapter 6.

25. LeBoeuf, "Case Study No. 3," 497. The "devil in the details" is providing sufficient resources to TRADOC to permit these kinds of initiatives.

26. E-mail correspondence from Lt. Gen. David Petraeus to Frederic J. Brown, October 13, 2006.

27. Ibid.

28. The ARFORGEN Road to Deployment for units is now being applied to the preparation of advisor teams (MiTT) for Operation Iraqi Freedom. For an excellent explanation of ARFORGEN applied to reserve forces, see "Transforming the U.S. Army Reserve to an Operational Force," Torchbearer Issue Paper (Arlington, VA: Association of the United States Army, 2007), 4.

29. Absent sustained training opportunities and requirements, there can be disabling loss of essential leader expertise. About 40 percent of Armor Captains today have never trained tank gunnery in a unit environment.

30. A superb example of an innovative combination of these new capabilities is the Warfighters' Forum for SBCTs, centered at Ft. Lewis. See "Stryker Brigade Combat Team (SBCT) Warfighters' Forum: A New Army Paradigm for Home Station Unit Training," Torchbearer Issue Paper (Arlington, VA: Association of the United States Army, 2007), 4.

31. Initial operational fielding of Land Warrior occurs for one Battalion in a Stryker Brigade for OIF in 2007. See Matthew Cox, "Stryker Team Set to Be First to Use Land Warrior in Combat," *Army Times*, December 4, 2006.

32. This was established in important task migration assessments conducted by the Army Research Institute (ARI) in reviewing task distribution across enlisted grades.

33. This "training up" is likely to require substantial modification to structured training practices. Scheduling "sergeant's time" while leaders train themselves changes when Corporals and Sergeants are leaders too. The inevitable embedding of structured training has to be replaced with unexpected opportunities and risks that mold agile, adaptive leaders. Structured training remains necessary but can become insufficient. The ARFORGEN Road to Deployment is designed to correct these deficiencies.

34. For extended development of these domains, SKAs, and applications, see Brown, *Preparation of Leaders*; Brown, *Vertical Command Teams*; and Frederic J. Brown, *Building High-Performing Commander Leader Teams: Intensive Collaboration Enabled by Information Technology and Knowledge Management* (Alexandria, VA: Institute of Defense Analyses, 2006). SKA of teamwork and team decision-making needs to be prepared also.

35. One of the authors had the opportunity to command substantial Army installations for nine years in all (Baumholder, Ft. Knox, and Ft. Sheridan). Similar organizational SKA worked for each. Developing a shared vision in Baumholder was clearly beneficial to focus activity: USAREUR sports championships, a USAREUR Energy Conservation Award to secure resources for better facilities, and so on. "Effortless superiority"—an oxymoron—was developed by teams of increasingly competent leaders striving, as teams, to create a clearly high-performing community.

36. These are discussed at greater length in Chapter 7, and in Zeb B. Bradford, Jr., and Frederic J. Brown, "Teams of Leaders: The Next Multiplier," Landpower Essay 07-1 (Arlington, VA: Association of the United States Army, 2007).

37. Similar nets have been employed by following Divisions engaged in OIF. Various other applications are discussed throughout Brown, *Building High-Performing Commander Leader Teams*. For additional discussion of BCKS, see Chapter 7.

38. Digital natives are young leaders who have grown up with computers, television, and other content systems that develop important multitasking abilities.

39. Etienne Wenger, Richard McDermott, and William M. Snyder, *Cultivating Communities of Practice* (Boston: Harvard Business School Press, 2002), 18–21.

40. An avatar is a digital person representing or acting as a real person in a wholly digital world. The avatar can talk and act as the actual person would in life, but he or she is represented digitally in a digital environment.

41. Riggs, "Objective Force in 2015," 11.

42. Christopher Lee, "Volunteer Efforts Spark Push for Public Service Academy," *Washington Post*, May 3, 2006.

43. An excellent example was the military "basic training" provided to members of the media before they were embedded in military units during Operation Iraqi Freedom.

44. Richard G. Lugar and Condoleezza Rice, "A Civilian Partner for Our Troops: Why the U.S. Needs a Reconstruction Reserve," *Washington Post*, December 17, 2007; President George W. Bush, "Executive Order: National Security Professional Development," May 17, 2007. Available at: http://www.whitehouse.gov/news/releases/2007/05/20070517-6.html.

Chapter 6

1. An important breakthrough in offensive weapons, EFP can be fabricated locally to destroy various levels of armor protection.

2. This is discussed in Chapter 2.

3. Gina Cavallaro, "Schoomaker: Reset Funds Must Be Predictable," *Army Times*, July 24, 2006.

4. Brig. Gen. Mitchell Zais, "U.S. Strategy in Iraq," presented at the Honors Convocation, Newberry College, Newberry, SC, November 9, 2006.

5. Lt. Gen. Douglas Lute, "Army Readiness a 'Significant Strategic Risk,'" *Inside the Army*, November 20, 2006.

6. Terrorism as manifested in September 2001 through subverting artifacts of advanced civilization (transport aircraft and skyscrapers), as well as drawing on use of WMD.

7. These characteristics are discussed at length in Chapter 3.

8. Maj. Gen. David Grange, "Ready for What," *Armed Forces Journal International* (December 1999): 44.

9. This is an unfortunate side effect of a post–Cold War drawdown initiated by CSA Carl Vouno, executed through and beyond Desert Storm, and completed by CSA Gordon R. Sullivan. Although superbly executed with exceptional congressional support, years of reductions in force and shortfalls followed by years of Soldier and material combat losses nonetheless generate their own atmosphere of decline. The continued high-level performance of America's Army today is a testament to the strength and abiding dedication of Soldiers exceedingly well led.

10. U.S. Department of the Army, *The Army*, FM 1.0 (Washington, DC: U.S. Department of Defense, 2001), chap. 1.

11. Gen. Carl Vuono, Interview in *All We Could Be*, videocassette (First Person Productions for the Association of the United States Army, 1996).

12. This chapter updates and expands on Frederic J. Brown, "Imperatives for Tomorrow," *Military Review* 82 (September–October 2002): 81–91; and Frederic J. Brown, "Transformation under Attack," *Military Review* 82 (May–June 2002): 9–15.

13. U.S. Department of the Army, *The Army*, FM 1.0, chap. 3.

14. We applaud the national Project on National Security Reform, but it is top down. Decentralized "open source" conflict requires an equal or greater measure of decentralized bottom-up innovation to enable widespread collaboration.

15. See Chapter 9.

16. U.S. Department of the Army, Training and Doctrine Command Headquarters, Intelligence Support Activity, *The Contemporary Operational Environment* (Washington, DC: U.S. Department of Defense, 2007), 2.

17. Brig. Gen. Huba Wass de Czege and Richard Sinnreich, "Conceptual Foundations of a Transformed U.S. Army," Landpower Essay 40 (Arlington, VA: Association of the United States Army, 2002), 43.

18. U.S. Department of the Army, *Concept Paper for the Objective Force* (Washington, DC: U.S. Department of Defense, 2001), 20.

19. Wass de Czege and Sinnreich, "Conceptual Foundations," abstract.

20. For additional discussion of hedge forces, see Chapter 9.

21. U.S. Department of the Army, *The Army*, FM 1.0, chap. 3.

22. This is another context for grouping *D*octrine, *T*raining, *L*eader, *O*rganization, *M*aterial, *S*oldier, *F*acilities—DTLOMPF—as force hedges are developed. Hedges are the policies and programs required to restore a known deficiency in ready military capability. See Chapter 9.

23. Kevin Woods, *Iraqi Perspectives Project: A View of Operation Iraqi Freedom from Saddam's Senior Leadership*, Joint Center for Operational Analysis and Lessons Learned/Joint Advance Warfighting Program (Alexandria, VA: Institute of Defense Analyses, 2006), vii–viii.

24. A "blame game" remains likely between several echelons of national security decision makers, including the most senior chain of command, who didn't see "nation building"/COIN as a national mission in Iraq for several years. Once there was clear direction that a different response was required in OIF, America's Army—led by TRADOC—moved rapidly and effectively to rewrite doctrine and institutionalize effective training. In fact, the effectiveness of the response reinforces the hedge strategies discussed in Chapter 9.

25. "Investigation of the 800th Military Police Brigade [Taguba Report]," Hearing Article 15-6, August 17, 2004, part 3, paragraphs 4 and 5. Available at: http://www.globalsecurity.org/intell/library/reports/2004/800-mp-bde.htm.

26. Thomas E. Ricks, *Fiasco* (New York: Penguin Press, 2006), 71, 175.

27. Michael R. Gordon and Bernard E. Trainor, *Cobra II* (New York: Pantheon Books, 2006), 100.

28. There is good news: excellent examples exist of TRADOC functional proponents acting to synchronize imperatives. For an example from the intelligence community, see F. Patrick Filbert, "Task Force 165 Military Intelligence Battalion: Building a Capability," Land Warfare Paper 65 (Arlington, VA: Association of the United States Army, 2007).

29. Gen. Frederick J. Kroesen, "Tactical Nukes," *Army* (December 2006), 8.

30. These conceptual approaches to addressing change were introduced and discussed in Frederic J. Brown, "Perpetual Transitions," *Military Review* 82 (November–December 2002): 75–86.

31. Transitioning from one pattern of operations to another—such as offense to defense or vice versa, as in the Civil War for the Union Army after success at Gettysburg—is really difficult even when anticipated. It is much more difficult when unanticipated, except for a very experienced organization.

32. Samuel P. Huntington, *The Clash of Civilizations and the Remaking of World Order* (New York: Simon & Schuster Paperbacks, 2003).

33. Violation of this was precisely the concern about the cancellation of Crusader, an important fire system. "Wagons have circled" around Future Combat Systems (FCS).

34. Walter Russell Mead, *Special Providence: American Foreign Policy and How It Changed the World* (New York: Knopf, 2001).

35. *Profile of the U.S. Army*, 7.

36. For an examination of escalating KM practices, see Chapter 7. TRADOC has wholeheartedly supported KM through the Battle Command Knowledge System.

37. U.S. Department of the Army, Armor Center, "FCCV Family" (Ft. Knox, TN: U.S. Department of Defense, 1983). From this family, the Army moved to IBDE LAV vehicles in the late 1990s, and to FCS in 2003.

38. Richard McDermott, "Learning Across Teams: The Role of Communities of Practice in Team Organizations," *Knowledge Management Review* 2 (May–June 1999): 32–37.

39. U.S. Department of the Army, Training and Doctrine Command Headquarters, Combined Arms Center, Center of Army Lessons Learned, "Executive Summary," presentation, July 22, 2004.

40. Brown, *Preparation of Leaders*, IV-1.

41. Some packages may be unbalanced to instruct experientially the need to seek balance.

42. U.S. Department of the Army, *Mission Command: Command and Control of Army Forces*, FM 6.0 (Washington, DC: U.S. Department of Defense, 2003).

43. This is discussed in Chapter 9 and is a very tough issue. Beyond the remedial branch-functional task training that is required, there are cultural issues such as the reestablishment of the culture of the mounted warrior for Cavalry and Armor after extended combat experience away from armored fighting vehicles, and insufficient dwell-time between deployments to train for mounted midintensity combat operations.

44. This was successful in the Balkans and then Partnership for Peace. Iraq and Afghanistan remain to be determined as COIN challenges shift.

45. It has been suggested recently that the CTC model could be applied to JIIM, with proposed JIIM regional training centers as a "vehicle for coordination and execution of regional national security objectives across departments and agencies" and eventually "a multinational regional training center of excellence for SSTR operations with all elements of national power participating." See Gregory L. Cantwell, "Nation-Building: A Joint Enterprise," *Parameters* 37 (Autumn 2007): 54–68.

46. Bradford and Brown, *United States Army in Transition*, 18; U.S. Department of the Army, Office of the Chief of Staff, *2006 Game Plan*, enclosure 7, "Stationing."

47. The contractor record in OIF is mixed. The disturbing lack of effective oversight of contractors in recent years must be corrected before more diverse use of contractors can be planned. See Karen DeYoung, "State Department Struggles to Oversee Private Army," *Washington Post*, October 21, 2007; and Dana Hedgpeth, "Iraq Contract Documents in 'Disarray,' Inspector Says," *Washington Post*, October 23, 2007.

48. For various combinations, see Chapter 7.

49. U.S. Department of the Army, Armor Center, "FCCV Family," 8.

50. Kim Hart, "Not Quite a Prototype But Something to Play With," *Washington Post,* November 20, 2006.

51. The Soldier is addressed more fully in Chapter 4.

52. These values, attitudes, and skills of service beyond self to nation are pervasive across past and present Soldiers in America's Army. When veterans are added to retirees, the state and local presence is enormous. See the Appendix for a representative example of the Army's presence in one state.

53. "Army Family Covenant," *FLO Notes* 20 (November 2007): 2.

54. This conceptual approach comes from Brig. Gen. Huba Wass de Czege, "Lessons from the Past: Making the Army's Doctrine 'Right Enough' Today," Landpower Essay 06-2 (Arlington, VA: Association of the United States Army, 2006).

Chapter 7

1. U.S. Department of the Army, *Mission Command*, FM 6.0, B-2.

2. There is increasing recognition that teams are important contributors to the generation of knowledge. See Stefan Wuchty, Benjamin F. Jones, and Brian Uzzi, "The Increasing Dominance of Teams in Production of Knowledge," *Science*, May 18, 2007.

3. The discussion of ToL draws on and expands on Bradford and Brown, "Teams of Leaders."

4. A wiki is a Web site that allows visitors to add, remove, edit, and change content, typically without the need to register. It also allows for linking among any number of pages. This ease of interaction and operation makes a wiki an effective tool for mass collaborative authoring. More information is available at: http://en.wikipedia.org/wiki/Wiki.

5. Heather Green, "The Water Cooler Is Now on the Web," *Business Week*, October 1, 2007.

6. Gary Winkler, "SES Army Knowledge Management Initiatives," presented at the CIO/G6 GO Workshop: Enabling Battle Command, February 25 2006, slide 2.

7. The best current examples are companycommand.mil for Company Commanders, LogNet for the Army, and joint logisticians and FiresNet for joint fires supporters.

8. The imperatives of Doctrine, Training, Leader, Organization, Material, Personnel, and Facilities are discussed in depth in Chapter 6.

9. U.S. Department of the Army, "Overview and Capabilities Brief for Eighth (U.S.) Army," presentation, November 28, 2006.

10. U.S. Department of the Army, Training and Doctrine Command Headquarters, Combined Arms Center, Battle Command Knowledge System, "Battle Command

Knowledge System as the FORSCOM Knowledge Enabler," briefing for Gen. Charles C. Campbell, August 14, 2007. Available at: https://www.us.army.mil/suite/portal/index.jsp.

11. ARFORGEN is discussed in detail in Chapter 5.

12. U.S. Department of the Army, Training and Doctrine Command Headquarters, Combined Arms Center, Battle Command Knowledge System, "Battle Command Knowledge System as the FORSCOM Knowledge Enabler," slide 31.

13. Helmer, "The Poor Man's FBCB2."

14. *Leaders* is a broad description of those in positions of authority and responsibility, be they chief executive officers or subordinates in business, or ambassadors or subordinates in the Foreign Service or other government agency—usages well beyond the military.

15. For an extended discussion of these teams, see Brown, *Vertical Command Teams*.

16. See Bradford and Brown, "Teams of Leaders."

17. A similar example could be put forward for homeland security or homeland defense.

18. Excellent references are U.S. Department of Defense, Joint Forces Command, *Commander's Handbook for the Joint Interagency Coordination Group* (Washington, DC: U.S. Department of Defense, 2007); and U.S. Department of Defense, Joint Forces Command, *Interagency, Intergovernmental Organization, and Nongovernmental Organization Coordination During Joint Operations*, Joint Publication 3–08 (Washington, DC: U.S. Department of Defense, 2006)

19. This is explained more fully in Bradford and Brown, "America's Army as First Responder."

20. Paul Collier, *The Bottom Billion* (New York: Oxford University Press, 2007), 124–33.

21. Gen. Bantz J. Craddock, "Press Remarks," March 2, 2007. Available at: http://www.defenselink.mil/news/newsarticle.aspx?id=3244.

22. U.S. Department of the Army, *Army Leadership*, FM 6.22 (Washington, DC: U.S. Department of Defense, 2006), chap. 3.

23. See Chapter 9.

24. This discussion expands on Brown, "Transformation under Attack."

25. No explicit tie is intended to the previous Objective, Interim, and Legacy forces morphing into the current modular force—which will and should all evolve continuously—subject to availability of resources. But there will always be force modernizations resulting in various combinations of "new" and "old" in America's Army. Whatever terms future leadership may wish to employ, the necessary forces are future (visionary), experimental, and present forces. All three must be addressed, plus a credible hedge capability linked to quantity forces generated after extensive mobilization. Hedges are discussed fully in Chapter 9.

26. An excellent account is available in Gary Berntsen, *Jawbreaker* (New York: Three Rivers Press, 2005). For a more recent summary of SOCOM relevance to the conduct of Long War operations—in this case, COIN in Pakistan—see Ann Scott Tyson, "Pakistan Strife Threatens Anti-Insurgent Plan," *Washington Post*, November 10, 2007.

27. A timely post-9/11 example—but probably not the most demanding requirement on future land power, as operations in Iraq have indicated.

28. Blum, "Army and Air National Guard Core Capabilities."

29. The Reserve Forces are being asked to do more and more, but at what cost to the essential ethos of "citizen-Soldiers"—vital members of America's Army? How much time can you devote to USAR or ARNG and still hold a civilian job? Overemphasis on the use of reserve forces, however capable they are (and they are capable), is an example of "seed corn" consumption with potentially detrimental long-term implications, particularly as reserves become operational as well as strategic reserve forces.

Chapter 8

1. This discussion expands on Bradford and Brown, "America's Army as First Responder." Other serious deficiencies were evident, and they persist—reflecting continuing bureaucratic incompetence. See Spencer Hsu, "Tons of Food Spoiled as FEMA Ran Out of Storage Space," *The Washington Post*, April 13, 2007; and Spencer Hsu, "Immigration Agency Mired in Inefficiency," *Washington Post*, May 28, 2007.

2. U.S. House of Representatives, *A Failure of Initiative: Final Report of the Select Bipartisan Committee to Investigate the Preparation for and Response to Hurricane Katrina* (Washington, DC: U.S. Government Printing Office, 2006), 132. Available at: http://www.katrina.house.gov.

3. See Christopher Lee and Paul Lewis, "With Minor Exceptions, System Worked," *Washington Post*, August 3, 2007; "The Fires of October," *The Economist*, October 27, 2007; and Sheryl Gay Stolberg, "With Katrina Fresh, Bush Moves Briskly," *New York Times*, October 24, 2007.

4. In this chapter, we frequently refer to all major domestic disasters as "domestic weapons of mass destruction."

5. As AKO morphs into DKO, the breadth capabilities of all Department of Defense military services become available.

6. For discussion of Teams of Leaders, see Chapter 7.

7. ARFORGEN and the Combat Training Center learning paradigm are discussed fully in Chapter 5.

8. Blum, "Army and Air National Guard Core Capabilities."

9. Spencer Hsu, "States Feel Left Out of Federal Emergency Planning," *Washington Post*, August 8, 2007.

10. Rick Mazem, "New Federal Guard Rules Concern Governors," *Army Times*, May 8, 2007.

11. Expertise in such intensive federal, state, and local collaborations within the United States is a central development experience to leaders in America's Army, but not to leaders from the Sea Services or the U.S. Air Force.

12. For an excellent summary of current capability and practice, see Lt. Gen. Tom Turner, "U.S. Army North: We're Here to Help," *Army*, September 2007, 27–32.

13. This example is borrowed from Bradford and Brown, "America's Army as First Responder," 10–11. There has been no attempt to reconcile this conceptual example with the current National Response Plan, or with the National Strategy for Pandemic Influenza Implementation Plan (NSPIIP). Our purpose is conceptual/future; they are practical/present—although as mentioned earlier, serious work has to be done to develop better federal–state collaboration. For a description of another persuasive contingency—a 10-kiloton nuclear attack on Indianapolis killing 14,000 and injuring 21,000—see Ann Scott Tyson, "Many Lessons in Disaster Drill," *Washington Post*, May 14, 2007.

14. Of course, there are comparable leaders prepared by the other military services who would also be both willing and available.

Chapter 9

1. It is noteworthy that Army Chief of Staff Gen. Ric Shinseki, essentially fired for not accepting the seriously flawed Defense Department estimate of force requirements for the war in Iraq, was the senior force commander in Bosnia. He knew requirements, as did the fired Secretary of the Army.

2. These considerations require significant revisions to the original argument in Frederic J. Brown, "Quality over Quantity—and Hedges," *Military Review* 82 (July–August 2002): 64–69.

3. Gen. Peter Schoonmaker, Annual Army Chief of Staff Address to the Eisenhower Luncheon, Annual Meeting and Exposition of the Association of the United States Army, Arlington, VA, October 10, 2006.

4. Lt. Gen. James Campbell, presentation at the Army Force Management Seminar, Ft. Belvoir, VA, December 2005.

5. See Sullivan and Brown, "America's Army."

6. Common usage is "go" or "no go" with respect to task performance to standard. It is increasingly possible to establish and measure very high levels of performance drawing on various forms of simulation linked to proven Combat Training Center learning practices, such as Opposition Force, Observer Controllers, After Action Reviews, and an Instrumentation System to record operations.

7. In contrast to erosion-of-effectiveness perceptions of U.S. forces due to exceptional U.S. force protection measures to avoid casualties in the Balkans, there is currently a clear U.S. willingness to fight and take casualties in both Iraq and Afghanistan. Restrictions now rest with some European NATO allies who are unwilling to position their national forces to fight in Afghanistan. Is the employment of NATO as a credible hedge force now compromised as a result? Might the situation be similar for Japan and India in addressing threats in Asia?

8. One of the authors, observing bitter religious/ethnic cleansing in Bosnia in 1995, subsequently designed the Bosnian Federation Army to protect Bosnia from a resurgent Serbian Army. Revisiting in July 2007, he observed both armies combining into one—success beyond anyone's expectations in the Implementation Force or later the Stabilization Force, even as enduring ethnic tensions persist. Given resources, time, and sensible policy direction, America's Army produces!

9. This is based on personal experience in an Infantry Battalion in Vietnam and on subsequent observations in other units as a Division G3, the Division Operations Officer.

10. See Chapter 5.

11. For additional discussion of the profound future potential of TRADOC and SOCOM, see Chapter 7.

12. Perhaps a comparable "wake-up call" has existed for several years, with Israel "fighting" on five fronts across the spectrum of conflict simultaneously—information warfare through weapons of mass destruction.

13. Balanced DTLOMPF is discussed in Chapter 6.

14. See Chapter 7.

15. For a profound appreciation of these characteristics of the United States, see Mead, *Special Providence*, particularly the discussion of the Jacksonian tradition.

16. Robin M. Frost, *Nuclear Terrorism after 9/11*, Adelphi Paper 378 (London: International Institute of Strategic Studies, 2005), 65.

17. Donald Kagan and Frederick W. Kagan, *While America Sleeps* (New York: St. Martin's Press, 2000).

18. Self-defeating ethnic animosity persists in Bosnia. See Jonathan Finer, "New Highway Bogs Down in Bitterly Divided Bosnia," *Washington Post*, September 1, 2007.

19. It is noteworthy that police and firefighter losses in New York appear to have far exceeded military personnel losses since Desert Storm. Only after several years of OIF conflict have losses exceeded 9/11.

20. U.S. National Intelligence Council, *The Terrorist Threat to the U.S. Homeland*, National Intelligence Estimate (Washington, DC: U.S. National Intelligence Council, 2007), 6.

21. International Institute of Strategic Studies, "Table 38: International Comparisons of Defense Expenditures and Military Manpower, 1985, 1998, and 1999," in *The Military Balance, 2000–2001* (London: International Institute of Strategic Studies, 2000), 297.

22. It does seem fair to accuse the United States of "snoozing" or, at a minimum, a lack of attention in the face of an increasing terrorist threat after the first World Trade Center attack.

23. Sullivan and Brown, "America's Army," 3–6.

24. This is in contrast to the situation in 1940–1942, when there had to be a massive changeover of unit leaders to accompany the rebuilding.

25. The extraordinary strategic value of quality Soldiers was evident in the success of the Partnership for Peace. Even better, citizen-Soldiers reinforced and in time led the effort as various states teamed with Partnership for Peace nations, such as the U.S. state of Georgia with the Caucasian Republic of Georgia.

26. This was German practice in the Reichswehr in the 1920s.

27. Excellent learning innovation was applied in this area in the Interim Brigade Combat Team nested-leader preparation.

28. There is a clear need to establish highly flexible personnel management policies enabling early vesting of retirement and lateral entry. See Chapter 4.

29. The "five-year rule" refers to the interval prior to likely employment when a decision to expand from quality to quantity in land power capability needs to be made by the national leadership.

30. James Dobbins, "Who Lost Iraq?" *Foreign Affairs* 86 (September–October 2007): 61–74.

Chapter 10

1. Notwithstanding the extremely serious failure of leadership to "care for our own" at Walter Reed Hospital, major corrective programs were instituted almost immediately. For an excellent summary, see "Army Medical Action Plan," Defense Report 07-2 (Arlington, VA: Association of the United States Army, 2007).

2. Ricks, *Fiasco*, 162.

3. See, e.g., Robert Kagan and William Kristol, "Bush Must Call for Reinforcements in a Deteriorating Iraq," *Financial Times*, November 13, 2007; and Zeb B. Bradford, Jr., "Why More Troops Will Not Solve Crisis in Iraq," *Financial Times*, November 16, 2007.

4. We are struck by the current imbalance in military expertise at the most senior levels. As we contemplated ground operations to kill Bin Laden in the territories of Pakistan bordering landlocked Afghanistan in late summer 2007, the CENTCOM Commander was an admiral, the SOCOM Commander was an admiral, and the outgoing and incoming CJCS/DCJCS duo are from the Sea Services (Navy and Marine Corps, respectively). Curious.

5. Mark D. Rocke and David P. Fitchitt, "Establishing Strategic Vectors" (Arlington, VA: Association of the United States Army, 2007), 11–12.

6. It is notable and disturbing that the Army has only 27 percent of its strength in the supporting institutional Army—in contrast to the Navy and Air Force, with about 50 percent so assigned. Sen. Joseph Lieberman, "Statement to Airland Subcommittee5," *AUSA News*, July 2007.

Bibliography

Army Times. February 7, 2005–July 16, 2007.

Berntsen, Gary. *Jawbreaker*. New York: Three Rivers Press, 2005.

Blum, Lt. Gen. Steven. "Army and Air National Guard Core Capabilities: Talking Points." Presented at the Army War College/George Washington University Homeland Defense/Eisenhower Series Homeland Security Symposium, Washington, DC, November 13, 2006.

Bradford, Zeb B., Jr., and Frederic J. Brown. "America's Army as First Responder." Landpower Essay 06-1. Arlington, VA: Association of the United States Army, 2006.

———. "Teams of Leaders: The Next Multiplier." Landpower Essay 07-1. Arlington, VA: Association of the United States Army, 2007.

———. *The United States Army in Transition*. Beverly Hills, CA: Sage Publications, 1973.

Brown, Frederic J. "America's Army: Expeditionary and Enduring—Foreign and Domestic." *Military Review* 83 (November–December 2003): 69–78.

———. "The Army and Society." *Military Review* 72 (March 1972): 3–7.

———. *Building High-Performing Commander Leader Teams: Intensive Collaboration Enabled by Information Technology and Knowledge Management*. Alexandria, VA: Institute of Defense Analyses, 2006.

———. "Imperatives for Tomorrow." *Military Review* 82 (September–October 2002): 81–91.

———. "Leaders for America's Army." *Military Review* 83 (May–June 2003): 68–78.

———. "Perpetual Transitions." *Military Review* 82 (November–December 2002): 75–86.

———. *Preparation of Leaders*. Alexandria, VA: Institute of Defense Analyses, 2000.

———. "Quality over Quantity—and Hedges." *Military Review* 82 (July–August 2002): 64–69.

———. "Three Revolutions: From Training to Learning/Teaching and Team Building." *Military Review* 83 (July–August 2003): 54–62.

———. *Training Third-Wave Landpower: Structured Training*. Alexandria, VA: Institute of Defense Analyses, 1993.

———. "Transformation under Attack." *Military Review* 82 (May–June 2002): 9–15.

———. *The U.S. Army in Transition*. Vol. 2, *Landpower in the Information Age*. McLean, VA: Brassey's, 1993.

———. *Vertical Command Teams*. Alexandria, VA: Institute of Defense Analyses, 2002.

Bush, George W. Graduation address at West Point. June 1, 2002. Available at: http://www.whitehouse.gov/news/releases/2002/06/20020601-3.html.

Campbell, Lt. Gen. James. Presentation at the Army Force Management Seminar, Ft. Belvoir, VA, December 2005.

Collier, Paul. *The Bottom Billion*. New York: Oxford University Press, 2007.

Craddock, Gen. Bantz J. "Press Remarks." March 2, 2007. Available at: http://www.defenselink.mil/news/newsarticle.aspx?id=3244.

Desch, Michael C. "Bush and the Generals." *Foreign Affairs* 86 (May–June 2007): 97–108.

Dobbins, James. "Who Lost Iraq?" *Foreign Affairs* 86 (September–October 2007): 61–74.

Frost, Robin M. *Nuclear Terrorism after 9/11*. Adelphi Paper 378. London: International Institute of Strategic Studies, 2005.

Gates, SMA (Ret.) William. Interview. *All We Could Be*. Videocassette. Produced and directed by Rob Kirk, 45 min., First Person Productions for the Association of the United States Army, 1996.

Grange, Maj. Gen. David. "Ready for What?" *Armed Forces Journal International* (December 1999): 44.

Helmer, Capt. Daniel. "The Poor Man's FBCB2: R U READY 4 the 3G Celfone?" *Armor* 115 (November–December 2006): 7–10.

Huntington, Samuel P. *The Clash of Civilizations and the Remaking of World Order*. New York: Simon & Schuster Paperbacks, 2003.

———. *The Soldier and the State*. Cambridge, MA: Belknap Press, 1959.

Installations as Flagships for Soldier and Family Readiness and Quality of Life. Torchbearer National Security Report 23. Arlington, VA: Association of the United States Army, 2007.

International Institute of Strategic Studies. "Table 38: International Comparisons of Defense Expenditures and Military Manpower, 1985, 1998, and 1999." In *The Military Balance, 2000–2001*. London: International Institute of Strategic Studies, 2000.

Kagan, Donald, and Frederick W. Kagan. *While America Sleeps*. New York: St. Martin's Press, 2000.

Korb, Lawrence J. "Political General." *Foreign Affairs* 86 (September–October 2007):

Kroesen, Gen. Frederick J. "Tactical Nukes." *Army* 56 (December 2006): 8.

Lute, Lt. Gen. Douglas. "Army Readiness a 'Significant Strategic Risk.'" *Inside the Army*, November 20, 2006.

"Married in America–The Frayed Knot." *The Economist,* May 24, 2007.

Mead, Walter Russell. *Special Providence: American Foreign Policy and How It Changed the World.* New York: Knopf, 2001.

Myers, Richard B., and Richard H. Kohn. "The Military's Place." *Foreign Affairs* 86 (September–October 2007): 147–49.

Nye, Joseph S., Jr. *The Paradox of American Power.* New York: Oxford University Press, 2002.

Nygren, Col. Kip. "Emerging Technologies and Exponential Change: Implications for Army Transformation." *Parameters* 32 (Summer 2002): 86–99.

Owens, Mackubin Thomas. "Failure's Many Fathers." *Foreign Affairs* 86 (September–October 2007):

Profile of the U.S. Army: A Reference Handbook. Arlington, VA: Association of the United States Army, 2005.

Resetting the Force: The Equipment Challenge. Torchbearer National Security Report 19. Arlington, VA: Association of the United States Army, 2005.

Schoonmaker, Gen. Peter. Annual Army Chief of Staff Address to the Eisenhower Luncheon, Annual Meeting and Exposition of the Association of the United States Army, Arlington, VA, October 10, 2006.

Sharra, Michael. *The Killer Angels.* New York: Ballantine Books, 1975.

Silber, Mitchell D., and Arvin Bhatt. *Radicalization in the West: The Homegrown Threat.* New York: New York City Police Department, 2007.

Snider, Don M., and Gayle L. Watkins. *The Future of the Army Profession.* New York: McGraw-Hill, 2002.

Steele, Lt. Gen. William. "Training and Developing Leaders in a Transforming Army." *Military Review* 82 (September–October 2001): 2–11.

Sullivan, Gordon R. "America's Army into the Twenty First Century." National Security Paper 14. Washington, DC: Institute for Foreign Policy Analysis, 1993.

Sullivan, Gordon R., and Frederic J. Brown. "America's Army." *Military Review* 82 (March–April 2002): 3–8.

Tichy, Noel M. *The Cycle of Leadership.* New York: HarperCollins, 2002.

A Transformed and Modernized U.S. Army: A National Imperative. Torchbearer National Security Report 31. Arlington, VA: Association of the United States Army, 2007.

Turner, Lt. Gen. Tom. "U.S. Army North: We're Here to Help." *Army* 57 (September 2007): 27–32.

The U.S. Army in 2004 and Beyond: Strategically Agile and Adaptive. Torchbearer National Security Report 25. Arlington, VA: Association of the United States Army, 2004.

The U.S. Army's Role in Stability Operations. Torchbearer National Security Report 27. Arlington, VA: Association of the United States Army, 2006.

The U.S. Army's Transformation to the Objective Force. Vol. 3, *Key Issues.* Torchbearer National Security Report 11. Arlington, VA: Association of the United States Army, 2003.

U.S. Department of Defense. *Military Support for Stability, Security, Transition, and Reconstruction (SSTR) Operations.* DoD Dir 3000.05. Washington, DC: U.S. Department of Defense, 2005.

———. *Quadrennial Defense Review Report.* Washington, DC: U.S. Department of Defense, 2006.

U.S. Department of Defense, Joint Forces Command. *Commander's Handbook for the Joint Interagency Coordination Group*. Washington, DC: U.S. Department of Defense, 2007.

———. *Interagency, Intergovernmental Organization, and Nongovernmental Organization Coordination During Joint Operations*. Joint Publication 3–08. Washington, DC: U.S. Department of Defense, 2006.

U.S. Department of the Army. *The Army*. FM 1.0. Washington, DC: U.S. Department of Defense, 2001.

———. *Army Leadership*. FM 6.22. Washington, DC: U.S. Department of Defense, 2006.

———. *Mission Command: Command and Control of Army Forces*. FM 6.0. Washington, DC: U.S. Department of Defense, 2003.

———. *The Objective Force 2015 Concept Paper*. Washington, DC: U.S. Department of Defense, 2002.

———. *Training the Force*. FM 7.0. Washington, DC: U.S. Department of Defense, 2002.

U.S. Department of the Army, Armor Center. "FCCV Family." Ft. Knox, TN: U.S. Department of Defense, 1983.

U.S. Department of the Army, DAPE-MPW-PD. "Information Paper." *Army Retention*, September 7, 2006.

U.S. Department of the Army, Office of the Chief of Staff. *2006 Game Plan—United States Army*, Washington, DC: U.S. Department of Defense, 2006.

U.S. Department of the Army, Training and Doctrine Command Headquarters, Combined Arms Center, Battle Command Knowledge System. "Battle Command Knowledge System as the FORSCOM Knowledge Enabler." Briefing for Gen. Charles C. Campbell, August 14, 2007. Available at: https://www.us.army.mil/suite/portal/index.jsp.

———. "Overview and Capabilities Brief for Eighth (U.S.) Army." Presentation, November 28, 2006.

U.S. Department of the Army, Training and Doctrine Command Headquarters, Combined Arms Center, Center of Army Lessons Learned. "Executive Summary." Presentation, July 22, 2004.

U.S. Department of the Army, Training and Doctrine Command Headquarters, DCG IMT. "The Human Dimension in Full Spectrum Operations." Presentation, 2006.

U.S. Department of the Army, Training and Doctrine Command Headquarters, Intelligence Support Activity. *The Contemporary Operational Environment*. Washington, DC: U.S. Department of Defense, 2007.

U.S. House of Representatives. *A Failure of Initiative: Final Report of the Select Bipartisan Committee to Investigate the Preparation for and Response to Hurricane Katrina*. Washington, DC: U.S. Government Printing Office, 2006. Available at: http://www.katrina.house.gov.

U.S. National Intelligence Council. *The Terrorist Threat to the U.S. Homeland*. National Intelligence Estimate. Washington, DC: U.S. National Intelligence Council, 2007.

Vuono, Gen. Carl. Interview. *All We Could Be*. Videocassette. Produced and directed by Rob Kirk, 45 min., First Person Productions for the Association of the United States Army, 1996.

Wallace, Gen. William. "TRADOC Commander's Perspective." Presented at the 2007 Armor Warfighting Conference, Fort Knox, KY, May 2, 2007.

Washington Post. March 12, 2003–November 9, 2007.

Wass de Czege, Brig. Gen. Huba. "Lessons from the Past: Making the Army's Doctrine 'Right Enough' Today." Landpower Essay 06-2. Arlington, VA: Association of the United States Army, 2006.

Wass de Czege, Brig. Gen. Huba, and Col. Richard Sinnreich. "Conceptual Foundations of a Transformed U.S. Army." Landpower Essay 40. Arlington, VA: Association of the United States Army, 2002.

Wenger, Etienne, Richard McDermott, and William H. Snyder. *Cultivating Communities of Practice.* Boston: Harvard Business School Press, 2002.

Winkler, Gary. "SES Army Knowledge Management Initiatives." Presented at the CIO/G6 GO Workshop: Enabling Battle Command, February 25 2006.

Woods, Kevin. *Iraqi Perspectives Project: A View of Operation Iraqi Freedom from Saddam's Senior Leadership.* Joint Center for Operational Analysis and Lessons Learned/Joint Advance Warfighting Program. Alexandria, VA: Institute of Defense Analyses, 2006.

Wuchty, Stefan, Benjamin F. Jones, and Brian Uzzi. "The Increasing Dominance of Teams in Production of Knowledge." *Science*, May 18, 2007, 1036–39.

Zais, Brig. Gen. Mitchell. "U.S. Strategy in Iraq." Presented at the Honors Convocation, Newberry College, Newberry, SC, November 9, 2006.

Index

About the Authors

ZEB B. BRADFORD, JR. (Brig. Gen., U.S. Army, Retired), is a business consultant and national security analyst. A graduate of West Point, he taught politics and economics at the Military Academy. He is also a graduate of Harvard University's Graduate School of Government and of its Senior Executive Seminar on National and International Security. He was Senior Military Fellow at the Council on Foreign Relations and a Resident Scholar at the Woodrow Wilson International Center for Scholars. A highly decorated Infantry officer, he served in numerous command and staff positions in the United States, Vietnam, Korea, and Europe, including service as head of strategic planning at NATO headquarters in Belgium. He is a widely published author on national security affairs, co-authoring with Frederic Brown the influential *United States Army in Transition* on the rebuilding of the Army after Vietnam. In his business career he held executive positions with United Technologies Corp. and Citigroup.

FREDERIC J. BROWN (Lt. Gen., U.S. Army, Retired), Ph.D., is currently Senior Mentor for establishing Knowledge Management in the U.S. European Command. He received his doctorate, as a West Point Olmsted Scholar, from the Graduate Institute of International Studies in Geneva, Switzerland. As a military officer he commanded army units at virtually every level in the United States, Germany, and Vietnam, including as Chief of Armor and Cavalry where he was deeply involved in rebuilding the American armored forces prior to Desert Storm. He has also served in the Office of the Army Chief of Staff, the Office of the Joint Chiefs of Staff, the National Security Council Staff and the West Wing White House staff. He is co-author, with Zeb Bradford, of *United States Army in Transition* and author of the subsequent *The United States Army in Transition II: Landpower in the Information Age.*